THE
MYSTERY
STORY

THE MYSTERY STORY

JOHN BALL, EDITOR
ROBERT E. BRINEY
MICHAEL GILBERT
E.T. GUYMON, JR.
ALLEN J. HUBIN
FRANCIS M. NEVINS, JR.
OTTO PENZLER
JAMES SANDOE
MICHELE SLUNG
AARON MARC STEIN
HILLARY WAUGH
PHYLLIS A. WHITNEY
DONALD A. YATES

A PUBLICATION OF UNIVERSITY EXTENSION
UNIVERSITY OF CALIFORNIA, SAN DIEGO

IN COOPERATION WITH
PUBLISHER'S INC. DEL MAR, CA

PN
3448
.D4
M98

Library of Congress Cataloging in Publication Data
Main entry under title:

The mystery story.

  Bibliography: p.
  1. Detective and mystery stories—History and criticism—Addresses, essays, lectures. I. Ball, John Dudley, 1911–
PN3448.D4M98   813'.0872   76-7110
ISBN 0–89163–019–8

5 4 3

TABLE OF CONTENTS

VI	PREFACE	*William D. McElroy*
VII	INTRODUCTION	*Martin N. Chamberlain*
1	MURDER AT LARGE	*John Ball*
29	THE MYSTERY STORY IN CULTURAL PERSPECTIVE	*Aaron Marc Stein*
61	THE MYSTERY VERSUS THE NOVEL	*Hillary Waugh*
83	THE AMATEUR DETECTIVES	*Otto Penzler*
111	THE PRIVATE EYE	*James Sandoe*
125	WOMEN IN DETECTIVE FICTION	*Michele Slung*
143	THE ETHNIC DETECTIVE	*John Ball*
163	THE POLICE PROCEDURAL	*Hillary Waugh*
189	LOCKED ROOMS AND PUZZLES: A CRITICAL MEMOIR	*Donald A. Yates*
205	THE SPY IN FACT AND FICTION	*Michael Gilbert*
223	GOTHIC MYSTERIES	*Phyllis A. Whitney*
235	DEATH RAYS, DEMONS, AND WORMS UNKNOWN TO SCIENCE	*Robert E. Briney*
291	PATTERNS IN MYSTERY FICTION: THE DURABLE SERIES CHARACTER	*Allen J. Hubin*
321	THE GREAT CROOKS	*Otto Penzler*
343	NAME GAMES: MYSTERY WRITERS AND THEIR PSEUDONYMS	*Francis M. Nevins, Jr.*
361	WHY DO WE READ THIS STUFF?	*E. T. Guymon, Jr.*
365	THE LITERATURE OF THE SUBJECT: AN ANNOTATED BIBLIOGRAPHY	*Robert E. Briney*

PREFACE

Quite apart from the distinction it derives from the calibre of its contributors and contents, THE MYSTERY STORY is unique among books: It is the first appreciation of the detective story ever published under the auspices of a major university.

For more than half a century, the American reading public has chosen the mystery story, in its numerous guises and disguises, as its favorite form of fiction. One estimate claims that more than 50,000 detective tales already have been published. Relatively few have achieved fame, and perhaps even fewer stand out as literary achievements. Nonetheless, it is no longer possible to ignore the enormous impact which this form of creativity has had on public tastes since that day in 1841 when Edgar Allan Poe launched the genre with his "Murders in the Rue Morgue."

University Extension of the University of California, San Diego is renowned nationwide for its innovative programs in the field of continuing education. THE MYSTERY STORY is the pilot volume in Extension's newest—and perhaps most imaginative—project, The UCSD Extension Mystery Library, about which Extension Dean Martin Chamberlain has more to say in the pages which follow.

W D McElroy

Chancellor
University of California, San Diego

INTRODUCTION

MARTIN N. CHAMBERLAIN
Dean of University Extension
University of California,
San Diego

The basic concept for this work, and for THE MYSTERY LIBRARY of which it is the pilot volume, was generated under the auspices of University Extension, University of California, San Diego, by John Ball, a mystery writer of world renown, and C. David Hellyer, an Extension teacher who was then Public Affairs Officer of the University.

A considerable role in the completion of this unique volume was played by Extension's Director of New Media Programs, Caleb A. Lewis, who helped to develop it from the conceptual stage and who nurtured the project through several difficult periods.

As editor of THE MYSTERY STORY, Mr. Ball invited a dozen of the most distinguished personalities in the world of the mystery story to join him in creating this volume. Many of these same authors accepted membership on the Editorial Board of THE MYSTERY LIBRARY. The great classics chosen by this Board will be reissued by THE MYSTERY LIBRARY, under University auspices, and these volumes will be made available, under a modified book-club plan, to students and to the general public at reasonable cost.

With one exception, all of the material in this volume is new and was prepared especially for THE MYSTERY STORY. Professor Sandoe's listing of the definitive "private-eye" literature was published earlier in a very limited edition. He has revised and augmented this highly praised work for the much wider readership it will now enjoy as a chapter in THE MYSTERY STORY.

Lovers of the mystery genre scarcely need an introduction to such authors, editors and critics as John Ball, Robert E. Briney, Allen J. Hubin, Francis M. Nevins, Jr., Otto Penzler, Aaron Marc Stein, Hillary Waugh, and Phyllis A. Whitney, all of whom contributed to this volume and now serve as members of THE MYSTERY LIBRARY Board.

E. T. Guymon, dean of all mystery-story collectors in the United States (if not the world), is also a Board member. Mr. Guymon has been persuaded to contribute to THE MYSTERY STORY the first essay he has ever written about the field in which his name enjoys worldwide fame. Students of the genre are forever in his debt: Mr. Guymon has donated his collection of some 15,000 volumes of mysteries to Occidental College for scholarly investigations.

(Also serving on THE MYSTERY LIBRARY Editorial Board, though not contributors to this volume, are Ellery Queen [Frederic Dannay] and Howard Haycraft, two of the foremost world authorities on mystery and detective fiction.)

John Ball is a novelist whose works in both the mainstream of fiction and within the mystery field have been published throughout the world in many languages. He is the winner of both the Edgar (Allan Poe) Award of the Mystery Writers of America and the Golden Dagger Award given by the British Crime Writers' Association for the best novel of the year by a non-British author, perhaps the most prestigious and difficult to obtain honor available to a mystery writer. The film version of Mr. Ball's book, IN THE HEAT OF THE NIGHT, received five Academy Awards including the one given for the best picture of the year. Mr. Ball serves as chairman of our Editorial Board in addition to his responsibility as editor-in-chief of THE MYSTERY STORY.

In the field of mystery scholarship and appreciation, Robert E. Briney enjoys international stature. In addition to chairing the mathematics department at Salem (Mass.) State College, Dr. Briney is the first authority on the exotic aspects of mystery fiction, a frequent contributor to the literature, and the editor and publisher of THE ROHMER REVIEW.

Despite the fact that he has a full-time law practice in the city of London, Michael Gilbert has achieved a reputation as a mystery novelist that can hardly be surpassed. Mr. Gilbert is, among other achievements, the author of GAME WITHOUT RULES, a work that has been described as one of the two best books of spy stories ever written (the other being W. Somerset Maugham's ASHENDEN; OR, THE BRITISH AGENT). Mr. Gilbert's unbroken string of successes places him in the front rank of mystery authors of world category.

Allen J. Hubin, at one time mystery reviewer for THE NEW YORK TIMES, is founder and editor of the outstanding scholarly journal in the mystery field, THE ARMCHAIR DETECTIVE. He is also the owner of the largest known library of mystery literature still in private hands, numbering some 25,000 volumes.

Francis M. Nevins is Associate Professor of Law at St. Louis University. A mystery novelist of distinction, Mr. Nevins has also made many important contributions to the literature, notably ROYAL BLOODLINE (devoted to the career of Ellery Queen) and THE MYSTERY WRITER'S ART, a publication of Bowling Green University. Together with Dr. Briney he edited MULTIPLYING VILLAINIES, a compendium of the mystery reviews written by the late Anthony Boucher.

Otto Penzler, author and lecturer, together with Chris Steinbrunner, compiled and edited the monumental ENCYCLOPEDIA OF MYSTERY & DETECTION. This important work, which was many years in preparation, is found today in the reference department of most general libraries of stature and in the hands of many aficionados of the genre. Mr. Penzler is also noted as a lecturer on Sherlock Holmes.

James Sandoe, professor emeritus in English and Humanities of the University of Colorado, twice won the Edgar Award over a twelve-year period for his mystery criticism in the NEW YORK HERALD TRIBUNE. He is also an anthologist of distinction and has contributed introductions to many compendia of mystery writing.

Michele Slung, despite her youth, is already established as the first authority on women in detective fiction. Her book, CRIME ON HER MIND, is an important contribution to the study of the detective story.

Aaron Marc Stein is the author of some ninety works of fiction in addition to his contributions to THE PRINCETON REVIEW and other media. He served recently as president of the Mystery Writers of America. In addition to works under his own name, Mr. Stein is also widely known under two pen names: George Bagby, and Hampton Stone. His own interest in and knowledge of archaeology have added much to his published work.

Hillary Waugh, another MWA past-president, also has a considerable number of works to his credit. He is widely read, particularly in the specialized field of the police procedural, in which he is an acknowledged expert. He has also extended his talents into the field of the Gothic novel. Particularly admired are his books concerning homicide detectives of the New York Police Department.

Phyllis A. Whitney enjoys international fame in the field of the Gothic story. She is a most active member of THE MYSTERY LIBRARY Editorial Board and also devotes much time to the Mystery Writers of America and other activities bearing on the field of literature in which she is preeminent. During the year in which THE MYSTERY STORY was in preparation, Miss Whitney was president of the Mystery Writers of America.

Donald Yates, of Michigan State University, has achieved a much-deserved reputation as an authority on the classical puzzle stories that make up so much of detective literature. Professor Yates has made frequent contributions to THE ARMCHAIR DETECTIVE and other journals, and is well-known also within the ranks of THE BAKER STREET IRREGULARS.

THE MYSTERY STORY is not a "how-to" book, although anyone who reads it will almost certainly improve his or her chances of success as a mystery author. But its true purpose is aimed somewhat higher.

A great university is required by its charter to reach out in many directions in its efforts to enrich the human experience. While it is true that a handful of American universities already are offering courses related to the mystery story, this facet of literature is still largely neglected and ignored by institutions of higher learning.

We at Extension believe that the time has come to include the mystery story in our curricula as a subject worthy of serious study.

The present volume, and THE MYSTERY LIBRARY of which it is the bellwether, are efforts in this direction.

Acknowledgement is due to several members of the Extension staff for their roles in bringing this project to fruition. Among them are Dr. Mary Walshok, Assistant Dean for Academic Affairs, and Mrs. Ann Porterfield, Program Assistant.

Appreciation is due as well to Richard L. Roe, President of Publisher's Inc., publisher of THE MYSTERY STORY, for his unflagging encouragement and support throughout the project.

THE MYSTERY STORY

ONE   JOHN BALL

*John Ball launched his career as
a mystery-story writer with
a work which won him immediate
worldwide fame, and several
coveted awards: IN THE HEAT OF
THE NIGHT. This novel, which
received five Academy awards
in its screen version, also
launched Ball's series detective,
Virgil Tibbs, whose exploits
thus far have been recounted in
five novels. HEAT . . . also
was honored with an Edgar, and
with the British Golden Dagger
Award. Mr. Ball presently is
published in eighteen languages,
in twenty-six countries. When
not at his typewriter, he involves
himself in a variety of interests
including flying and aikido (he
holds the Black Belt).
To Mr. Ball goes the major credit
for conceiving THE MYSTERY
LIBRARY, and its pilot volume,
THE MYSTERY STORY.*

MURDER AT LARGE

It may well be that when the historians of literature come to discourse upon the fiction produced by the English-speaking peoples in the first half of the twentieth century, they will pass somewhat lightly over the compositions of the "serious" novelists and turn their attention to the immense and varied achievement of the detective writers.

W. Somerset Maugham

On 30 September 1840 a gentleman who is remembered only as S. Maupin wrote a letter which is today preserved in the Boston Public Library. In that letter, which was addressed to Edgar Allan Poe, the terms were set down under which C. Auguste Dubouchet could be engaged to teach French in the city of Richmond, Virginia. That particular letter would have passed very quickly into limbo except for one interesting fact: In the April 1841 issue of the Philadelphia publication *Graham's Magazine*, Poe published "The Murders in the Rue Morgue" featuring a private detective known as C. Auguste Dupin, and thereby fired a literary shot heard 'round the world.

That Dupin story, and two others that followed, founded a form of literature that was to grow and develop during the next century and a third into overwhelming worldwide popularity. There had been previous writings approaching the same vein, just as Americans had played various sorts of stick-and-ball games before Abner Doubleday, but it was unquestionably Poe who first defined the form and breathed into it both life and a strong measure of immortality.

He did it so well that the subsequent passage of more than thirteen decades has only added to his popularity and the stature of the work he produced. Over the years millions of readers have experienced vicariously the thrill of finding buried treasure as they stalked through the pages of "The Gold Bug," and there are certainly few readers of American literature who have not had their blood chilled by the fascinating, frightening tales of horror that flowed from Poe's pen.

Possibly conscious of the fact that he was venturing into unexplored literary territory, Poe began "The Murders in the Rue Morgue" with a considerable windup before he pitched. But in spite of the flowery language common in his day, and the need to display learning by providing quotations in the original Greek (as in "The Man of the Crowd"), he could, when he chose, get down to business in a hurry. His immortal story "The Cask of Amontillado" begins with one of the greatest opening sentences in the English language: "The thousand injuries of Fortunato I had borne as I best could, but when he ventured upon insult, I vowed revenge." In twenty-one words Poe set the stage, introduced the two principal characters, supplied a powerful motive, and began the action. Such is genius.

The way having been pointed, detectives in literature began to be fruitful and to multiply, but they had not yet found their Eden. The creation took place in the British publication *Beeton's Christmas Annual* for 1887, which was made available to the public at one shilling per copy. Those who invested a little less than a quarter for some entertaining reading discovered a story that had been rejected several times before it had landed on the desk of Professor G. T. Bettany, the chief editor of Ward, Lock and Co. Although he had not been able to see any way to use it for at least a year, he had offered twenty-five pounds for all rights to the short novel.

The author had not been pleased, either with the amount of the offer or the long delay before publication, but he had had very little choice—a situation with which authors are all too familiar to this day. He finally accepted both. That was in 1886. Something over a year later the story, in the words of Dorothy L. Sayers, was "flung like a bombshell into the field of detective fiction." Unfortunately, the brilliant Miss Sayers was not available to publish her opinion, her age being minus six at the time, and the public was not yet aware that a titan had been born. Or, to be more accurate, two of them. The story, called *A Study in Scarlet,* was by a young physician whose medical skills were under-appreciated by potential patients who, in invisible droves, failed to consult him. He therefore spent his otherwise unoccupied time in writing. The hand that held the pen was that of (Sir) Arthur Conan Doyle, but the words that flowed on paper were the words of Dr. John H. Watson, M.D. By this means Dr. Watson, physician and man of letters, gave to the world the greatest detective of all time, his friend and companion Mr. Sherlock Holmes.

The immediate impact was limited. Prior to Dr. Watson, the mystery story had yet to attain respectability; it had already been typecast as something weighed in the balances and found unimportant. The Sherlockian scholar, Dr. Julian Wolff of New York, has exhumed a review which appeared in *The Graphic* (London) for 1 September 1888, and which stated in part: "There is no trace of vulgarity or slovenliness so often characteristic of detective stories." The reviewer did concede that "he (Doyle) has actually succeeded in inventing a brand new detective."

Indeed he had, and long before the days of Lord Peter Wimsey, Dr. Gideon Fell, Nero Wolfe, Sam Spade, Philip Marlowe, Hildegarde Withers, Miss Marple, Gideon, Dr. Thorndyke, Hercule Poirot, Perry Mason, Father Brown, Maigret, and Inspector Napoleon Bonaparte, to cite only a few of those who have achieved world fame.

Before very long Sherlock Holmes and his physician friend rose to international acclaim and, well within Doyle's own lifetime, to immortality. A very good case could be made that Sherlock Holmes is the best-known and most read-about Englishman of all time, despite the formidable competition of William Shakespeare, Sir Winston Churchill, and several of the distinguished monarchs who have occupied the throne. Obviously no one would challenge the Olympian stature of *Macbeth* or dare to propose that Doyle, even at his sterling best, could approach such a literary level, but on the plane on which he wrote he too knew how to turn a majestic phrase.

> "He said that there were no traces upon the ground round the body. He did not observe any. But I did—some little distance off, but fresh and clear."
> "Footprints?"
> "Footprints."
> "A man's or a woman's?"
> Dr. Mortimer looked strangely at us for an instant and his voice sank almost to a whisper as he answered:
> *"Mr. Holmes, they were the footprints of a gigantic hound!"*

The paralyzing chills that that scene has created for uncounted millions of readers make it very nearly as memorable as Lady Macbeth's *"Out, damned spot."*

Meanwhile, who were the authors whose detective stories were characterized, in one reviewer's opinion, by "vulgarity and slovenliness"? Some bad ones surely, but it is not so easy to dismiss Emile Gaboriau, Honoré de Balzac, Eugene Sue, Wilkie Collins, Victor Hugo, and Charles Dickens, not to mention Poe himself.

In this connection Dickens deserves a special word. In *Bleak House* he created the celebrated detective Inspector Bucket, about whom much has been written, and deservedly so. But *The Mystery of Edwin Drood* remains to this day one of the most remarkable of all crime stories, and one of the most discussed. It could hardly be otherwise. It is a gripping story full of the kinds of characters that put their creator among the immortals. Durdles, the drunken stonemason, is a good example. For twenty-three compelling chapters the mystery unfolds and then it ends—unfinished. Dickens had a fatal seizure and did not live to complete the story. Unfortunately for posterity, he had not told anyone who survived him what the outcome was to be. As a result, the mystery-without-a-solution has challenged some of the most formidable intellects of the literary world to try and resolve it. There are tantalizing clues in certain illustrations prepared for the book-to-be that depict scenes not in the text. Hints of disguises are present, as is a heroine with the remarkable name of Rosa Budd, an appellation that is topped only by Gilbert and Sullivan's Japanese ingenue Yum-Yum.

Many authors have attempted to finish *Edwin Drood* and to resolve the mystery. An outstanding event was the "trial" of John Jasper, one of the suspects in the story, which was staged in London in January 1914 with a sterling cast that included G. K. Chesterton as the judge and George Bernard Shaw as the foreman of the jury. Other distinguished writers and attorneys appeared during the "trial" as jurymen and characters in the story. The proceedings were as lively and arresting as might be expected, particularly when the presiding judge fined Shaw and the entire jury panel for contempt of court. It was Mr. Chesterton's private opinion that the mystery of Edwin Drood was insoluble without Dickens to tell where his supremely gifted imagination was to take him. The jury disagreed; its members returned a verdict that found Jasper guilty of murder.

Where did it all begin, the fascinating recounting of crime and detection? It would be easier to identify an alley cat's grandfather than to be definitive on that point. The Bible has been cited as containing crime stories and an early mention of spies. Régis Messac has made the suggestion that the account of Archimedes' discovery of the principle of liquid displacement, while investigating a possible crime, may properly be regarded as a detective story. It certainly qualifies insofar as a sensational ending is concerned, with one of the greatest intellects of the ancient world running naked through the streets shouting *Eureka!*

If a starting point must be chosen, then the story of the three princes and the missing camel is an important landmark. During their travels three Persian princes were asked if they had seen a camel that had wandered away and become lost.

They reported that they had not seen it, but by any chance was it the one that was blind in one eye, had a tooth missing, and was lame?

Despite their noble rank, the three princes were brought before the monarch and accused of stealing the animal that they had described so accurately. If they were innocent, His Majesty wanted to know, how had they acquired all that information?

The princes then explained. The camel had grazed on only one side of the road, despite the fact that the grass was better on the other. They had observed partially chewed clumps of grass that were just the size of a camel's tooth scattered along the way and marks in the dust that clearly showed that the animal had been dragging one foot.

The story has been told many times, but what is quite possibly the original version appears in *The Arabian Nights*.

During the forty-six years between "The Murders in the Rue Morgue" (what a title!) and *A Study in Scarlet* quite a bit occurred. In 1843/44 Sir James Graham, the British Home Secretary, added a new and pungent word to the English language. He selected a few of the most capable and intelligent officers of the London Police, formed them into a special unit, and called them *The Detective Police*. It is regrettable that the word "detective" had not been coined a little sooner, as Poe could have made good use of it.

A note must also be inserted concerning the first professional detective to enter the pages of history, the flamboyant Eugene Francois Vidocq, who was in full cry during this period. The career of M. Vidocq is probably unmatched in history, which is perhaps just as well. He was a dashing detective who produced one sensational exploit after another; he founded the *Sûreté* and served as its chief for two terms, a total of twenty-eight years. His sensational successes and natural flair for publicity made him a great celebrity. He was a master of disguises, had a phenomenal memory for faces and events, and an unerring sense of the dramatic. At the climactic moment of capture he was known to cry "I am Vidocq!", paralyzing his quarry into terrified submission. Which was not a bad performance for a several-times escaped convict and perhaps the only man known to have risen to such prominence following earlier employment as a galley slave.

M. Vidocq did not rest on his laurels. He became an author and published his *Memoires* which kept the bedroom candles of Paris burning far into the night. To call them exciting reading would be an understatement. He became the subject of stage dramas and his career was the basis of the exploits of Balzac's famous Vautrin. There was even one memorable occasion when the great detective and the great author set out to solve a mysterious crime together. What an event *that* would have been to witness!

Obviously Balzac profited from the association in more ways than might be obvious. In his *Maître Cornélius* he scored a formidable first by introducing a resourceful detective who was none other than King Louis XI of France. In Balzac's account, His Majesty takes on a knotty problem and by means of an ingenious device successfully identifies a totally unsuspected criminal. Later on, in "The Adventure of the Golden Pince-Nez" the same technique was employed by Sherlock Holmes himself.

A major event occurred in 1862 when Victor Hugo wrote *Les Miserables*. The cordial Gallic hatred of the police, which had been well instilled for decades, was given additional spiritual nourishment. France was not yet prepared for Maigret, but its citizens cheered for Vidocq largely because the former convict headed a separate bureau that constantly embarrassed the police by beating them at their own game.

The first French novelist to risk presenting a police officer in a favorable light was Alexandre Dumas. The creator of *The Three Musketeers* and *The Count of Monte Cristo* published *Les Mohicans de Paris* in 1854/55, a book which introduced the police detective Monsieur Jackal. He is not a very important personage, but he did have his moment in history when he first uttered the immortal phrase *Cherchez la femme!* It unquestionably set a style, and femmes have been assiduously cherched ever since.

In England Wilkie Collins, lawyer, painter, and novelist, wrote a number of books which are today all but forgotten, except for two detective stories notable for their immensely complicated plots. *The Woman in White* introduced Count Fosco, who became the prototype for uncounted numbers of despicable villains yet to come. This 1860 work, which was based on an actual case in France, used the now familiar device of confining a perfectly sound person to an insane asylum simply to keep him or her out of the way. It was dramatized with great success, and may well have influenced Collins's very close and good friend, Charles Dickens, in his subsequent works.

Eight years later, suffering acutely from gout and frequently under the influence of the opium he used to kill the pain, Collins dictated *The Moonstone,* one of the best detective novels ever written and one of the longest. In it he introduced Sergeant Cuff, a detective whose place in history is secure. He was drawn from an actual individual, Inspector Whicher of Scotland Yard. The inspector, who was well known at the time, enjoyed a unique distinction: He served as the model for two different detectives created by two internationally celebrated authors. Dickens also depicted the inspector under a thin alias as Sergeant Witchem in "Three Detective Anecdotes."

Then came Baker Street and the status, stature, and format of the detective story was altered for all time to come. Sherlock Holmes created an enthusiasm that rose like a tidal wave and has not abated to this day. The world's greatest detective's fame reached to even the most remote areas of the globe; his career was followed with intense interest over decades and no one since his retirement has ever ventured to challenge his preeminent position. The Canon left us by Dr. Watson includes a total of sixty works, fifty-six of which are short stories. The literature about Holmes and Watson, apart from the Canon itself, is astonishingly vast and continuously growing. It is, in itself, a miracle without parallel; were Sir Arthur here to view it, he would probably be overcome, particularly because he was himself one of the few great literary lights of the world who did not regard Sherlock Holmes as an incredible achievement. In fact, Sir Arthur once made an earnest effort to get rid of Holmes so that he could turn to "more serious work."

More serious work indeed! Despite the claims of the sponsors of Tarzan of the Apes, who might be said to represent a voice crying from the wilderness, Sherlock Holmes is undoubtedly the most world-celebrated personage ever to emerge from the pages of literature. He is also responsible for the Baker Street Irregulars.

Early in the career of the Baker Street sage we meet this band of street urchins who go forth in a pack to do their master's bidding for a payment of a shilling each per day. They were useful while Holmes was in active practice and they are even more so today. They publish *The Baker Street Journal,* a learned quarterly to which some of the most august by-lines in the world have contributed. They hold meetings, notably on the Master's birthday (January 6th), and read scholarly papers, some of which are astonishingly profound. Almost every aspect of the Canon has been explored in depth by the most distinguished living experts in various fields of specialization. As an example, in "The Musgrave Ritual" Holmes recovers the ancient crown of England that had been lost for generations. This raises the logical question: *Which* crown?

The Irregulars were fully equal to that one; in *The Baker Street Journal* for April 1953 (Vol. 3, No. 2 [New Series]) the distinguished Sherlockian, Nathan L. Bengis, identified the crown in question as the ancient one of St. Edward the Confessor. This essay was by no means the first on the subject; a number of other crowns had been proposed by various scholars and their findings were vigorously researched through every kind of available source material. However, Mr. Bengis firmly established that: "Not only does this crown fit all the requirements of the Canon, no other crown does." He then launched into some highly technical data concerning the various crowns of England which fully supported his conclusion.

That, however, is not the end of the story. Mr. Bengis, who is nothing if not thorough, wrote to the Keeper of Her Majesty's Jewel House, Major General H. D. W. Sitwell, C.B., M.C., and asked his opinion on the matter. General Sitwell responded from the Tower of London with a superbly written historical account entitled "Some Notes on St. Edward's Crown and the Musgrave Ritual," one of the most exciting pieces of reading that has ever graced the *Journal*. This astonishing revelation of British history is filled with fiery action and proves for all time that Sherlock Holmes did indeed recover for the Throne the priceless crown of St. Edward. General Sitwell's magnificent contribution was later endorsed, according to reliable report, by Her Majesty the Queen Mother.

President Franklin D. Roosevelt was a member of the Baker Street Irregulars while in office and despite the enormous weight of his responsibilities, he too found time to write for the *Journal*. It was the President who designated the Secret Service areas at Shangri-La (Camp David) as Baker Street. The headquarters is, of course, 221B—a London address even more famous than 10 Downing Street.

Students of the Canon, the 660,382 authentic words concerning the life and career of Mr. Sherlock Holmes, are acutely aware of the fact that Dr. Watson set them some very tricky little problems. Dates are supplied that don't work out. Facts are given that appear directly to contradict one another. Key individuals are concealed behind pseudonyms. It is obvious that the Illustrious Client is King Edward VII but it is less easy to decipher the precise identification of a piece of deep blue eggshell pottery of the Ming period, loaned from His Majesty's own collection, particularly when Sir Eric MacLaglan, the director of the Victoria and Albert Museum, stated while addressing the Sherlock Holmes Society of London that there is *no* Ming eggshell pottery of anything like that color.

Mrs. Hudson, the immortal landlady at 221B Baker Street, once was replaced without warning by a lady of another name, but that difficulty is as nothing compared to the occasion when Mary Morstan Watson addressed her husband as "James" when the entire world knew that his name was John.

There are hundreds of these apparent inconsistencies, all of which the Irregulars have taken it upon themselves to explain. No problem in the Canon is more renowned than the matter of Dr. Watson's wound. It is absolutely definite that Dr. Watson was struck by a Jezail bullet during the Battle of Maiwand while serving as assistant surgeon with the Fifth Northumberland Fusiliers. In the doctor's own words:

"There I was struck on the shoulder by a Jezail bullet, which shattered the bone and grazed the subclavian artery. I should have fallen into the hands of the murderous Ghazis had it not been for the devotion and courage shown by Murray, my orderly, who threw me across a packhorse, and succeeded in bringing me safely to the British lines."

Praise and gratitude forever to the house of Murray!

However, in "The Sign of the Four" (sometimes rendered "The Sign of Four") Dr. Watson speaks of his wounded *leg*. "I had had a Jezail bullet through it some time before, and though it did not prevent me from walking it ached wearily at every change of the weather." Later, in the same account, Holmes asks if Watson's leg will prevent him following the trail of the criminals.

The plot thickens. Early in their acquaintanceship Holmes himself refers to the wound as being in the *arm*. Then, again in "The Sign of the Four" the wound is back in the leg. "What was I, an Army surgeon with a weak leg . . ." We later learn, in Watson's words, that he is "a half-pay officer with a damaged tendo Achillis" (which is in the ankle). All this sounds very much like two wounds, but that absolutely cannot be, because in the famous episode in "The Resident Patient" where Holmes apparently reads Watson's thoughts (as Dupin did for his unnamed companion—presumably Poe) the Master said, "Your hand stole toward your own old wound."

Where, then, was Watson wounded?

The explanation: Out on the open battlefield, with complete disregard for his own safety, Dr. Watson was kneeling, bent over a fallen comrade and ministering to him, when he was shot in the left buttock. Any suggestion of cowardice in that he was not "facing the foe" is an unwarranted slander; he was ignoring the presence of the enemy. When he later wrote *A Study in Scarlet,* the excessive restraints of the Victorian era compelled him to bowdlerize the historical facts and he conveniently relocated his wound in his shoulder, both in referring to it himself and in reporting Holmes' observation of his condition.

For this yielding to expediency he was definitely upbraided by Holmes during the Master's criticism of *A Study in Scarlet,* quoted in "The Sign of the Four." Immediately thereafter Watson refers to his wounded leg, which is materially closer to the truth. Perhaps too close, hence the second evasion when he mentioned the tendon of Achilles. It is, of course, virtually impossible to imagine a bullet lodged semipermanently in that area.

How do we know this? Read again Dr. Watson's account of his rescue from the battlefield. Note that Murray threw him *across* the packhorse. A man wounded in either the shoulder or the ankle would most certainly have been *seated* on the horse, permitting him to retire to the hospital with some measure of dignity. If he had been wounded in the shoulder, a position across the horse would have been disastrous; the pain would have been multiplied many times over, the injury would certainly have been compounded, and the bleeding greatly intensified. Dr. Watson was thrown across his horse for the very good reason that he had been shot in the buttock, and therefore a normal seated position would have represented the acme of discomfort. With this single honorable, if undignified, wound he was removed from the arena of conflict and saved for his appointment with destiny.

Incidentally, it is known that the bullet was later surgically removed, because during the final pursuit in "The Hound of the Baskervilles" Dr. Watson is discovered to have recovered the full use of his limbs, enabling him to follow the climactic events of the tragedy on the dead run. In "The Adventure of Charles Augustus Milverton" Watson was in a physical condition that permitted him to scale a six-foot wall and then run for two miles without undue difficulty. (Ref: *Leaves From the Copper Beeches*, Livingston Publishing Co., Narberth, Pa., 1959, pages 121–126 inc.)

It should be added that the Irregulars have long agreed that the true author of the stories is Dr. Watson; the fact that the name of the good doctor's literary agent appears as author has also been explained (The Second Collaboration; *The Baker Street Journal*, April 1954, Vol. 4, No. 2 [New Series], page 69). In this exclusive company Sir Arthur is always referred to as the Agent: a higher tribute than any other author of so-called popular literature has ever been paid.

The makeup of the Baker Street Irregulars is notable: some of the most distinguished men and women of science, literature, business, the arts, and politics, make up the roster of this extraordinary fan club devoted to the careers of Sherlock Holmes, Dr. Watson, and the Agent. When considered sufficiently qualified by reason of service and achievement, a member may receive an investiture—at which time he is awarded the canonical recompense of one shilling. The Irregular Shilling has been treasured by some of the greatest names in America.

From their beginning, mystery stories have not lacked endorsement from high levels. In the words of Howard Haycraft: "Abraham Lincoln . . . was the first of the countless eminent men who have turned to the detective story for stimulation and solace." He is reported to have reread Poe's Dupin stories regularly every year. President Woodrow Wilson particularly enjoyed J. S. Fletcher's *The Middle Temple Murder* and praised it publicly. The success of the James Bond stories by Ian Fleming was substantially enhanced when President John F. Kennedy told how much he enjoyed reading the adventures of this larger-than-life superspy. President Franklin D. Roosevelt provided the plot for *The President's Mystery Story.* President Roosevelt was seldom topped, but in this instance he was by Baron Tweedsmuir, the governor general of Canada, who as John Buchan (his correct name) wrote one of the classic spy stories of all time, *The Thirty-Nine Steps.* The work was also memorable because it represents one of the few instances where the motion-picture version (the original one with Robert Donat and Madeleine Carroll) is superior to the original. *Topkapi,* which was made from Eric Ambler's *The Light of Day,* is another.

During much of the Victorian era, and beyond, a novel was not considered to be of satisfactory length unless it ran to a full three volumes—the celebrated three-decker. This requirement caused many authors to indulge in a good deal of stretching, including providing detailed biographies of the characters in the story and explanations of how they got into the mess they were in when the story began. This exposition naturally slowed up the action and imposed a considerable strain on the detective-story writers who were required to maintain suspense and mystery for so long a time. Gradually this need for length lessened until, by 1920, it had passed from the scene. Sherlock Holmes continued to triumph in short stories and in a novel of lesser length, *The Valley of Fear.* Then, not abruptly but visibly, a considerable change took place.

A whole new generation of mystery writers appeared and began to produce work that once again revitalized their medium. The parade of mystery writing never stopped, but there was a period of relative doldrums around the turn of the century until the new wave of talent began to make itself felt. At that point the modern detective story, as it is currently known, came into its own and the position that it occupied has never been relinquished.

Earl Derr Biggers produced the Chinese-American detective of the Honolulu Police Department, Charlie Chan, who subsequently became the central character in numerous motion pictures. His Japanese counterpart, but an altogether different personality, appeared when Mr. Moto bowed into the picture. The variety of detectives, official and otherwise, multiplied, with sheer novelty sometimes the only discernable motive for their creation. Several were blind, the most notable being Max Carrados, who was introduced by Ernest Bramah (a pseudonym). One was more than a hundred years old. Many were women of various ages and occupations. Out of a near maelstrom of entries certain authors and their detectives emerged into permanent world fame.

A complete list of the great detectives and their creators is far beyond the scope of this chapter, but among them can be mentioned—after Sherlock Holmes, of course—such international figures as the late Hercule Poirot (Agatha Christie); Dr. Gideon Fell (John Dickson Carr); Father Brown (G. K. Chesterton); Ellery Queen (Ellery Queen); Jules Maigret (Georges Simenon); Inspector Schmidt (Aaron Marc Stein as George Bagby); Superintendent Gideon (John Creasey as J. J. Marric); Lord Peter Wimsey (Dorothy L. Sayers); Nero Wolfe (Rex Stout); Detective Inspector Napoleon Bonaparte (Arthur W. Upfield); Dr. John Thorndyke

(Richard Austin Freeman); Miss Hildegarde Withers (Stuart Palmer); Sam Spade (Dashiell Hammett); Chief Fellows (Hillary Waugh); Perry Mason (Erle Stanley Gardner); Lew Archer (Ross Macdonald); Philip Marlowe (Raymond Chandler), and many more. All of the above have appeared in long series of stories, but there are others who have made virtuoso appearances that have been all too brief. This regrettable list is headed, obviously, by the Chevalier C. Auguste Dupin. But where there is life in the author there is hope, and we may yet hear more from some highly significant, relative newcomers who have appeared during the past several years.

By the time that the United States was girding up to celebrate its bicentennial, the detective story was firmly established as the most popular form of entertainment reading ever offered to the public. But it had achieved considerably more than that. Admittedly much that was published was of little consequence and quickly disappeared, but a great deal more attained the status of enduring literature. The Father Brown stories of Chesterton are celebrated because of their own merit, not because their author is a great name in English letters. If the novels and stories of Dashiell Hammett are currently receiving fresh attention, it is because they reveal within themselves far more than the cops-and-robbers type action which was their first excuse for being.

Some critics have contended that the mystery story is something that is worthless once read and the secret learned. They fall into the same category as those savants who predicted unfailingly that Robert

Fulton's steamboat would not be able to move upstream. Not every mystery story deserves to be regarded as literature, but just as the Sherlock Holmes stories give a fascinating contemporary view of the Victorian age in London, so the Inspector Napoleon Bonaparte novels of Arthur Upfield provide a compelling overview of the Australian outback.

Much of the time the detective story tells of murder. This is a long established tradition that has Madame L'Espanaye and her daughter Camille as the first victims, a not unlikely consequence of their having taken up residence in the Rue Morgue. And let no purist complain that they were not murdered in the strict technical sense of the term; they were not only murdered, they were done in within a locked room and thus one of the great traditions of the genre was born. But murder within the pages of the detective story is not done so that the readers may fulfill their lust for gore; murder is done because it is an ultimate crime, one which cannot be reversed and for which restitution cannot be made. Even the traitor may in some way, perhaps, manage to undo the effects of his terrible crime, but when the murderer has struck the deed is done and there is no calling it back this side of the Day of Judgment.

It has been pointed out that while there is only one means of getting born, there are unlimited ways in which to die. Therefore the hidden criminal may strike in many different manners, such as the unique means employed in Dorothy Sayers's *The Nine Tailors*. And there are also innumerable places in which to expire against every imaginable background. Many authors of the murder mystery take pains to see that while their victims die, no blood is spilled. Very often, as in most of Hildegarde Withers' adventures, the deceased has already attained that status before he or she is introduced into the story. Only very rarely is the victim someone whom the reader has come to know well, to admire and to like, before demise sets in. This has sometimes happened in the Colonel Hugh North stories of F. Van Wyck Mason, but it is a rarity. Also, the reader for a considerable time was spared attending autopsies, funerals, or interments. More recently these events have been given greater attention and the TV watcher is often taken on trips to the morgue to view the remains.

The comment has frequently been made that the public has a definite taste for violence and enjoys seeing it depicted on the printed page and on the screen. Some movie producers are fond of pointing out that "everyone stops to look at a bad traffic accident." Unfortunately, both statements are probably true, but it does not follow that the fictional detective needs to litter his trail with an array of dismembered corpses in order to attract the reader's attention. One of the happier aspects of murder is that the victim cannot sit up after a suitable interval, assist his revival with a quick brandy, and then give evidence concerning who did him in, why, and how. Dead men (and women) can tell tales, but they must do so passively and therefore give the detective on the case something to challenge his powers.

Violence for its own sake has appeared in detective literature—Mickey Spillane is noted for this—but the detective story does not exist for the purpose of appeasing the reader's Dracula-like tendencies. The true detective story requires the reader to think, to match his wits with those of the investigator in the narrative, and to participate, as it were, in the events as they unfold. If the tale is simply one of smash-bang violence with none of the elements of the classic mystery story, it is likely to die a quick and deserved death. Nick Carter has been kept alive largely by continuous transfusions of printer's ink, but none of the almost countless stories about this well-known character stands out enough to be remembered by name.

The mystery story does have certain limitations, but they are not severe. The development of character, of background, and of human actions, offers unlimited scope. These are prime ingredients of story telling, no matter what format has been chosen or how distinguished the author. The restrictions imposed are those that enhance the mystery story itself and widen its appeal. The author must play fair with his reader; he cannot say, "At that moment Graspingham Featherkill bent over and picked up a small object that lay all but hidden on the rug; after studying it carefully for a moment, he slipped it covertly into his side pocket." If the detective saw the object, the reader must see it too and be given the same chance to apply it as a clue to the solution of the mystery.

The murderer may turn out to be a highly unlikely person, and frequently does, but it is *verboten*, for example, to disclose that the supposed victim in actuality committed suicide. These rules are fundamental although like all rules, they are occasionally broken.

Sometimes the reader may penetrate the mystery; if he does he usually feels quite happy about his achievement. If he is misled, the chances are he will enjoy it even more. There are generally two types of readers who have been through the pages of *The Agony Column* by Earl Derr Biggers: those who were completely fooled, and those who have disgraced themselves by peeking in the back—an unforgivable sin. Another book famous for its surprise ending is *The Murder of Roger Ackroyd* by Agatha Christie, and there is a notable bomb waiting for the reader as he nears the conclusion of *Murder Down Under* by Arthur Upfield. (This superb story was all but ruined by its British title, which virtually gives away the ending.)

Mystery stories of the classic kind are filled with memorable characters, and they constitute the most compelling ingredient. Sherlock Holmes' personality alone would have carried him to international fame. Another detective whose presence dominates every scene in which he appears is Nero Wolfe, who resides at a frequently revised address on West 35th Street in New York.

Probability is not an essential ingredient; some of John Dickson Carr's best locked-room puzzles depend on solutions that are somewhat beyond the edge of likelihood. One of them, at least, was literally done with mirrors, but the best of them display such ingenuity that the fact that it *could* have been done that way is enough. It is a little surprising that the chief of police in a small Connecticut community would have quite as many baffling cases spreading gore on his doorstep as does Chief Fellows of Stockford, but this in no way diminishes the enjoyment of Hillary Waugh's stories of this quietly competent policeman who draws inspiration from the display of fetching nudes that decorates one wall of his office.

Of what use is the mystery story, and how does it advance the world's work? Of what precise practical use is a nocturne by Chopin except as something to play or to listen to? What is the international significance of the all-star game? What is the point of spending extra money to go out on New Year's Eve? And why should a woman buy another dress when she already owns one that fits her reasonably well?

It is possible to fabricate a whole host of reasons why the mystery story is a significant contribution from an entirely practical standpoint, but such rationalizations are not needed. There is no requirement that literature be boring, or confined to reporting the sufferings of various segments of humanity as they endure their wretched lives. *Tom Sawyer* is literature; it is also immensely entertaining. Sufficient to say that the mystery story has more than come of age, and the public has so willed it by providing millions of readers, generation by generation, to be instructed, baffled, and entertained. The standards have steadily risen and the quality of the product continues to improve as men and women from every facet of life turn to it for relaxation, mental stimulation, and escape from endless pressures. They can find the same thing in the inspiration of great music, and they sometimes do both at the same time.

Living—except as a hermit—imposes so many strains and requirements that the human organism and intellect are forced to work under pressures they were not meant to endure. And in modern society the pressures grow worse, not better. We now have dental anesthetics, but we have also gained smog and the Internal Revenue Service. We have Social Security, but it is increasingly difficult to find a little patch of land on which to live.

There is much to be gained by feeling the texture of soil and learning from it that nature still does exist, no matter how distorted and suppressed. There is relief in a good dinner and dancing, in almost any activity that successfully shunts aside the bitter realities that force themselves upon almost everyone as the computers pour out their deluge of bills, regulations, requirements, credit ratings, and harassments of every description. Occasionally the distressed human may lie down to rest, hoping to find some peace within himself. Then how glorious it would be to be awakened by a hand on the shoulder, to look up into the eager, alert face of Sherlock Holmes revealed in the darkness, and hear the blood-pounding words:

"Come, Watson come; the game is afoot!"

TWO

AARON MARC STEIN

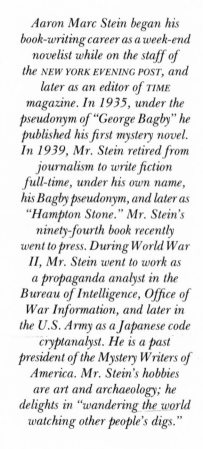

Aaron Marc Stein began his book-writing career as a week-end novelist while on the staff of the NEW YORK EVENING POST, and later as an editor of TIME magazine. In 1935, under the pseudonym of "George Bagby" he published his first mystery novel. In 1939, Mr. Stein retired from journalism to write fiction full-time, under his own name, his Bagby pseudonym, and later as "Hampton Stone." Mr. Stein's ninety-fourth book recently went to press. During World War II, Mr. Stein went to work as a propaganda analyst in the Bureau of Intelligence, Office of War Information, and later in the U.S. Army as a Japanese code cryptanalyst. He is a past president of the Mystery Writers of America. Mr. Stein's hobbies are art and archaeology; he delights in "wandering the world watching other people's digs."

THE MYSTERY STORY IN CULTURAL PERSPECTIVE

Although it is generally agreed that the detective story had its beginnings with the tales of Edgar Allan Poe, it must be recognized that any work of art, if it is not to be "born to blush unseen and waste its sweetness on the desert air," needs more than a creator. It needs as well an audience to which it can speak, one that is prepared to receive it. In the long history of the arts there have been, it is true, occasional prophetic creations which by some miracle survived the indifference of their contemporaries to surface later into recognition, but it can be argued that even such works were not truly before their time. It was not that there was no contemporary audience prepared to listen, but rather that there was an audience not yet aware that it was so prepared.

In his own time Poe and his works were held in relatively low esteem in his native country. It has been suggested that his American contemporaries considered him to be overly preoccupied with death, therefore morbid and unhealthy. It has further been suggested that disapproval of Poe's private life may have also been a factor in the shaping of contemporary attitudes toward his work. Romantic preoccupation with the nonconformist antics of *la vie bohême* belongs to the end of the nineteenth century. The beginning of its fifth decade was too early for such titillations.

Be that as it may, the detective story, despite its American birth, had its earliest post-Poe development in France. This is not to say that the French of the mid-nineteenth century were less concerned with mental health than the Americans of that time, but that they probably defined it differently. It was a Frenchman, after all, who said *cogito ergo sum,* and it would be difficult to find a Frenchman, if not since the time of Pascal at least since the time of the Eighteenth-Century Enlightenment, who, whatever the evidence to the contrary, does not conceive of himself as a thinking man. To the sons of Voltaire and Diderot this new form of fiction in which a reasoned story line led to a neat and inevitable QED was irresistible.

The times in the English-speaking world were also ripe for it; it was only a short time before the word had crossed the channel and English authors avidly began to take up the detective story. From Britain it quickly made the return journey across the Atlantic to reroot itself lustily in the land of its birth.

Why then should this form of fiction have been so long in making its appearance? Why did it have to wait for Poe and the closing years of the first half of the nineteenth century? Tales of crime and its aftermath, and indeed of murder and its aftermath, are as old as the art of storytelling. One does not need to dig far into the works of the ancients to find examples of crime narratives which contain detective-story material.

Before exploring any of these it is well to establish some necessary distinctions. Any work of the imagination in which crime is a major factor may be placed in the broad category of crime fiction. That crime fiction ever since the beginnings of storytelling has constituted a large part of all forms of narrative literature is obvious.

Only recently, however, a matter of a century or less, has crime fiction, or at least some part of it, been institutionalized into a separate genre—that which is called mystery fiction. Although this is something of a misnomer, the term nevertheless has become firmly embedded in the language to cover all varieties of crime fiction which publishers for commercial reasons choose to present in a separate category and which critics, for possibly whimsical reasons, choose to regard as belonging to this separate category.

The border lines in this area have never been sharply defined. *An American Tragedy, The Great Gatsby, The Postman Always Rings Twice, Rebecca,* and *Lolita,* for example, were published not as mystery novels but simply as novels. *The Franchise Affair* and *A Kiss Before Dying,* on the other hand, were placed in the mystery category. Any argument that the distinction is based on considerations of literary merit is not supported by the evidence. Nobody could possibly contend that all, or even much, of what is published under the undepartmentalized label of the novel is of conspicuous literary merit. Among the works that have been published under the mystery label may be found a similar proportion of gold to dross.

Within the broad category of mystery fiction, furthermore, there is a more sharply defined subdivision called detective fiction, a distinct literary form originated by Poe. Detective fiction is a dramatization of a reasoning process concerned with assembling and interpreting data to arrive at the truth that underlies the events of a crime.

Since the detective story is a clearly definable form, it did come to be classified as a separate department of fiction writing. To a considerable extent, furthermore, it drew into its orbit other forms of crime fiction included in the broader category of the mystery, infusing them to a greater or lesser degree with elements of the reasoned search and in that way established the broader and vaguer catchall genre, the mystery story.

A brief examination of some ancient crime stories which contain detective-story material will clarify the distinction.

In the story of Cain and Abel, Genesis provides a passage of Q and A and even an example of that characteristic device of detective-story dialogue in which a suspect seeks to evade an incriminating response by countering question with question: "Am I my brother's keeper?" However, the account of Cain and Abel is not a story of detection. The Interrogator is omniscient. He questions Cain not in an effort to uncover the truth, but only to give the criminal an opportunity to mitigate his guilt by confessing to it. By definition, omniscience has no need for detection.

Sophocles in the *Electra* presents a passage of great detective-story writing. After a long absence Orestes returns to home and homicide. He has come incognito and if he is to hope to accomplish his bloody purpose, he must remain unrecognized. However, his sister, Electra, is on the home scene and she is potentially a valuable ally. He wants to make himself known to her and to her alone. We have, therefore, the recognition scene—a passage of dialogue in which brother and sister like a pair of strange dogs circle one another with equivocal questions until they make the breakthrough and arrive at the recognition.

This episode must be the envy of every detective-story writer, but it is only the one scene. The *Electra* as a whole is not a story of detection. It is not difficult to multiply such examples. Many centuries after Sophocles, though still much predating Poe, we have Shakespeare's *Hamlet,* a work that comes much closer to the form of detective fiction.

If we permit ourselves the barbarism of stripping *Hamlet* of its manifold riches and baring it down to a crude outline of its plot, it can be recognized as a story of detection. It is not, however, a detective story; in modern publishing-house jargon it would be called a suspense story.

Many years ago I encountered *Hamlet* so stripped. It was an early German version—whether it was a tale known to Shakespeare and used as the outline of his tragedy, or just a crude paraphrase of the Shakespearean text is, I believe, not known. It is called *Bestrafte Brudermord,* in English, *Fratricide Punished.* In the event that someone might be offended by the mauling of a masterpiece, let us say that we are discussing *Bestrafte Brudermord,* a work nobody could call untouchable.

In the play the audience is expected to accept the ghost as genuine, to have no doubts of the ghost's veracity, and never to question Claudius's guilt. The suspense hangs not on learning who committed the murder, but on the uncertainty of the outcome of the struggle between Hamlet and Claudius. Who will emerge the winner? Who will be damaged along the way? Who will die?

If we undertake to determine what could be done to convert the plot into a detective story, we can in the process uncover part of the answer to the question we have posed: Why did the detective story have to wait for Edgar Allan Poe and almost the midpoint of the nineteenth century?

A detective-story writer, of course, cannot permit himself a ghost. He must build his proof entirely on hard, physically verifiable fact without any recourse to supernatural assistance. Assuming, however, that when *Bestrafte Brudermord* was written ghosts were accepted as unassailable facts, let us permit the ghost.

There must, however, be a simple shift in what is assumed to be a ghost's supernatural knowledge if we are to start the tragedy off as a detective story. The play's assumption is that the ghost knows what happened to him just before he died, who caused his death, and how the murder was done. If we assume that a ghost's supernatural knowledge is not retroactive to even a moment before the spirit was separated from the body, then we can have the ghost tell Hamlet that he was asleep in his garden. He felt a trickle of liquid in his ear, a sensation which woke him. Someone had stolen up behind him while he slept. As the man bent over him, he could feel the man's hot breath on his skin. He tried to struggle, he tried to turn his head to see the man, but even in his moment of waking he was already under the effect of the poison. He couldn't move. He couldn't cry out. He couldn't turn his head to see his killer. He couldn't even raise his eyelids. The poison had paralyzed him.

That would be the whole of his information. He had been murdered. By whom he wouldn't know. It would then be Hamlet's job to determine that and to bring the killer to justice.

That's good enough for a beginning, but where can we go with it? An unsuspecting Hamlet takes the information to Uncle Claudius? The king, whom we must keep in character, would pretend to be shocked and concerned. He would tell Hamlet that this terrible thing touches him even more deeply than it does Hamlet. The dead king was Hamlet's father, but he was Claudius's brother, and more than that, murder is a crime against the state. Regicide is the most serious crime against the state, and Claudius, now king, is the state.

"Justice is my responsibility. Rest assured, my boy. I shall leave no stone unturned. The murderer will be found. He will be brought to suitable punishment."

Claudius would then choose from the court some unfortunate he would just as soon have out of the way. The poor man would be taken into custody and put to the torture. His agony would wring from him a confession to the crime he had not committed, or failing that, it would continue until he died under it. There isn't much story there.

It is, however, not necessary to do it that way. Hamlet is no fool. Even on his way to see the king he would be thinking about the most likely suspects. It would occur to him that Claudius was the man who had profited most from the untimely death. He would recognize that the official approach wouldn't do, that he would have to go it alone.

So then we are back with the suspense story. There is, however, something to be learned from a quick look at Hamlet's methods of detection. He makes no search for a witness who may have seen Claudius on his way to the scene of the crime, or making his getaway afterward. He makes no attempt to discover the source of the poison. He doesn't question the friendly neighborhood alchemist. He doesn't so much as take a look at the strange old crone down at the end of the lane to whom people have been going for philtres and potions.

He follows the accepted methods of detection of his time. Circumstances, of course, make it impossible for him to put the king to the torture; he cannot haul his royal person off the throne and stretch him on the rack. The hand that holds the scepter cannot be fitted to the thumbscrews, but he does employ the one method of torture available to him—mental torture— and through it he attempts to torment Claudius into a confession, or at least into a damaging admission.

Here then lies part of the reason why the detective story did not make its appearance until the nineteenth century had been almost half-run. As long as the officially practiced, universally accepted means of crime detection was torture, the detective story was impossible.

A modern novelist could attempt a detective story set in some earlier century. A good man is suspected of a crime. The king's agents are searching for him. If they find him, he will be put to the torture. If no confession is wrung from him, the torture will continue until the good man has died under it. His friends spirit him away and keep him in hiding while they do the detection that leads them to the true criminal. By turning the culprit over to the king's agents, they clear their friend. Such a story would be the equivalent of one of those modern detective stories in which the evidence piled up against an innocent man has satisfied the police; he is saved only through the efforts of an amateur sleuth or a private eye who sets the police straight by uncovering the truth.

It is to be doubted that such a story could be done without attributing to characters of an earlier day modes of thought that might not have been possible for them. If we go all the way, however, and assume that such a story could have been written in that earlier day, there is a strong likelihood that it would have been suppressed. A society that looked askance at Beaumarchais' *Figaro* because it called into satiric question the morality of the ruling class, might well have reacted violently to a work that called into doubt the basis of its system of justice.

By Edgar Allan Poe's time there had filtered down into the popular consciousness some of the philosophic thinking of the Eighteenth-Century Enlightenment and with it the political thinking of the American and French Revolutions. Torture had fallen into disrepute, not only because it was cruel; but also because men of the Age of Reason had come to recognize that it wasn't good enough. Torture guaranteed only that punishment would follow crime; it offered no guarantee that it would fall on the right man.

The nineteenth century was a time of optimists. It was thought that if torture had not already disappeared from human societies, it was at least in the process of disappearing. In the twentieth century, one would like to believe that its disappearance has been accomplished, but there is too much evidence to the contrary.

Modern times, however, have brought an important difference: the universal public acceptance of torture is gone. When torture is practiced today it is either concealed and denied, or it is covered by apology. Nobody is advocating it as a good thing. At most it is presented as a disagreeable necessity. We are told that law and order demand it and that our own safety depends on it.

There was also another change crucial to the conception of the detective story. The nineteenth century saw the first organized police forces that were to be responsible only to the law. They displaced the agents of the king who had been responsible only to the royal will. The British bobby and the American cop appeared as ordinary citizens who were doing a job for the protection of the people. It could be believed that they were working in our interest and not for the advantage of someone in power who had hired them to molest us and tyrannize over us.

Earlier crime literature—if it did not deal with crime in high places, the violent deeds of gods and heroes and kings, if it did not in the words of Shakespeare's Richard II "sit upon the ground and tell sad stories of the deaths of kings"—was most likely to be on the side of the criminal. He emerged as the free man, the man who dared to stand up to tyrannical authority. He was Robin Hood. He was the hero of the picaresque novel.

At the level of less serious crime he was the beloved rogue or the merry clown. Plautus and Terence filled Roman comedy with scheming slaves who victimized their brutal owners with clever little dodges. Boccaccio built laughs on the witty confidence games worked by servants on their powerful and dull-witted masters. Although the small triumphs of the underdog and the entertaining antics of the turning worm persisted in literature through the nineteenth century, and still engage the talents of fiction writers to the undiminished delight of their audiences, the centuries-old automatic alignment with the lawbreaker was shaken where it was not destroyed.

Prior to the eighteenth-century emergence of free societies, crime could essentially be defined as any act that threatened the authority or prerogatives of the ruler. It was the commission of an act by a person whose station in life did not grant him the right to that act. In the face of the *droit du seigneur*, rape was not defined entirely by the act itself. Its criminality was at least to some extent determined by who committed the act. In societies where one class exercised an absolute and arbitrary power over life and death, murder could be regarded as the usurpation by someone of the lower orders of the ruling power's right to kill. The highwayman was a robber. The robber baron was a baron. Undertaken by the man up in the castle, kidnapping was high finance.

In any society where police authority is seen to be the protector of the powerful in their privileges, the sympathy of most men would tend to lie with the criminal. No man could be sure that one day he might not fall afoul of the royal whim.

It was only with the emergence of free societies that there developed in the consciousness of most men the concept of a delinquent class, a concept of clear separation between ourselves, the law-abiding, and the criminals. In such societies with the replacement of the agents of the king by an organized detective police force that operated under a body of law instead of under royal command, popular attitudes toward the police power changed. The bobby or the cop was seen to be on our side. He became an acceptable hero.

This new attitude became dominant, but it never completely displaced the old. It was a factor in making the detective story with its basically pro-establishment orientation possible, but in parallel development the anti-establishment, criminal-as-a-free-man, beloved-rogue story persisted.

Without these changes in political and social climate the detective story could never have evolved, but there was yet another event that more than any other was central to the invention and development of the form. It was a change in intellectual attitudes. Out of the Age of Reason there had come into the general consciousness a new hero, the man of science.

Out of his efforts there was to be created a better world, a world from which crime, want, inequity, and injustice would disappear. Consider, for example, that most optimistic of nineteenth-century philosophies that predicted the ultimate withering away of even the supreme criminal, government itself. It was, of course, the emergence of the man of science as the new hero that brought about science fiction.

The detective story developed as a form of science fiction. In its classic form, it is still a fictional celebration of scientific method, of the process of inductive reasoning. Nineteenth-century man was not blinded by his optimism. He recognized that in the brave new world the men of science and the men of reason were to create, some substitute for torture would be needed if crime was to be detected and controlled.

The new hero was to be the man who did the job. Proceeding by scientific method, he would examine the available data with the eye of a trained observer. The fact that in the work of the detective the data would be called evidence was a difference only of language. From the available data he would form a hypothesis. In accordance with Occam's razor it would be the simplest hypothesis that could contain the known facts. Guided by his hypothesis, he would search for additional data, new evidence. He would keep his hypothesis fluid, reshaping it as necessary to contain new evidence as it emerged. By this process he would accumulate all the evidence and would reason from it the final proof, the one and only hypothesis capable of containing all the evidence.

The nineteenth-century conception of science was far broader than the laboratory-oriented view of it commonly held in our time. The natural sciences were looked upon only as parts of the whole; philosophy, ethics, and law, for example, were also to be transformed by the application of scientific method. Vestiges of this attitude are still to be found in our university curricula. Courses are still given, for instance, in political science.

Central to this attitude was total reliance on observable fact and logical processes. The Eighteenth-Century Enlightenment had transformed men's minds, and men now were in the process of transforming their world. The detective-story hero, therefore, emerged as this nineteenth-century man, the devotee of fact, the child of reason. Of just such stuff Sherlock Holmes was made.

However, if the detective story was to have the tension it required, this genius of detection had to be opposed by a worthy adversary, a genius of crime who would provide a proper challenge through his skill at concealing the data, or masking them, or scrambling them into deceptive patterns. Holmes needed his Moriarty.

The detective story, accordingly, developed into a double contest. There was the battle of wits waged between the detective and the criminal, and there was also the contest of wits played between the author and his readers. The reader was drawn into competition with the detective in observation of the data and in reasoning from them.

Insofar as it was a game, it was necessary that it have rules, and the detective story developed as a highly structured, formal art. Robert Frost remarked of free verse that it was like playing tennis without a net; not necessarily a bad game, only a different one. A detective story that does not observe the rules, however, is like playing tennis with neither a net nor a court. It would degenerate into an aimless batting about of balls.

The rules are simple. All the data must be presented to the reader. When he is confronted with the solution, he must be left with the conviction that if he had not failed to take notice of a piece of evidence when it was given to him, or if he had reasoned properly from the available data, he would have achieved the solution on his own. If the surprise of the solution depends on information not offered to the reader, then the author has violated the form. If misleading data are offered and are not counterbalanced by the presentation of other data that would identify the earlier evidence as irrelevant, then again the author is violating the form.

As the form developed, it inevitably departed more and more widely from the actualities of crime and detection. The genius detective, whether a police officer, a private operator, or a brilliant amateur, has seldom existed in the flesh. In the actual world the great scientific mind did not often apply itself to a career of crime detection. A young person of suitable potential, confronted with the choice between a university scholarship to study mathematics or physics and the opportunity to enroll in a police academy where he could earn while he learned, invariably would choose the university.

Why? Because the academic career is more prestigious? The acclaim that would come to a detective able to operate at the level of a Sherlock Holmes, a Nero Wolfe, a Hercule Poirot, or a Lord Peter Wimsey would be great enough to satisfy even the most immortality-hungry individual. Out of consideration for personal safety? Consider the scientific researchers who have pursued dangerous experiments, pressing forward in magnificent disregard of dangers to their health or even to their lives. It would be difficult to conceive of a moment of hazard that could exceed the one when Enrico Fermi gave the signal for the movement of the control rods that initiated the first chain reaction. The young who combine a lust to meet danger with a capacity for science aspire not to be detectives, but to be astronauts.

The choice of a career in one of the scientific disciplines over a career as a detective is made because the scientist is guaranteed a continuing challenge. The detective can expect to go through his whole career and rarely, if ever, be confronted with a case that will fully test his powers. He has little hope of ever confronting a worthy antagonist.

Criminals in the actual world are stupid people. Those who seem clever are merely the skilled practitioners of their specialties. Hotel thieves are glib. Pickpockets are manually dexterous. Confidence men are persuasive. None of these is a great brain. If one considers violent crime, one is likely to arrive at a picture of inverse proportion. The greater the level of violence, the lower the level of intelligence.

Of all criminals, the greatest dullards are likely to be the murderers. In cases where a murderer appears to be a person of any considerable mental capacity, during the commission of murder he is likely to be at least temporarily stupified by the emotional impact of his act. He will be in no condition to play intricate games of move and countermove with a genius of detection.

Any writer of detective stories must at some time have been haunted by the thought that out there in the real world there must be perfect crimes, murders that have never been solved because it was impossible to recognize them as murders; deaths that have successfully been staged to present the unassailable appearance of suicide or accident. If there are any such, they have been successful, not because they presented evidence that could not be unscrambled, but because they presented no evidence at all.

A New York City Police Department detective defined the difference. "The detective of fiction," he said, "depends on clues. The police officer depends on informants."

Most actual murder cases that are solved solve themselves. In the event that a difficult one is handled successfully, it is probably because somebody talked. If the murder is not a family affair or the result of obvious hostilities in the victim's immediate circle, and if there is nobody to talk, the case will probably remain unsolved. The difference between a detective-story case and a baffling actual case is the difference between the difficult but complete jigsaw puzzle and the puzzle that can never be done because too many of the pieces are missing.

It must be conceded that there have been examples of successful police work in cases which at first sight did not solve themselves. At the simplest level a persistent mugger who kills and robs and leaves the scene unobserved might eventually be brought to justice if he works one area regularly, and if the police department can spare the manpower to play the patient game of keeping the area under surveillance until the mugger is caught in the act.

Valuable as such police work unquestionably is, it does not make a detective story. It is a story of patience, of dogged pursuit, and to a great extent, a story of luck. It cannot be converted into a celebration of the process of inductive reasoning.

For an illustration of the difference we can consider an actual murder case in which detectives, both professional and amateur, did attempt to operate at the detective-story level.

Some years ago in Manhattan's fashionable upper East Side the Wylie-Hoffert murders electrified the affluent and eminently respectable neighborhood. Three young women shared an apartment. One of the three came home late in the afternoon to find in one of the bedrooms the murdered and mutilated bodies of her two fellow tenants.

The police, surveying the scene, arrived at the hypothesis that the killings were the work of a sex maniac. The nature of the mutilations inflicted on the two young women so indicated.

The police made all the available moves. They questioned the neighbors. Nobody had seen anything; nobody had heard anything. They inspected the apartment building and learned that inadequate security left the service entrance unprotected for considerable periods of time. They questioned the young women's office associates. They took a hard look at all the young men the two victims had been dating, investigating most assiduously those gentlemen whose hair lengths or life-styles were not in accordance with what police officers of that day considered suitable. They brought in for questioning all known sexual deviates they could locate. But on all sides they came up empty-handed. There were simply no clues.

While they were so engaged, across the river in Brooklyn a woman reported to the police that a youth had attempted to molest her sexually on a public street in the morning hours well before dawn. The police scoured the neighborhood and picked up a young man, physically ill-favored, mentally deficient, unemployed, and aimlessly on the loose.

When they arranged for the complaining woman to view the youth, she identified him as her molester. The method used by the police to set up the viewing for identification was later called into serious question, but at that point the matter stood with the accused identified by the complainant.

Since in Manhattan the New York County police were looking at sexual deviates and the Kings County police in Brooklyn had in custody a man accused of odd sexual behavior, a detective who had worked on the Wylie-Hoffert murders came to look at the accused.

Among the objects found in the young man's pockets at the time of his arrest was a snapshot of a pretty, well-dressed, well-groomed young woman. In the opinion of the Manhattan detective the photograph looked very much like the late Miss Wylie. He questioned the young man about it and all he could elicit was a statement that it was a photograph of his girl friend. The youth refused to divulge her name or her whereabouts.

Since the Manhattan crime was by far the more serious, the young man was turned over to the Manhattan police for questioning. He was soon charged with the murders and assigned a court-appointed attorney. The attorney examined the photograph. To his eye it was anything but an overwhelmingly convincing likeness of the murdered Miss Wylie.

He questioned his client about it, but he was unable to draw from the young man anything more than the story he had already given to the police. Not satisfied, the lawyer began to do some detective work. He learned that at the time of his client's arrest, the young man had only recently arrived in Brooklyn from a small town on the New Jersey shore.

The attorney then visited the town, and since he was a sound man, assiduous on behalf of his client and the proper administration of justice, and since the town was small, he succeeded in finding the young woman of the photograph. She identified it as a snapshot of herself, but was unable to explain how it could have come into the possession of the murder suspect.

He was not, and had never been, her boyfriend. She had never known him, had never seen him, and had never so much as heard of him. She had not liked the photograph. In her opinion, it did not do her justice. The last time she had seen it had been when she had thrown it away in the trash.

The lawyer also succeeded in locating a group of young men who had known the accused before he had left for Brooklyn. They knew the photograph. The young man had shown it to them and had boasted that it was a picture of his girl friend. They had never believed him. He was homely, he was not bright, and he spent most of his time scavenging in the garbage of the town dump. In the opinion of his peers it was hardly credible that he could have any girl friend, much less one who was clean, well-dressed, and well-groomed.

The attorney returned to New York. When he confronted his client with the information he had picked up in the youth's hometown, the young man broke down and admitted that the snapshot was just something he had salvaged from the dump. All the other fellows had girls. All the other fellows could boast of their conquests. He alone was different. He never had had a girl. With the picture he had only been trying to establish himself as one of the boys.

The lawyer took this information to the District Attorney's office. The prosecutor agreed that the one item of evidence, the photograph, had been eliminated. It was his contention, however, that under questioning the accused had made damaging admissions. Although the youth's attorney was convinced that his dull-witted client could be manipulated into saying almost anything, it made no difference. The murder charge against the youth was not dropped.

While the unfortunate young man was in custody awaiting trial, an unsolicited informant appeared. He was a drug addict, who had been arrested for the killing of another addict. To save himself, he volunteered the information that an addict friend of his had killed the two girls. The police bugged the informant's apartment and the informant led his friend into conversations which on tape convinced the jury.

The Wylie-Hoffert case had solved itself, and the poor lad who had never had a girl friend was returned to Brooklyn to stand trial on the lesser charge still pending against him there.

Any reader of the works of Erle Stanley Gardner will recognize that the court-appointed attorney in this case attempted to operate as both Perry Mason and Paul Drake. The Paul Drake part of the job he did and did well. The Perry Mason part—taking the information into court, blowing the case wide open, and confounding the prosecution by producing the true killer—he was unable to do.

It was, however, through no lack of will or lack of ability that he could not do it. It was because the evidence was not available. Furthermore, when it did become available, it was not through the efforts of anyone connected with the investigation or through the exercise of anyone's investigatory skills.

The detective story, therefore, developing as a celebration of scientific method through the dramatization of the process of inductive reasoning, created worlds of its own, worlds only tenuously connected to the world as we experience it. Before it may be condemned on these grounds, however, it is well to remember that in the total history of the arts, as men have practiced them through the millennia of historical record, and through earlier periods that are recorded for us only by their artifacts, naturalism, *verismo,* and slice-of-life representation speak for only one band of the great and various spectrum.

If one accepts the dictum that art, if it is to have any relation to truth, must be aleatory, operating as life appears to operate, pulled along by blind chance from chaos to chaos, then obviously the detective story does not qualify. But by this measure, virtually everything else man has called art will fall with the detective story, eliminated because it is contrived, an artifice, untrue.

If, therefore, we may except the aleatory, we must recognize that even the most naturalistic works are made with contrivance and artifice. If we accept that a work of art creates its reality through the cosmic organization of whatever piece of the chaos of actuality the artist has chosen to organize, we must recognize that the simple act of selection, as it lifts out of the surrounding chaos and isolates for representation one chosen piece, is a contrivance and an artifice.

The relationship of actuality to artistic realities can most easily be examined in the visual arts. On superficial acquaintance with painting and sculpture some people are inclined to assume that anything that diverges at all from the most literal naturalistic representation so diverges from a lack of skill on the part of the artist. On a slightly more sophisticated level there might be some recognition of the limitations of tools and of materials. Whether the artist alone is faulted, or whether he is permitted to share the fault with his tools and his materials, the judgment remains that for a work to fall at all short of literal naturalistic representation does constitute a fault. It is reasoned that if he had been good enough at his job, he would have created a likeness.

Exploration of the visual arts, however, quickly begins to chip away at this judgment. Works that make little or no concession to naturalistic literalness in representation frequently display such consummate skill and competence in other aspects of the art that it is difficult to believe that the artist could not have accomplished anything he chose to do. If he has produced no likeness, it would have to be concluded that doing a likeness had been no part of his purpose.

More direct evidence of the artist's intent is often available. Consider Byzantine mosaics where, with a dazzle of light and color, the artists delineated in rigidly schematized, highly formal style the characters of Old and New Testament stories and the figures of saints, of kings, and of queens. There are such mosaics where, along with the sternly schematized eminences, the artists chose to put in some ordinary people as observers of the scene. These little nobodies are represented with a high degree of naturalism. They have the look of portraits done from life.

Since the artists demonstrated their ability at handling this greater degree of naturalism, why did they deny it to the major characters in the stories they depicted?

It was done by intention. They were creating a deliberate distinction. There was the world of appearance and the ordinary people who inhabited that world, but there was also this other world the artists had created, the world of the divine personages. That kings and queens were included in this world of the divine was no anomaly. It was widely accepted that royal personages ruled by divine right.

Similarly, at Wells Cathedral in Somerset the great Gothic sculptures of the Holy Company are highly schematized. Where the South transept joins the crossing, however, there are carved capitals that show a woman drawing a thorn out of her foot and boys stealing apples—little naturalistic scenes of genre portraiture. Here again it is the deliberate establishment of a distinction between the world as it appears to be and a world as it doesn't appear to be, the contrast between the earthly and the divine.

There is no need to multiply examples. Artists select whatever aspect or segment of the actual world they choose to explore and celebrate. Through the process of isolation and development they convert what they have chosen into a world of their own invention. Through this world a successful work of art has something to say about actuality and reality.

The choice made by the detective-story writers was the exploration and celebration of the process of inductive reasoning. For this purpose the detective, no matter how naturalistically he is characterized, is necessarily transferred to a world as it is not.

His world, so far as the progress of his own operations is concerned, has to be free of chance and accident. If there are to be lucky breaks, they will break only for his antagonist because the detective represents an abstraction, namely scientific method, just as the characters in the old mystery plays represent abstractions—Patience, for example, or Greed or Chastity or Folly.

As the puzzle-detective story developed, it took on more and more of the character of abstract art. By the end of the first quarter of this century it was moving toward the extremes of abstraction, but in that respect it was no more than moving in step with other arts of the time. Pablo Picasso and Georges Braque with the fragmentations of their analytical cubism were creating a world of their own for the exploration and celebration of the geometry of forms. Composers were well into the mathematical constructions of the twelve-tone row.

Among the arts involved in this move toward abstraction the detective story, however, was the only one that was truly a popular art. A painter could keep going with a few patrons. Composers fared less well but there were some funds for the subsidization of performances. The detective-story writers on the other hand, were producing entertainments, and entertainments were expected to be self-supporting.

The reading public that followed the detective story into this, its most formal and abstract phase, was enthusiastic and faithful, but its numbers were decreasing. As an example of this type of story, there is the Agatha Christie novel that appeared under three different titles but is perhaps most widely known as *And Then There Were None.* As an antidote to its abstraction it whipped up an atmosphere of unremitting menace and suspense, but at the cost of its validity as a detective story.

The game it played with its readers was essentially a fraud in that it engaged its audience in the detective-story contest to detect the killer and at its conclusion it failed to detect him, but instead aborting the puzzle by offering a confession in place of a reasoned solution.

In such stories the form was approaching the place where it would be almost totally cerebral, with characters recognizable only as symbols moved about in a game of wits: bloodless people, carrying bloodless corpses through the maze of a formal garden.

The detective story never quite reached that ultimate, since in that direction lay no wider public. It took instead the direction of a return toward a higher degree of naturalism. It emerged from those isolated country houses designed not so much for habitation as for the satisfaction of an Aristotelian unity of place. It fleshed out the characters who had been thinning down to symbols that were free of all vice but murder.

Despite these changes, however, it has remained at the heart of the matter what it had been, still a formal work in celebration of scientific method. Even though the detective might now be required to soak up in all the likely and unlikely parts of his anatomy a multitude of blows, even though his survival may have come to a large extent to depend on his ability to slug and shoot, he is still in there assembling the data and reasoning from it. That his cerebration may be taking place under a rain of bullets makes it no less a dramatization of the logical process.

Such changes reflected in the detective story, as similar changes did in other forms of the novel, a popular readiness to take a less limited view of the nature of man, to recognize him as possessed of not only mind and heart, but also of muscle, bone, blood, and the full assortment of glands and organs.

In the detective story, however, further changes appeared and are still appearing. Although that first post-Poe development did take place in France, it was writers in English who took the form to its full flowering. However much French writers may have been enamored of the logical story line, since they were working out of a culture that subscribed to the Code Napoleon, they were somewhat hampered in the processes of plot development. At the heart of the classic detective story lies that admirable eccentricity of Anglo-Saxon justice, the presumption of innocence. If you are to have readers who will take the side of the detective, you must either have detectives who are devoted to the presumption of innocence, or detectives who are working counter to the established system of justice.

Lawyers will object that in practice the presumption of innocence does not come into play as any part of the process of detection. It is instead an obligation on jurors when in their hearing of the evidence and in their deliberations on the proffered evidence, they must assess its validity.

In the detective story the presumption of innocence appears as a quality of the detective's mind. It is a corollary of his devotion to fact, to all facts. Georges

Simenon's Inspector Maigret, even though he does operate under the Code Napoleon, is in this fashion so much dedicated to the presumption of innocence that again and again he contrives to hold his investigations away from the public prosecutor and the magistrates until he has assembled all the facts and has fitted them into an inescapable pattern of proof.

All through the period when the development toward extreme abstraction was taking place, there were other writers who took a tougher and more cynical view of the processes of crime and detection. They found justice in free societies not so much changed from the old ways when it was an instrument for the protection of the powerful. Their work appeared among the dime novels and the penny dreadfuls and in the pulp magazines. Although these outlets did run heavily to hack work, but perhaps no more heavily than did the hardcover product that was accepted as respectable, there was much good writing done at this level, and it was here, possibly, that the twentieth-century crime story first developed social and moral sensitivity.

It was here that the so-called hard-boiled school took its shape, and from here it emerged into what was considered respectable publishing, coming as an alternative to the extremes of abstraction. It has been the strongest American contribution to the form, and it has had worldwide influence and popularity.

Dashiell Hammett's Continental Op can serve as an example. He is a dirty fighter engaged in a dirty game. He operates as he does because in a totally corrupt society there is no other way to operate, and the dirty game is the only game in town. His only loyalty is loyalty to his job and he is aware that in doing it he is also corrupted, but he never pretends that he stands apart from the corruption in which he lives.

Ever since the time of the turning away from the extremes of abstraction, the two styles—the classic whodunit and the more free-wheeling hard-boiled story—have coexisted, and have enjoyed a symbiotic relationship. The celebrations of the process of inductive reasoning have never disappeared. They have gained force and credibility insofar as they have been influenced by the hard-boiled school. On the other hand, the private eyes and the vigilante-minded individualists are also in some part men of reason.

The faith and the optimism out of which the detective story was born are, however, no longer as strong as they had been. The governments of free men that were to be created out of the Age of Reason are now found to be flawed. Faith in the perfectibility of man through intellectual processes has been shaken. Questions arise about the police and other government investigatory agencies. Are they, as we had thought, dedicated to our service, or have they become latter-day equivalents of the agents of the king, engaged to molest us and tyrannize over us?

These doubts and these questions, earlier manifested in the pulps, are increasingly reflected in the detective story today. We have the private eye or the embattled citizen. He does the job because the police are ineffective, or because through corruption they have moved over to the side of the criminals. We have had the rogue cop, but we are also having the one honest cop who battles single-handedly against a rogue system. The spy story has moved from recounting the activities of incorruptible gentlemen in pursuit of international careers of derring-do to explorations of double-dealing where trust is folly and there is no wisdom that is not suspicion.

We also now have the city-street vigilante. He sees himself as detective, prosecutor, jury, judge, and executioner because he is convinced that the whole system has broken down and that there will be no justice but that which he metes out with his own hand. Where now is the presumption of innocence?

Whether we like these developments or not, they must be recognized for what they are: reflections of the malaise of our own time, just as the beginnings of the detective-story form were reflections of the faith in reason of the nineteenth-century inheritors of the thought of the Enlightenment.

THREE

HILLARY WAUGH

Hillary Waugh writes because, in his own words, he cannot NOT write. Though he aspired to make a career of art (cartooning) and music (popular songs), Mr. Waugh first tried his hand at mystery writing while flying in World War II as a Navy pilot. His first effort sold, and Mr. Waugh was hooked on writing. Since then, he has published some thirty-four novels in the United States and abroad, most of them in the crime and mystery fields. One of his novels, LAST SEEN WEARING . . . , was chosen by the LONDON TIMES as one of the one-hundred best mysteries ever written. Mr. Waugh writes under his own name and two pseudonyms: Harry Walker and H. Baldwin Taylor. He is a pioneer in the field of police procedurals, and a past president of the Mystery Writers of America.

THE MYSTERY VERSUS THE NOVEL

There is an awareness on the part of most readers that the mystery per se is something separate and distinct from the novel itself. This fact of fiction is acknowledged both by the devotees of the mystery form and by its detractors; the term "mystery" is applied to a specific type of novel to set it apart from the so-called "straight" or "serious" novel.

There is a difference, that is true, but the degree of difference depends upon how we define the term "mystery." Time was when "mystery story" meant "*detective* story"; then the tale was a puzzle and little else. More and more, however, the parameters of the genre have broadened and where they now lie is more a matter of personal viewpoint than of any objective line of demarcation. Nowadays suspense stories have come under the umbrella of mystery fiction so that Harper & Row even labels each book in its mystery line as "A Harper Novel of Suspense." Spy stories are called mysteries; chase and adventure yarns come under the heading. Gothics, those tales of romance and suspense, are a part of the field, and even some ghost stories can be included. Anything that involves crime or the threat of crime is eligible. So is anything that pits the forces of good against evil—and evil can mean anything from Count Dracula to Hitler's minions.

This covers, we might note, a rather broad area. In fact, not much is left over for the field of straight fiction. Mystery writers induct into the fraternity not only the likes of Edgar Allan Poe, but also Dostoevski *(Crime and Punishment)*, Shakespeare (any tragedy with the possible exception of Lear), Victor Hugo *(Les Miserables)*, and anyone else who has produced a work of fiction involving criminous activity.

Quite obviously, if we are going to use this broad type of criterion, then we will have to say that the only difference between mystery fiction and straight fiction is that the former involves criminal wrongdoing and the latter doesn't—a distinction too meaningless to acknowledge.

Yet there is a difference, and everyone knows it. Shakespeare wrote about crime, but he was not a mystery writer in the sense that Agatha Christie was a mystery writer. Inasmuch as the mystery novel, especially in America, has traditionally been regarded as second-class fiction and its top practitioners as less worthy of note than the most hapless of straight novelists, the insistence of mystery writers in embracing the literary giants of history as kissing kin may well be nothing more than an attempt to overcome an ill-begotten inferiority complex.

If we are to separate the mystery from the novel and recognize the similarities and the differences, we must more adequately define our terms. We must find the areas of distinction that identify one and not the other. We must construct a discriminatory sieve that will firmly hold the likes of Earl Derr Biggers' *Charlie Chan Carries On* in the mystery genre and turn loose such as Theodore Dreiser's *An American Tragedy*.

Is it a matter of length? Mysteries, in all their recognized forms, are pretty standard in this regard. Generally speaking, the range is from 185–225 pages, or 60,000 to 70,000 words. Gothics are longer and a reader expects closer to 300 pages or 110,000 words in that form. The moment a book gets into the 350-pages-and-up range, even if it deals with crime, it will be accepted by editors and public alike as "more than a mystery."

Length, though indicative, is not a valid measure; quite obviously length does not determine greatness and we must not pretend that extra pages are a hallmark of distinction. There are too many gems of classic fiction—*The Red Badge of Courage* for one—that deliver their message in beautiful brevity.

Another totem that is supposed to identify the mystery is that it is read for "entertainment." The mystery is supposed to be light reading, something that doesn't require serious involvement; a piece to be ingested for relaxation, for fun, for pleasure.

But what does this tell us? Are we to conclude that books of merit are literary spinach: ("You won't like it, but it's good for you")? That argument won't wash. Shakespeare, Dickens, Austen, Hardy—the list is long—were, and are, enormously popular. Dull novels are bad novels and will not sell, but dull mysteries won't sell either. So it is not a matter of bad writing versus good writing, or fun reading versus dull reading, short books versus long books, or crime stories versus non-crime stories. The subgenre of the mystery is isolated from the rest of fiction by other criteria.

To make the distinction, we need to dig deeper and realize that the mystery has been growing and expanding, maturing, and almost leaving its old self behind. In fact, the more the mystery probes into character and issues and the makeup of the human animal—and it is doing this—the more it is departing from its original format and outgrowing its original aims. If the spy is no longer fighting the forces of evil to rescue the kidnapped scientist, but is, instead, coping with the cynicism of his trade and his own expendability, or learning to live with the realization that his life is a cipher, then we are leaving what used to be the mystery form and entering into the field of the straight novel. Even if the spy is rescuing the scientist while he's having his self-doubts, we are dealing with a different kind of book. The original essence of the mystery is becoming hidden beneath additional layers of what would be called "serious" writing. (How serious the writing actually is, of course, depends upon the talent and insight of the author.)

To lay bare the bones of the mystery itself, we should turn back in time to the point of greatest separation, to the period when the distinction between a mystery story and a novel was the most unmistakable. We must return to the era of the puzzle story, to the fantasyland of mystery—before Hammett and Chandler moved murder out of the prim neatness of the drawing room and into the blood and guts of the back alley, which more closely approximates where actual murders occur and what they are like. We must get away from the subsequent *approachment* toward "realism" that led to the private-eye and the gangsters *cum* nightclub, which gave way to the later world of the detective squad and the police procedural. We should return to the artificial world of Hercule Poirot and Philo Vance, of Charlie Chan and Ellery Queen, to the heyday of the intellectual detective when every murder was compound-complex and ratiocination was all.

We use for our model those long-ago stories and their never-never world because those tales, for all time, represent the essence of the mystery. They were tales from which everything else had been distilled. Here lay, for all to view, the artifacts of the pure mystery, the articulated skeleton of the whole art form. Whatever has since happened to the mystery—and much has—is overlay. Flesh, nervous systems, muscles, blood, and clothing of various kinds have been added, but the true mystery today still has the same old skeleton deep down underneath. It's just a little harder to find and therein lies a tale—but there are several tales to be told about this particular skeleton.

In those bygone days of the classical detective story, when the skeleton first stirred itself in permanent form, the puzzle was the thing. The reader was presented with a crime, a handful of clues, a cast of suspects, and a detective against whom to match wits. The object of the game was to beat the detective to the solution. Quite obviously, under those conditions, the difference between reading a mystery story—"detective" story in that context—and a straight novel was equivalent to the difference between doing a newspaper crossword puzzle and reading the columnists. Yet, despite the obviousness of the difference, there is more kinship here—as we shall shortly discover—than meets the eye. It is this kinship that has enabled the mystery to develop to the point where it successfully challenges straight fiction on the best-seller lists and enjoys an everbroadening base of popularity. Let us examine these bones, then, and determine why this form of literature, the mystery story, is to the novel what the sonnet is to poetry.

Let it be recognized first that the skeleton that structures the classical puzzle story is nothing more or less than a series of ironclad rules. These rules became essential in order to present the puzzle properly and also in the interests of fair play. The book, remember, was a battleground between author and reader—with the reader trying to outguess the detective and beat him to the criminal, and the author trying to waylay, bemuse, and trick the reader so the detective would get there first. Since the author was in control, his efforts to win had to be restricted to make sure that the reader had an equal chance.

The first and most obvious rule of fair play was the requirement that *every clue discovered by the detective had to be made available to the reader.* The author could try to discount it as a clue, misconstrue its meaning, or hide it amid a lot of inconsequential garbage—but he had to show it. It had to be there so that at the end of the book, when the detective revealed its true nature, the reader would be able to say, "You beat me that time," but he could not say, "You left out a piece of the puzzle."

Rule two was: *Early introduction of the murderer.*

Obviously it would be unfair for the author to introduce a totally new character on page 214 and name him as the murderer on page 215. All suspects must be prominent throughout—known if not shown.

Rule three: *The crime must be significant.*

To elicit reader involvement, the problem in question had to be of sufficient seriousness for the reader to want to see it solved—to want to solve it himself. Since murder is the most serious crime of all, most mystery stories are murder mysteries. By choosing murder as the crime, the mystery writer automatically fulfills that requirement.

Rule four: *There must be detection.*

The crime in a detective story doesn't solve itself, nor does it go away. An effort must be made to solve the crime. In fact, the *raison d'etre* of these early detective stories *is* the solving of the crime.

Rule five: *The number of suspects must be known and the murderer must be among them.*

This is the fair-play element again and the method generally adopted in obeying this injunction was the construction of an enclosed universe inhabited solely by victims, suspects, murderer, and detective. One of the commonest such universes was the mansion full of guests, cut off from the outside world by a storm or other expedient, thus insuring that when the murder occurs, the killer must be among those present.

So far these requirements, while restrictive, do not seem onerous. But lastly there comes the one that does draw the binding tight. Since the story is a puzzle and a contest of wits between author and reader, the reader, as part of the game of fair play, has the right to expect that nothing will be included in the book that does not relate to or in some way bear upon the puzzle.

This is, incontrovertibly, a logical request and one that cannot be denied. It is, however, a crushing liability to the author. It is demanded of him that there be nothing extraneous in his story. All scenes, all events, all effects (and this includes red herrings) are to relate to and bear upon the puzzle—the creation and solution of which is the story.

The author is not allowed to rhapsodize over Renaissance art or the poetry of Keats—if that be his fancy. He is not to go into irrelevant detail on the workings of the Palomar telescope or the Gatun locks. Relevant details, yes, but not irrelevant.

It is a brutal blow. The author of the highly disciplined detective story is tightly fenced, his limitations severe. Admittedly, to the writer who has the wit and the relish, the strictures offer challenge. First, he must learn how to work within these disciplines and, thereafter, when he has mastered that art, how to maximize whatever opportunities he is afforded. Finally, he must learn to make the disciplines work for *him*.

Nevertheless, the boundaries are narrow. The mystery writer does not have the freedom to digress into his philosophy of life while the action stands still. This does not mean philosophy is not permitted, nor does it mean that Renaissance art or Keats cannot be evaluated, nor that background cannot be given on 200-inch telescopes or canal locks. It only means that he must create plots and story lines of such nature that they will be furthered and developed through such discussion.

It is a harsh stricture. But all of the requirements of the detective story are harsh strictures. Certainly, the writer of a mystery novel is working under a much tighter rein than the straight novelist who can roam pretty much at will—or at least he thinks he can—over the whole landscape of his intellect.

These, then, are the emblems which identify the mystery novel and set it apart from the rest of fiction. Times have changed, of course, and the mystery has changed with them. No longer is it deemed sufficient to present the puzzle in a vacuum. No longer are characters made of cardboard, distinguishable from each other only by name and by sex. No longer do they serve merely as tokens to be moved on the puzzle board. Background can, without betraying the nature of the genre, add spice and purpose to the tale. The stories can come out of their closed universe and take place in the real world. Schools of the mystery can develop: the hard-boiled school, the private-eye school, the cute young couple, the blood and sex, and the police procedural. These things can happen. All kinds of flesh can be laid upon the bones.

Many variations of the theme can also be played: Whodunit? Howdunit? Howcatchem? Stories can be told backwards and sideways. Yet, through it all, the same distinguishing bones lie underneath, only slightly modified over the years—and then only in response to the changing view of the readership. If the disciplines are not as rigidly restrictive as they used to be, it's because the reader is no longer being approached as nothing more than a puzzle-solver. Today's aficionado is more interested in being entertained than puzzled—

perhaps he always was—and a little relaxation of the codes is permitted to serve the aim of entertainment. But the codes are all still in force and a mystery novelist who sits down to plot a book today automatically obeys the rules.

One might now ask, since it is time to direct our attention to the straight novel, is there any advantage to the above? Let the mystery writer learn his craft; let him become facile in plot manipulation, clue planting, and the rest. Does this serve him any useful purpose above and beyond his own specific subgenre in the field of fiction? If one aims to write novels, is the mystery in any way a training ground?

An obvious advantage in writing mysteries lies in the disciplining of a talent. The greatest genius in any field, from athlete to concert pianist, will, to the degree that he develops and trains his talent, be greater than before. The demands that are made upon a mystery writer, if he is to flex his muscles within that framework, will hone his talent.

A counterreply can also arise. If the field of the mystery is so firmly structured, does one need talent to become competent? Is there not a difference between craftsmanship and talent? And would not craftsmanship be a sufficient commodity with which to work successfully in this medium? On the other hand, does not talent rise above rules? Would not a great talent be thwarted and stifled trying to cope with such narrow limits?

Let us return to and amplify the earlier statement that the mystery is to the novel what the sonnet is to poetry. The sonnet is a stylized form of poem which makes rigid meter, length, and rhyme scheme demands upon its practitioners. In like manner, the mystery is a stylized form of fiction which makes rigid storytelling demands upon *its* practitioners. To this extent they share the same bed. Does the relationship go further?

The sonnet is a discipline. Those who would meet its demands must shape, manipulate, and refine their message so that it fits into fourteen iambic pentameter lines totaling exactly 140 syllables, no more, no less. That is no mean task. Add to these limitations the further requirements of rhyme scheme, and the sonnet becomes a honing strop of awesome proportions. Any poet who masters the sonnet form takes with him into the broader field of poetry sharp skills indeed.

What of the mystery story? Does it, in like manner, refine an author's skills for other forms of fiction?

It does, indeed! For, it turns out, the disciplines that govern the mystery are actually the rules—masquerading incognito—which structure the whole art of fiction! Truly revealed, they form the complete training ground in the art of communication through storytelling. Let us view them with their masks off:

Rule one: *All clues discovered by the detective must be made available to the reader.*

In its broader sense, this rule is saying that all stories should be tied together, and the tying requires that coming events cast their shadows before. The clues to the future are planted in the present. The reader is not to be cheated, surprised, or upset by the story's taking a sudden, irrelevant course. In no way can Hamlet and Ophelia walk off, hand in hand, into the sunset. Nor may Petruchio not tame Katharina. The omens promise a different future.

The course of clue-planting is broader and deeper than just mood. The lottery ticket must be bought before the prize can be won, the ice must be known to be thin before the child falls through. The way must be paved. The reader may be caught unawares—and, indeed, it is a part of storytelling to catch the reader unawares—but he should never be caught in *ignorance*. All surprises must stem from within the universe of the story; they may not be introduced from outside. There should be that totality in a tale which pulls it together as a whole so that the reader is always comfortable. His credulity is never strained because whatever happens can be related to what has gone before. *The clues have been fairly planted.*

Rule two: *Early introduction of the murderer.*

This is only another way of saying that the sooner the cast is assembled, the better. It is not required, of course, that all hands be on deck at the launching, but it is required that the way is paved for the arrival of those who aren't. This again relates to the enclosed universe of the story and proper concern that the reader is not unfairly and uncomfortably surprised.

Rule three: *The crime must be significant.*

This is the warning any novelist must heed—that the events and concerns of his tale must be sufficient to grasp the interest of the reader. For all that an author should write to please himself, it must never be forgotten that he is writing to be read. If, in arrogance, a writer takes a "public be damned" attitude, and writes for himself alone, he reveals himself as failing to understand the nature of his craft. Writing is communication. The purpose of words and of language is to transmit as accurately as possible what is in the mind of one person into the mind of another. An author must always write with his reader as well as himself in mind. The more successfully he involves his reader, the more successfully he is communicating. He must create interest in his purposes. Therefore his purposes, like the mystery writer's crime, must be significant.

Rule four: *There must be detection.*

In its broader application, this rule means that something must happen. An author, whatever kind of story he may seek to tell, whatever message he may want to deliver, or whatever emotion he may want to share, should couch it in a developing tale. There should be form to the novel, there should be shape and direction. Characters should act and react. They must not drift at the mercy of the fates.

Rule five: *The number of suspects must be known and the murderer must be among them.*

This is the matter of the enclosed universe which we have mentioned before. Every story must operate in such a system. It is necessary, for purposes of orientation, to help the reader feel comfortable and aware of his parameters. To put it another way: Only the characters in a story can have impact upon other characters in the same story. Consequently they've all got to be there.

Rule six: *Nothing extraneous may be introduced.*

This is the final fence that pens the mystery writer so tightly. This is the discipline that makes the highest demand upon such a writer in terms of skill, economy, and artistry.

What it is saying with regard to fiction as a whole is that an author should not wander or meander. He should have purpose and he should stick to his purpose; everything he puts into his stories should relate to that purpose. Quite obviously, the purposes in a straight novel can be quite different from those of the mystery and they will generally embrace far vaster areas. The lesson, however, is the same. Do not be sloppy, do not be verbose, do not be irrelevant. Writing is communication, and it's not enough merely to use the right words to transmit the message; one should also take pains to see that the form of the message is not garbled.

What we have been talking about until now has been, actually, the areas of similarity between the mystery and the novel, and what we have been saying, in effect, is that the mystery makes a good training ground for the novel. The claim has been made, and I would give it much truth, that a good mystery writer can write a better novel than a good novelist can write a mystery. This is because the mystery writer has had to develop the disciplines of the novel form to a far higher degree than is required of the straight novelist. The mystery is a craft within a craft and all that pertains to the art of the mystery pertains to the art of the novel.

There is, however, a whole universe beyond the tightly fenced realm of the mystery, a universe wherein only the straight novelist roams. In this vast otherworld lie challenges not available to the mystery author, and demands of craft that are not imposed upon him. Herein resides the fact that the great names in literature belong to the novel, not to the mystery!

But why? What is this forbidden land wherein the mystery writer may not tread? What is it that makes these straight-fiction books, even if they deal with crime and punishment, more than mysteries? What can a novelist do that a mystery writer cannot? What is the *difference* between the mystery and the novel?

One distinction is pure and simple. The mystery novel does not contain the equipment to carry messages. It is too frail a box to hold the human spirit. It allows an author to speak, but not to explore and instruct. The credo can be expressed as follows: "If you want to write and have nothing to say, write a mystery." If you have other ambitions, the mystery form had best be eschewed.

Why do we say this? Why is the mystery form inadequate?

The first and most obvious reason is that the mystery is, in actuality, a morality play. Though evil threatens, justice emerges triumphant. Goodness is honored, sin is vanquished. Portia wins and Shylock loses. (But, mark you, *The Merchant of Venice* is a vehicle that would burst into a thousand fragments if it tried to encompass a Lady Macbeth!)

The real world does not behave as tidily as the make-believe world of mystery. Justice, all too often, suffers defeat. Right does not always make might, and one who would deal with the ills of the world and the lessons to be learned therefrom, cannot use the mystery as a soapbox.

There is a deeper reason too. Its inadequacy is not merely because it holds up a slanted mirror to nature — for sometimes nature does conform to the image. The roots of the problem are more sinuous and penetrating than that, for the inability of the mystery to deal with matters of serious concern lies in the nature of the animal itself.

In the mystery novel, the story is the core, the be-all, the end-all, the Heart of the Matter. This is its glory, and its liability. This is what sets it apart from the straight novel. This is why it doesn't serve the purposes of the straight novelist.

The author of a straight novel has other fish to fry. His aim is not to puzzle the reader or tell him stories. His basic aim isn't even to entertain. He writes for all the other reasons: to save himself, to objectify his life, to express his preoccupations and concerns with the human condition. He writes, more often than not, because he *has* to write, to get the monkey off his back. Sometimes he is consciously trying to send messages, to argue a cause, put forth a concept, or present a viewpoint, but for the most part his statements are not consciously expressed. The insights he puts forth, for however much or little they are worth, lie hidden in the depths of his prose. They are sought for and argued over by critics, if the ore that is found is deemed worth the mining.

Story is not this author's goal. It serves instead as the vehicle through which he expresses himself. If he is wise, disciplined, and makes his talent work for him, he will pay attention to his story and obey the injunctions we have been talking about. If not, he will suffer a corresponding loss of effectiveness. In either case, however, story is a sideline; expressing whatever it is inside of him that must come out is the guiding fire of his book.

How does he present his case, then, if not by story? He does it through character. It is people working upon people that is the heart of his novel. Characters, or a character, form the core of the work and everything else is structured around them. The story is created to show off the characters rather than, as in the mystery, the characters being created to show off the story.

But, one may ask, does this claim lie above challenge? Is it indeed true that, in the mystery novel, the story is the heart and core? Are not the adventures of Sherlock Holmes mere vehicles devised for the purpose of putting Holmes on stage? Isn't Holmes, really, the center, the core, the *raison d'être?* Don't we read Maigret for the sake of Maigret and never mind what he's up to in this particular case? How can it be said that "the play's the thing"?

It is true that people, generally, write and read about series detectives for the sake of the detective. The point is, however, that the detective is not touched by the series. If Philip Marlowe mellows, it is only because Raymond Chandler mellows, not because Marlowe has been tempered by experience. Perry Mason and Della Street bore the same relationship to each other in 1963 that they did in 1933. They were no more affected by the times and tides of thirty years than Little Orphan Annie.

Admittedly, the Ellery Queen of *Double Double* is a different person from the Ellery Queen of *The Chinese*

Orange Mystery, but this is not due to growth of character, it is due to tailoring and updating him to suit the times.

The mystery writer is a storyteller. He may use the same character over and over, but it doesn't change the fact that all he is doing is telling stories.

To an author who tries his hand in both fields, the needed shift of cores from story to character hits with the unexpected impact of an express locomotive. It is not a decision the author makes, it is a realization that is thrust upon him.

To the reader, the essence of the difference is still vivid. The characters in a novel are *affected*. They think, they feel, they are touched. The working of people upon people produces alteration and what happens to these people—not to their bodies, but to their psyches—is where the author lives. In the novel, people grow, people shrivel, people change. Jean Valjean is not Raffles.

Can not one, at this point, broach a second challenge? It has been acknowledged that flesh, muscle, blood, and clothing have been added to the bones of the mystery over the years. Valjean is, admittedly, not Raffles, but do not the characters created by today's mystery authors more closely approximate Hugo's creation than Hornung's? Is not Raffles irrelevant by modern standards?

It is true that the mystery more and more approaches this aspect of the straight novel. It was, in fact, for just this reason that it was deemed necessary to look to the classical age of the mystery form, when it was more appropriately called the detective story, in order to make clear the difference. Over the years the fuzzing of the line of demarcation has increased. More and more, mystery writers are either growing out of that form—like Graham Greene—or being recognized as having overflowed the field even when they were writing within it—like Hammett, Chandler, and James M. Cain.

In fact, there are top practitioners in the field today who will argue that there is no "forbidden land" for the mystery novelist. They claim there is nothing straight fiction can do that the mystery novel cannot also do.

What this is saying, and what it means if it is true, is that there is no longer any difference between the straight novel and the mystery. This is, in effect, suggesting that "Mystery Story" is nothing but a label put on or not put on a book by the publisher according to the public relations department's assessment of its sales value.

The mystery has grown a lot. It has come a long way, but in my own opinion it has not—and never can—come quite that far. Let us harken back to the core business again. If it is an author's aim to write a mystery novel, it must be conceded that his purpose is to confound, puzzle, scare, bewilder, or horrify the reader and, generally speaking, to keep him in a constant state of suspense. This, by definition, has to be what he is up to, otherwise he is not writing a mystery.

If this be his purpose, then, it is up to him to invent a story that will elicit these results. To present this story effectively, he must create characters who will make it happen. Now it is true that he can show these characters in as much depth as he is capable—which is what most modern mystery writers give attention to and the ancients did not—and he can make them work upon each other, penetrating as many of their seven veils as he can manage. To this extent, the mystery writer can match the straight fiction writer and, if the mystery writer has greater insight, can exceed his counterpart. But the fact remains that his characters were created for the purpose of telling a story. The story is central and upon anyone who would fly from it, it weighs like a lump of lead.

If, on the other hand, an author chooses to write a novel for the purpose of studying the impact of avarice, or jealousy, or love upon the human condition, he does not start with a story. He starts instead with a character, a symbol, a means of conveyance through which his message on these subjects will be made manifest. He will then construct a story created for the purpose of delivering this message.

In short, the one ultimate distinction between the mystery and the novel, and the one which, it seems to me, must always mark the difference, is the question of—appropriately—*motive*. If the motive is "mystery," then the story (suspense, of course) is the core, and a mystery it is. If the motive is otherwise, then story (no matter how gory) is not the core, it is the means, and a mystery it is not.

FOUR   OTTO PENZLER

*Otto Penzler, a free-lance writer
whose articles appear in a
wide range of American
publications (including a column
in ELLERY QUEEN'S MYSTERY
MAGAZINE), won world-wide
plaudits among mystery fans as
coeditor with Chris Steinbrunner
of the 300,000-word
ENCYCLOPEDIA OF MYSTERY
& DETECTION. Mr. Penzler is also
founder of The Mysterious Press,
a publishing house devoted
to mystery fiction; a member of
the advisory board of
FIRST PRINTINGS OF AMERICAN
AUTHORS, and the author of ten
children's books. He was compiler
and editor of RAFFLES
REVISITED, by Barry Perowne,
and WHODUNIT? HOUDINI?, an
anthology of magic and mystery.
Mr. Penzler is also coauthor
of DETECTIONARY, a biographical
dictionary of famous fictional
detectives and crooks.*

THE AMATEUR DETECTIVES

There is a strange magic to the word "amateur." It is often used as the strongest (clean) epithet when one wishes to express contempt for another's ability. Yet, in the proper context, the description suggests more than a hint of admiration for the subject. In the sports world, for example, a note of awe slips into a commentator's voice when he mentions that the third leading scorer in the U.S. Open Golf Championship is an *amateur* (gasp!) and there is a tendency to root for an amateur tennis player in a match with a professional. There is an implicit reverence for the fact that a mere amateur is good enough to challenge an honest-to-goodness professional. Also implied is "just think how good he could be if he turned pro and devoted all his time to the game."

Although it is unfashionable to admit it (particularly since the nightmare of World War II), in this era of alleged *égalité*, supermen have a strong appeal. It tickles the imagination to know that a novice, a pure innocent who had never been inside a boxing ring in his life, could challenge the world champion and knock him on his nape. The intellectual equivalent is The Thinking Machine, Professor Augustus S. F. X. Van Dusen, sitting down to play chess with the world champion. Never having seen the game before, he has the rules explained to him and, applying the rules of logic to the situation, annihilates his adversary. It's all nonsense, of course, just as it is when Holmes straightens out a bent poker with his bare hands and with apparent ease, but it's nice to believe it's all true nonetheless. The history of fiction abounds with myths and legends that illustrate the universal wish for powers that stretch the boundaries of human potential, often going absurd distances beyond those limits, ranging from Merlin removing the great stones of Stonehenge from Ireland to the Salisbury Plain to the blind detective Max Carrados reading newspaper headlines with the touch of his fingertips.

The myth of the amateur cracksman is a puzzling one. Raffles was the first gentleman crook to be described as an amateur. Certainly his skill and unblemished string of successes mark him as absolutely top calibre. So his abilities are not amateur. Since he made his living by stealing, with no supplemental income of any kind, and had fairly expensive tastes requiring a steady acquisition of pounds sterling, he cannot be called an amateur befitting the definition of one who is not paid for his activities. Surely, then, the amateur cracksmen of mystery fiction are professionals—in every sense of the word.

But the amateur detectives are something else again. They blunder into situations, or are asked for help, and solve crimes purely for the love of it, or the sport of it, or because the crime outrages their moral or social sensibilities. They receive no pay, and often no thanks, for their efforts.

The number of amateur detectives is substantial because they have always been popular. If the first amateurs had been unwelcome, few would have followed. Publishers would have seen to it. Their popular appeal can probably be attributed to that superman syndrome. The pompous member of the official police force, a man who earns his living by solving crimes, has finally come up against an insoluble puzzle, or a criminal far more brilliant than he. Sometimes a small army of professional helpers—lab experts, fingerprint experts, ballistics experts, medical experts—are baffled as well. All the genius of modern (even in a turn-of-the-century story, the methods were modern for their day) technology and criminology has failed to apprehend the criminal—or, more likely, thrown an innocent into the slammer. Suddenly, lacking only a white stallion, along comes SuperSleuth, with only his wits to assist him, and he correctly finds the elusive clue, solves the riddle, deduces the motive, frees the innocent, and clamps a firm hand on the shoulder of the guilty person.

Some amateur detectives feel (and act) as if they are performing a worthwhile service to humanity, working very hard toward a solution and taking the whole adventure quite seriously. Others treat the exploit as a grand game, enjoying the thrill of the chase, with a superior attitude that indicates they already

know the identity of the killer, but they want to pro-
long the process for just a little longer because they are
having such a ripping good time.

Perhaps the most exasperating of this type of
amateur detective is Philo Vance, of whom the poet
Ogden Nash once wrote perceptively: "Philo Vance/
Needs a kick in the pance." If you were involved in
a murder case, you would not want Vance to be involved—whether you were the murderer or an
innocent bystander. The supercilious Vance has the
irritating and unwholesome habit of solving the case
almost immediately, then trailing Sergeant Heath of
the New York City Police Department as the ineffec-
tual policeman tries to conclude the investigation.
While Vance smugly watches, others are often murdered, in some instances in fairly substantial numbers.

In *The Greene Murder Case* (1928), for instance,
almost all members of the wealthy old Greene family
are slaughtered. The author of the Vance novels,
S. S. Van Dine (pseudonym of Willard Huntington
Wright) was an aesthete who passed his esoteric knowledge on to his detective. Vance finally concludes the
Greene case by recognizing that the killer has developed his *modus operandi* from a German reference book on criminology, Hans Gross' *Handbuch für
Untersuchungsrichter*.

The first in the 12-book series, *The Benson Murder
Case* (1926), sees Vance solve the case almost at once,
only to refrain from divulging the killer's name because he enjoys the pitiable efforts of Heath as he
arrests, on circumstantial evidence, one suspect after
another. In perhaps the best novel of the opera, *The*

Bishop Murder Case (1929), a series of murders based on nursery rhymes eliminates all but three suspects before Vance does away with the killer. As one of the more convincing manifestations of his Nietzschean philosophy, Vance avoids being murdered by switching poisoned drinks with the killer.

When District Attorney Markham learns what Vance has done, he is stunned and outraged. "But it was murder!" he bellows in indignation.

"Oh, doubtless," said Vance cheerfully. "Yes—of course. Most reprehensible. . . . I say, am I by any chance under arrest?"

He was not, and returned in future cases with his endless cheerfulness, his frequent lectures on inconsequential subjects, dropping his g's with irritating regularity.

Similar to Vance in many ways is Ellery Queen. Just as the official law enforcement agencies of New York enlist Vance's aid in solving difficult murder cases, Ellery Queen's father, Inspector Richard Queen, often seeks help from his highly intelligent son.

The young Queen has vast stores of knowledge on a wide variety of subjects, and he is generally willing (well, anxious, actually) to show it off on the slightest pretext. Arrogant, vain, brilliant, condescending, and generally irritating, he is a worthy successor to Philo Vance. The adventures of America's most famous detective began in 1929 with *The Roman Hat Mystery*. Cousins Manfred B. Lee and Frederic Dannay took the name of their detective for their by-line and collaborated on 40 books about the intellectual detective. Fortunately, Queen (the detective) changed considerably through the years. While he was introduced as a writer, he never seemed to write in the early books. Later, he was often found at the typewriter, agonizing over a deadline and snatching badly needed time from his work to help his father. He developed a greater social consciousness as he grew more mature, and he treated his father with more respect as well, without the revolting condescension of the early titles.

Queen (the author) did not deny that he was influenced by Van Dine (who was a best-selling author in the late 1920s and early 1930s) and that his detective was very closely patterned after Vance. Just as the reading public quickly tired of Vance, Dannay and Lee soon tired of their detective. Instead of retiring him or killing him, and creating someone new, they changed him. Apart from the name, the Ellery Queen character of the 1940s and beyond bears little resemblance to the early character. He became less of an intellectual dilettante, became tougher, and actually showed some interest in women!

Although Ellery opens his own private detective agency in one novel (*The Dragon's Teeth*, 1939) and serves as special investigator to the mayor in *Cat of Many Tails* (1949), his mystery-writing career plays a major role throughout the series.

He is not the only writer who has added luster to his name by solving crimes as well. LeRoy King, the creation of James Holding, is a parody caricature of Queen. A long series of books by Lenore Glenn Offord features the adventures of Todd McKinnon, a pulp-magazine writer of mystery stories.

Perhaps the most unusual literary detective is no less majestic a figure than Samuel Johnson. Lillian de la Torre once claimed that Dr. Johnson possessed the correct personality and abilities to be a fine detective, and supported her claim by writing more than two dozen pastiches about the major literary figure of the second half of the eighteenth century. She also felt that he had the perfect "Watson" to assist him and chronicle his cases in James Boswell. Most of the stories originally appeared in *Ellery Queen's Mystery Magazine* and were later collected in *Dr. Sam: Johnson, Detector* (1946), one of the most handsomely designed books of its time, and *The Detections of Dr. Sam: Johnson* (1960). The stories combine fact with fiction, in absolutely authentic historical settings, in the plush style of their time. Miss de la Torre said that Johnson and Boswell were "the only team fit to rival the Holmes-Watson combination."

Roger Sheringham begins as a rather offensive amateur detective and best-selling author. Created by Anthony Berkeley Cox under his Anthony Berkeley pseudonym, Sheringham was conceived as a deliberately offensive character because Cox thought it would be amusing. When the public took the stories (and the character) seriously, Cox toned down the irritating and unlikeable characteristics of Sheringham, particularly his rudeness and verbosity. Perhaps his finest feats of detection occur early and mid-career (when he also proves to be wrong more often than right) in such cases as *The Silk-Stocking Murders* (1928) and *The Poisoned Chocolates Case* (1929).

Peter Sargeant, the hero of three books by Gore Vidal (under the pseudonym Edgar Box) found himself a free-lance writer when his newspaper resented his request for a raise. After three years as a drama critic (ghostwriting for the alcoholic who had the by-line), he opened a one-man public relations firm.

There are almost as many journalists solving crimes as there are private detectives. The first, and perhaps the most important, is Joseph Rouletabille, the teenaged reporter created by Gaston Leroux for *Le Mystère de la Chambre Jaune* (1907; U.S. title: *The Mystery of the Yellow Room,* 1908) and the hero of four additional novels. As a precocious young crime reporter, Rouletabille virtually takes charge of the case. Ignoring the official police, withholding evidence, turning up clues and refusing to divulge the information to anyone (including his Watson, Sainclair), he nonetheless solves one of the greatest locked-room murders ever conceived (although the plot of *The Mystery of the Yellow Room* owes much to Israel Zangwill's *The Big Bow Mystery,* 1892).

Peter Styles, the crusading journalist in Judson Philips' *The Black Glass City* (1964) and other novels, lives in a high-crime neighborhood in Manhattan and his personal investigations of violence pull him into the center of several murders. David Alexander's Bart Hardin also lives and works in New York. Like Styles, Hardin is a former war hero, but there the resemblance ends. Hardin edits *The Broadway Times,* a racing and theatrical sheet that reflects his intimate knowledge of the seedy world of gambling and Times Square, where he has an apartment above a flea circus. The first of the novels about him is *Terror on Broadway* (1954).

Philip Trent, whose first case was published by E. C. Bentley (a lifelong newspaperman) under the title *Trent's Last Case* (1913; U.S. title: *The Woman in*

Black) was another journalist, of sorts. Actually an artist, he was offered a goodly sum to cover a crime story because of his past success with helping authorities uncover killers. Trent violates one of the old axioms of detective stories by falling in love with the leading suspect. His solution is a brilliant exercise in deduction that astounds those on the scene. It has only one weakness: it is wholly wrong.

Bentley's historic novel is generally lauded as the first example of a naturalistic detective novel and the beginning of the modern era of mystery fiction. Ironically, it was intended as a spoof of the genre, designed to show how silly readers were to accept the *dénouement* of the master detectives. Trent was so likable, and the problem so carefully constructed and baffling, that *Trent's Last Case* became one of the most popular of all detective novels, reprinted scores of times.

The pulp magazines of the 1920s and 1930s had a detective to fit every physical infirmity or peculiarity, every race, religion, and national origin, as well as every imaginable profession. Among the most popular jobs in which crime fighters found themselves was journalism, and among the most popular of these adventurers was Addison Francis Murphy, known as The Rambler because he is an itinerant newspaperman traveling throughout the United States during the Depression years. The author of the stories about The Rambler was Fred MacIsaac.

Also not to be forgotten is the most famous of all the journalist crime fighters (if detective is not exactly the right word): Clark Kent, the mild-mannered reporter for a great metropolitan newspaper, better known as the comic-book hero Superman. Like many other great comic-book heroes (such as Batman, Mandrake the Magician, The Phantom, and similar costumed characters), Superman is a pure amateur, receiving no remuneration for his efforts, presumably living on his modest salary as a reporter.

Some amateur detectives who work for newspapers use a camera instead of a typewriter. Herbert Brean's Reynold Frame is a personable young photographer for *Life* magazine (Brean was an editor for the once-popular pictorial) whose cases have such unusual ingredients as germ warfare. It was George Harmon Coxe, however, who created the most memorable crime photographers in literature: Flashgun Casey and Kent Murdock. Both Casey and Murdock work for Boston papers and have other striking similarities, although Casey is tougher and Murdock more cultured. Jack "Flash" Casey is the highest-paid photographer in Boston in a series that ran from the 1940s into the 1960s. The Murdock series ran even longer, from 1935 *(Murder with Pictures)* to 1965 *(The Reluctant Heiress)*. Both men have trouble in their relations with the local police, a problem also encountered by Stuart Palmer's retired newspaperman, Howard Rook, in *Unhappy Hooligan* (1956).

Leonidas Witherall is the pseudonymous author of the adventures of Lieutenant Haseltine. At other times, he is a dignified headmaster of an exclusive boys' school in Massachusetts. Phoebe Atwood Taylor, writing as Alice Tilton, recounts the humorous attempts of Witherall to maintain his scholarly reputation and proper appearance (he resembles William

Shakespeare, so his friends call him "Bill") while solving murder cases that appear with alarming frequency in a series of eight books that dates from 1937 *(Beginning with a Bash)*.

If there is an environment that practically begs for murders to occur all around it, surely it is an academic one. In addition to Witherall and the literally scores of other scholar-educators who have appeared in only a book or two, some of the most effective amateur sleuths have professorial backgrounds.

One of the most active crime-solving careers has been pursued by Dr. Lancelot Priestley, formerly a professor of applied mathematics at a renowned British university. Although universally esteemed in his profession, he nevertheless resigned from his chair because of a dispute with university officials. His favorite pastime, in retirement, is applying pure logic to the problems brought to him by Inspector (later Superintendent) Hanslet and Inspector Waghorn of Scotland Yard. He treats each problem as if it were no more than a mathematical formula in need of a solution, caring neither about the crime itself, the individuals involved, nor the justice ultimately meted out (or not). The dry, humorless Dr. Priestley is featured in 72 dry, humorless novels by John Rhode (pseudonym of Cecil John Charles Street), beginning with *The Paddington Mystery* in 1925.

Also a professor of mathematics, but far more colorful, is Prof. Augustus S. F. X. Van Dusen, who has more than a score of degrees and honors to his credit. Prof. Van Dusen once voiced the theory that a man totally unfamiliar with the game of chess could defeat the world champion—simply by applying a superior intellect to the laws of logic. After demonstrating the truth of the theory by roundly beating the world champion, he was told by his crushed opponent: "You are not a man; you are a brain—a machine—a thinking machine." The extraordinary achievements of Prof. Van Dusen are recorded by Jacques Futrelle, the most important being contained in *The Thinking Machine* (1907). The Georgia-born author died heroically when the Titanic sank.

Other professorial amateur detectives include Peter Utley Shane, the University of Chicago Professor of Sociology and Criminology, whose cases are recorded by Francis Bonnamy (pseudonym of Audrey Walz); Edmund Crispin's (pseudonym of Robert Bruce Montgomery) tall, lanky Gervase Fen, Professor of English Language and Literature at Oxford University, who is easily recognizable by his huge raincoat, incredible hats, jaunty little red roadster, and the fallible way in which he drives it; Arthur B. Reeves's Craig Kennedy, the Columbia University professor who was, for a time, called "The American Sherlock Holmes," who was primarily a scientist, chemist, and inventor but also worked as a consulting detective and unofficial advisor to Inspector Barney O'Connor of the New York Police; and Nicky Welt, the white-haired English Language and Literature professor of a New England college, who affects a pedagogical manner when explaining his solution to his friend, pupil, and chronicler, the District Attorney of Suffolk County, Mass.—even though he is only two or three years older than the professional crime fighter. The Nicky Welt stories were collected in *The Nine Mile Walk* (1967) by Harry Kemelman (also a white-haired English professor in New England).

Kemelman created an even more famous amateur detective, Rabbi David Small, who lives and works in the small New England town of Barnard's Crossing. In his first case, *Friday the Rabbi Slept Late* (1964), Small is suspected of murder himself, but he solves the crime and becomes the good friend of the local police chief, Hugh Lanigan, an Irish Catholic with whom he frequently discusses religion. The rabbi's familiarity with *pilpul*, the hairsplitting Talmudic method of logic, is an evident aid to his criminal deductions.

Rabbi Small is one of a huge flock of religious detectives. The most famous, of course, is G. K. Chesterton's cherubic Father Brown, who would rather save a criminal's soul than see him punished for a crime. Unlike most successful detectives, both professional and amateur, who rely on logical deductions, Father Brown relies on his instincts, his insights into human nature, and the practice of his personal style of psychology. He puts himself in the place of the criminal, goes where the criminal has been, thinks the way the criminal thinks, until, he claims, he *is* the criminal. Then, naturally, he knows who his man is. He views the wrongdoer as a soul in need of salvation, and often allows the crime to go unpunished, foiling official police efforts to apprehend the culprit. Father Brown (and Chesterton) often side with the criminal, and make the police into the villains. All the exploits of Father Brown are short stories, the first collection, *The Innocence of Father Brown*, appearing in 1911; *The Father*

Brown Omnibus (1951) contains all 51 tales (in its later editions).

One of the most dynamic priests in literature is Father Bredder, the creation of Leonard Holton (pseudonym of Leonard Wibberley, the author of *The Mouse that Roared*). Like Father Brown, Bredder is less interested in punishing criminals than he is in saving them and making them repent. As pudgy, soft, and benign-looking as Father Brown was, Bredder is tough and physical. A former Marine sergeant who saw action on Guadalcanal, he was also once an expert amateur boxer and looks as if he is still willing to go a few rounds with anyone. A priest in the Franciscan Convent of the Holy Innocents, Father Bredder encounters some of the most bizarre cases imaginable—perhaps not surprisingly, considering the locale of the convent: Los Angeles. The first book in the continuing series is *The Saint Maker* (1959).

Not an ordained member of the clergy, but equally motivated by religious principles, is Uncle Abner, who takes a harder stand on criminals than Fathers Brown and Bredder. He believes that the innocent and law-abiding residents of his community (in the mountains of Virginia) deserve protection from wrong-doers and those who live by the rules of the devil. Although not a member of any official police force, as a powerful country squire he assumes the responsibility of solving crimes and bringing justice to all because of his deep moral convictions and profound Biblical knowledge.

The first book about the rugged pioneer detective, Melville Davisson Post's *Uncle Abner: Master of Mysteries* (1918), ranks second only to Edgar Allan

Poe's *Tales* (1845) among all the books of detective short stories written by American authors, according to Ellery Queen (in *Queen's Quorum*) and many other critics. Incredibly, it took until 1974 for the remaining Uncle Abner stories to find their way into book form, in a slim but handsome volume entitled *The Methods of Uncle Abner,* published by The Aspen Press; it contains the novelette "The Mystery at Hillhouse" and three short stories.

In Montana, criminals must watch out for the benign-looking Reverend Martin Buell, the creation of Margaret Scherf, whose series of novels about the unorthodox minister have such amusing titles as *The Curious Custard Pie* (1950), *The Elk and the Evidence* (1952), and *The Cautious Overshoes* (1956). Two priests who combine religion with detection are dramatically different from each other, but operate similarly. Alice Scanlon Reach's Father Francis Xavier Crumlish is old and tired and just wants to relax as much as possible, preferably watching baseball on television, while Jack Webb's Father Joseph Shanley is a handsome, energetic young priest who emerged from a ghetto and is quite willing to get involved with the tough characters who still inhabit it. Both men are called upon for assistance by members of the police department— Crumlish by Lt. Tom Madigan and Shanley by Sgt. Sammy Golden of the Los Angeles Police Department. A different member of the L.A.P.D., Lt. Terence Marshall, reaps the benefits of the deductive abilities of a different member of the ecclesiastical world— Sister Mary Ursula of the Order of the Sisters of Martha of Bethany. The exploits of the tough-minded nun were recorded in such outstanding locked-room puzzles as *Nine Times Nine* (1940) and *Rocket to the Morgue* (1942) by H. H. Holmes (pseudonym of William Anthony Parker White, who also wrote as Anthony Boucher).

Sister Ursula is far from being the only member of her sex to turn to amateur detection, either out of necessity or as a hobby. The best-known of all female detectives is no doubt Jane Marple, Agatha Christie's long-lived spinster sleuth. Beginning with *Murder at the Vicarage* (1930) and continuing through the posthumously published *Sleeping Murder* (1976, but actually written in the 1940s), Miss Marple has been an unfailingly successful detective. Many readers see Miss Marple as a fictional representation of the author; Miss Christie did not deny it but also stated that the character was loosely based on her grandmother. A bit of a caricature, Miss Marple is generally quite likable, even though she spends an inordinate amount of time (especially in her early cases) snooping through bird glasses and gossiping with neighbors in her little town of St. Mary Mead. Miss Marple normally manages to solve crimes simply by finding analogies between the current problem and past events in the evidently colorful history of St. Mary Mead—every detail of which seems indelibly impressed upon her memory. Although she is as mid-Victorian as is possible for any inhabitant of the twentieth century, neither the most grisly murders nor the most scandalous behavior of her acquaintances can shock the genteel lady. Unlike most amateur detectives, who are asked for help by professional policemen or by victims, potential victims, or friends and relatives of victims, Miss Marple generally becomes involved in a case merely by being meddlesome.

The same hyperextension of the vertebrate olfactory organ afflicts Hildegarde Withers, who spends a great deal of time listening to calls on her police radio and forcibly assisting Inspector Oscar Piper of the N.Y.P.D. Despite the fact that he has referred to Miss Withers as "a meddlesome old battle-axe who happens to be the smartest sleuth I know," he once proposed to her (retracting it at the last moment). A no-nonsense type in her approach to solving crimes, Miss Withers wears the most outlandish hats outside the Mardi Gras. The lean, angular schoolteacher was largely based on Stuart Palmer's high school teacher, Miss Fern Hackett, and some of her idiosyncracies on his father; she makes her detectival debut in *The Penguin Pool Murder* (1931).

Other spinster sleuths with an inclination to assume their help is welcome by the police—sometimes with good reason, sometimes with no reason at all—are Rachel Murdock, the cat-loving creation of D. B. Olsen (pseudonym of Dolores Hitchens) in a series of novels in which she is assisted—somewhat reluctantly—by her sister Jennifer and which have the word "Cat" in the title, as *The Cat Saw Murder* (1939); Miss Emily Seeton, the opera, theatre, and ballet-loving creation of Heron Carvic who first appeared in *Picture Miss Seeton* (1968); and Miss Marian Phipps, another amateur detective who earns a living by writing and whose adventures are in short stories published by Phyllis Bentley in *Ellery Queen's Mystery Magazine*.

Considerably younger and prettier, but equally intrusive, is Mignon Eberhart's Susan Dare, also a writer (of mystery stories), whose only book appearance has been in *The Cases of Susan Dare* (1934). Mrs. Eberhart also created an older nurse, Sarah Keate, who has a similar capacity to find herself in the midst of crime problems. Considerable effort is usually expended in extricating her from a dangerous situation so that she can explain whodunit. Another interesting nurse/amateur sleuth is Mary Roberts Rinehart's Hilda Adams, affectionately nicknamed "Miss Pinkerton" by the police because of the frequency with which she becomes enmeshed in criminal matters. The largely autobiographical character appeared in two short stories in *Mary Roberts Rinehart's Crime Book* (1925) before her first book-length treatment in *Miss Pinkerton* (1932).

The medical profession has had too many amateur detectives to chronicle, but a few of the best are Dr. Mary Finney, the African missionary created by Matthew Head (pseudonym of John Canaday) for a series of four novels, beginning with *The Smell of Money* (1943); Dr. Daniel Coffee, the chief pathologist and director of laboratories at Pasteur Hospital in the fictional midwestern town of Northbank, in two books of short stories and a novel by Lawrence G. Blochman; Dr. Morelle, the sardonic psychiatrist in fourteen books by England's famous "Armchair Detective," Ernest Dudley; Dr. Basil Willing, not really an amateur because he is the medical assistant to the District Attorney of Manhattan, who has appeared in a dozen volumes so far produced by Helen McCloy, beginning with *Dance of Death* (1938); Dr. David Wintringham, the youthful, sports-minded creation of Josephine

Bell (the pseudonym of Dr. Doris B. C. Ball), who wrote thirteen novels about him, beginning in 1937 with *Murder in the Hospital;* (and while we're in 1937, and in the W's) Dr. Hugh Westlake, the poor, hardworking general practitioner in nine books by Jonathan Stagge (pseudonym of Hugh Callingham Wheeler and Richard Wilson Webb); warm and gentle Colin Starr, the wealthy young physician who appears in Rufus King's *Diagnosis: Murder* (1941); Anthony Wynne's (pseudonym of Robert McNair Wilson) snuff-taking Dr. Eustace Hailey of Harley Street (because of his great height, he is referred to as "the Giant of Harley Street"), whose adventures fill twenty-eight books, beginning with *The Sign of Evil* (1925); and Margaret Millar's distinguished psychiatrist-detective Dr. Paul Prye, who finds murders to solve in Illinois, where he has his practice, and in Canada, where he spends his summers (and where Mrs. Millar was born). There are three novels involving the tall (6'5") Dr. Prye, starting with *The Invisible Worm* (1941). There is also Reggie Fortune, the corpulent physician who also serves as advisor to Scotland Yard and who, irritatingly and frequently (if not constantly) exclaims "My dear chap!" or "Oh, my aunt!", in twenty-one books, mainly short-story collections.

Not all amateur detectives are writers, professors or doctors. It just seems that way. No job is too grand or too humble, too commonplace or too *outré;* these performers always appear to have the willingness and ability to solve crimes more expeditiously than the professionals who make a career of it.

The theatre, which attracts what one can only term a diverse assortment of personalities, has provided such amateur detectives as Peter Duluth, a producer, and his actress wife Iris. They met in an insane asylum. The nine books about their various acts began with *A Puzzle for Fools* (1936) by Patrick Quentin (pseudonym of Hugh Callingham Wheeler and Richard Wilson Webb). Drury Lane (loosely patterned after William Gillette) was a great Shakespearean actor forced to leave the stage because of deafness. From his Hudson River mansion, he solves cases for Inspector Thumm, beginning with *The Tragedy of X* (1932). The four novels were written by Barnaby Ross (pseudonym of Frederic Dannay and Manfred B. Lee, who also wrote as Ellery Queen).

Magicians, too, have been useful in solving crimes, particularly the "impossible" type that generally requires, for its success, the use of the magician's basic maneuver—misdirection. Clayton Rawson's The Great Merlini is the most famous of the stage illusionists to become involved in cases which have plagued a perplexed police department. Now the owner of a Times Square magic shop in which is displayed a sign reading "Miracles for Sale," Merlini's four book-length and several shorter cases are recorded by free-lance writer Ross Harte. All the tales deal deeply and knowledgeably with magic (Rawson was a member of the Society of American Magicians), but none more than the first, *Death from a Top Hat* (1938), in which the country's leading magicians are being murdered. Another Rawson character, Don Diavolo, appeared first in four pulp novelettes, later collected two to a book. These were written under the pseudonym Stuart Towne. The other great magician detective is Norgil, the creation of Maxwell Grant (pseudonym of Walter B.

Gibson). There were twenty-three long stories written about the handsome stage magician—the only other character (in additon to The Shadow) to have his exploits recorded by Grant. The special attraction of these adventurous tales of detection is the appearance in the stories of many of the country's most famous actual magicians, under thinly disguised pseudonyms. The first collection in book form of these stories did not appear until 1976.

The Shadow falls into that strange group of detectives who do not appear to have jobs at all. Some are fabulously wealthy, some are just plain "folks," and some are downright broke, but none ever seems to worry much about where the next forkful is coming from. The Shadow is not Lamont Cranston, of course, although he is often identified that way. He merely assumes the real Lamont Cranston's identity when the famed big-game hunter is away from the country. He has ample funds to hire a small army of assistants and associates, as well as whatever props they need in their war against crime, but it is not a simple matter to locate the source of the wealth. R. T. M. Scott's Richard Wentworth, known as The Spider (he uses the spider symbol as his trademark because "it strikes terror into the hearts of his enemies") also has lots of help and lots of money; he appears in *The Spider Strikes* (1933). The same is true of The Avenger, the underworld nickname for Richard Henry Benson, who appeared in a long series of pulp stories, subsequently issued as paperback novels, by Kenneth Robeson (pseudonym of Lester Dent).

One of the finer examples of living with wealth, and having the time, energy, and means to dabble in the hobby of solving murders, is the career of Lord Peter Wimsey, Dorothy Sayers' brilliant and popular detective. After a conventional beginning (Eton, Oxford, cricket, books, music, engagement to the charming girl he loved), Wimsey made *le grand geste* and postponed his wedding just before entering the service at the outset of World War I. He felt it would be unfair to marry a girl with the possibility of returning to her as an invalid. As a noble act on his part, it was magnificent. As a clever one, it left something to be desired: The girl he loved promptly married someone else. Wimsey thereupon threw himself into the fray with recklessness, inviting tragedy. Instead of being killed, he was decorated for extraordinary bravery, but the war left its mark and Lord Peter suffered headaches, nightmares, and a nervous breakdown when it was all over. He did get a gentleman's gentleman out of it, however: the impeccable Bunter, formerly his loyal sergeant. The first Wimsey book, *Whose Body?* (1923), was published seven years before Harriet Vane is introduced (in *Strong Poison*). The witty young aristocrat falls in love again, but it takes him five years and six books to get her to say "yes" (in *Gaudy Night*, 1935).

Another wealthy member of the nobility, of even loftier rank, is Prince Zaleski, M. P. Shiel's exiled Russian nobleman detective. The pure amateur and the pure armchair detective, Zaleski does not leave his fabulously rich and ornamented apartment except in a single case, and then not for long. Shiel (serving as both author and narrator) brings cases to him, whereupon the prince concentrates furiously, exercising his great intellect, apparently possessing "the unparalleled power not merely to disentangle in retrospect but of unravelling in prospect, and . . . to relate coming events with unimaginable minuteness of precision." The three short stories forming *Prince Zaleski* were published in 1895; the fourth tale, "The Return of Prince Zaleski," did not appear until 1955 (in *EQMM*).

Zaleski was much like Edgar Allan Poe's C. Auguste Dupin, who appeared in only three short stories, beginning with "The Murders in the Rue Morgue" (1841), followed by "The Mystery of Marie Roget" (1842), and concluding with "The Purloined Letter" (1844); all were collected in Poe's *Tales* (1845). More recently, Michael Harrison has written a series of successful pastiches of the great Dupin.

Just as he anticipated most of the vital elements of all subsequent detective fiction, Poe created Dupin as the first great amateur detective. Living extremely modestly at No. 33 Rue Dunot, Dupin had no visible means of support. He seemed to require little beyond books and tobacco, which he enjoyed smoking with his only friend, the anonymous chronicler of his adventures. Slow-witted and awed by the apparent omniscience of the erudite Dupin, this devoted associate establishes a prototype for most of the Boswells, or Watsons, of the future.

Dupin was never described physically, so it is impossible to know what he looks like—a deliberate attempt on Poe's part to stress the overwhelming importance of the intellectual process. Dupin seldom leaves his tiny apartment, except for nighttime strolls and under extreme exigencies, such as for the *dénouement* of a case.

Dupin is not as reclusive as Zaleski, nor as totally

an armchair detective as The Old Man in the Corner, Baroness Orczy's cerebral wonder. The Old Man can always be found sitting at a certain corner table in a tea shop, endlessly tying and untying the most complicated knots into a long piece of string. Polly Burton, a pretty young reporter, often reads newspaper accounts of a crime to him, which he proceeds to solve without leaving his booth. These milestone stories appeared in three short-story collections, the first, *The Case of Miss Elliott,* appearing in 1905.

Dr. Gideon Fell no longer earns a living. He is a retired schoolmaster, journalist, and historian. He lectures from time to time but mainly devotes his boundless energies to holidays; Fell always seems to be on vacation, or just returned, or on the way. He turns up in every corner of England, is promptly charmed by a pretty young thing up to her elbows in problems (generally involving a murder of some sort), so naturally he tries to help—with extraordinary success. John Dickson Carr's robust, beer-drinking, wheezing, joke-telling, Chestertonian, amateur solver of "impossible" locked-room murders appears in twenty-six books, beginning in 1933 with *Hag's Nook.*

Evan Pinkerton doesn't work, either, although he, too, once did. His domineering wife treated each farthing as if it were the Star of India, so when she finally died, Mr. Pinkerton inherited 75,000 pounds and had the leisure to devote his energies to the things he liked best—going to the movies three times a week, and helping his friend, Inspector J. Humphrey Bull of Scotland Yard, to solve crimes. The first of the eleven-volume series by David Frome (pseudonym of Mrs. Z. J. Brown) is *The Hammersmith Murders* (1930).

A wholly different sort of unemployed amateur detective is the adventurer, the sort of swashbuckler who actively seeks trouble, either in the service of a damsel in distress (a specialty of Simon Templar, The Saint), his country (Bulldog Drummond's domain), or his own purse (like Travis McGee). McGee, John D. MacDonald's recoverer of stolen property, lives on "The Busted Flush," a Florida houseboat he fittingly won in a poker game. He is not really an amateur detective, because he generally takes half the property he's recovered as his justly earned fee. He is honest, however, and spends much of his life searching for, and contemplating, the possibility of honorable relationships. The McGee novels are plentiful and, because of their recent commercial success in hardcover, and the loftier stature accorded MacDonald, some of the paper-covered works are being reissued in more permanent format.

Drummond had been a military man and, when the Great War ended, found himself bored and anxious to again taste adventure. Although he served England, and almost single-handedly saved her from Carl Peterson (who attempts world conquest through a series of four books, until Drummond eliminates him), he is not on his country's payroll. The enormously popular series about Drummond was begun by "Sapper" (the military term for engineer and pseudonym of H. C. McNeile) and continued, after his death, by Gerard Fairlie.

The Saint is a rogue of the type that has to be logged in the detective column as well. Leslie Charteris's handsome adventurer almost continuously finds himself matched in battles of wits, muscles, and guns with a villain or gang of villains. To extricate himself, a friend, a pretty girl, or some other person worth extricating, he must solve a crime and bring criminals to justice—the normal pursuit of detectives. But he also relieves them of their ill-gotten goodies—the normal pursuit of rogues. But it is not the profit motive that catapults Templar into action; it is his sense of justice, his desire for fair play, and a thirst for adventure.

A similar thirst does not motivate Pamela and Jerry North, a pair of amateur detectives that solved dozens of crimes together, generally in self-defense. In the looney, scatterbrained world of Pam North, nothing seems terribly clear—particularly to poor Jerry, a respectable book publisher who finds his wife in one imbroglio after another. The Mr. and Mrs. North characters were in a popular series of sketches for *The New Yorker* during the 1930s, but the Norths became detectives only after innumerable sketches and a full-length book had recorded their equally bizarre, if less lethal, adventures. The sketches had originally been written entirely by Richard Lockridge. When his wife, Frances, decided to write a detective novel and got bogged down, she asked her husband for help. The story finally became a Mr. and Mrs. North mystery novel, and a pattern had developed. For the subsequent novels, Frances plotted and Richard wrote. After Frances died, the series ended because Richard Lockridge felt he couldn't continue the series without his wife for inspiration as the Pam North character; he has since concentrated on two other series characters, Merton Heimrich and Nathan Shapiro, and written many books about them on his own.

The other famous husband-and-wife team who have been involved in crime as amateurs are Nick and Nora Charles. Dashiell Hammett's *The Thin Man* (1934) is the only book in which they appear. Nick is a former private eye who simply wants to be retired and drink, party, and thoroughly enjoy his wife's abundant wealth.

Amateur detectives, both the great and the merely good, have an endless number of motivations, ranging from self-serving to altruistic to no motivation at all—just a silly set of circumstances apparently conspiring to suck them into a nasty situation. They also come in ages, sizes, professions, and social standings varied enough to satisfy George Gallup. Whoever they are, and from wherever they come, they have provided readers with a delicious assortment of colorful, even bizarre, personalities.

The trend of contemporary fiction seems to be away from the amateurs, with all their idiosyncratic charm, to the professionals, with all their cool, meticulous procedure. Although the characters often are just as interesting and likable, their methods cannot be. In an era when the technocrats are taking almost complete control of most facets of human existence, we need—more than ever—the colorful, exotic, individualistic amateur detectives and their massive egos and unpredictable behavior. Give us enough morose Martin Becks, uncertain Nathan Shapiros, complaining Inspector Schmidts, dedicated Luis Mendozas, downtrodden Inspector Ghotes, and courageous Jose da Silvas, all operating—however brilliantly—within the restricting rules of their respective police departments, and it could almost make Philo Vance seem appealing again.

FIVE   JAMES SANDOE

*James Sandoe fell into the habit of
of reading mysteries at an early
age following an encounter
with Sherlock Holmes, and has
never broken the habit (nor
wished to). In 1940 his inquiries
into the genre turned more
systematic, and he began a period
of reviewing mystery fiction
which was to span fifteen years,
with contributions to the* CHICAGO
SUN-TIMES, *the* NEW YORK
HERALD TRIBUNE, *and the* LIBRARY
JOURNAL. *Professor Sandoe
(now emeritus, in English and
Humanities, from the University
of Colorado) was awarded two
Edgars for reviewing by the
Mystery Writers of America.
Since retirement from university
life, Professor Sandoe has —
in his own words —"begun to try
to write mysteries, one or
another of which might even
be published."*

THE PRIVATE EYE

Dupin, Holmes, Father Brown and Philo Vance are all, in one sense, private eyes in that their salaries do not come from city hall. But that is not the sense in which we understand the phrase. It begins in *Black Mask,* explodes into Dashiell Hammett, and probably dies out with Mickey Spillane. Lew Archer persists, so laden with laurels that they may account for his weariness. So does Travis McGee.* Scarred and given to bouts of meditation, McGee is a little bemused by his own knight errantry. ("Maybe I could be stirred only by the wounded ducklings." *Bright Orange . . . ,* Fawcett, 1969, page 51.)

There have been British imitators (all, so far as I know, negligible) and so few notable latter-day practitioners worth remembrance that the vein seems to have been worked out. Happily, such prophecy is dangerous. Witness the revival of the Gothic as Phyllis Whitney reports it, or the tolling of bells for the mys-

---

* And more the private avenger than the private eye, as Barzun and Taylor neatly remark in *A Catalog of Crime,* page 292.

tery as a whole which began, as Howard Haycraft shows, before the nineteenth century was out.

So, living, dead, or due for resurrection, what is a "private eye"? The Continental Op works for an agency (as Hammett worked for Pinkerton); Sam Spade has Effie see to the erasure of Archer's name from the door; Chandler's Philip Marlowe, like Macdonald's Archer, has been a cop but is now a loner. McGee is a "salvage expert" drawn past his reluctance into action against malefactors.

There are others who should and will be evoked but these are preeminent. So what makes them all, diversely, "private eyes"? After all, there is great disparity among them.

Perhaps they are all, in their diverse ways, knights errant. Even the Op whose heart (or sensibility) is engaged even when it's just another assignment ("It was a wandering daughter job") from the old man.

Describing the private eye is like executing a collage. Certain elements seem constant, for all that they actually weren't: the shabby office with buzzing flies—except for the dead ones on the windowsill—down the corridor from a creaking elevator with a sulky and aged operator, a bottle of booze in the desk drawer, a shabby restaurant nearby serving leaden eggs and greasy bacon, and the streets of San Francisco or Los Angeles stretching away toward the mountain and the ocean. A sense of used paper cups and of looks still sharp from tired eyes. Integrity, along with knight errantry, is their common possession—even with the awful Spillane. That, and a sense of operating alone. The Op may lean on the agency for special information, but in practice he works by himself. The entirely egregious Mike Hammer, whose sensibility was reflected in the title of his first novel *I, the Jury* is a poor relation, smug and priggish even when cutting his killers, preferably women, to slow death.

But there has to be more than flyblown offices, integrity, and a California setting to distinguish the private eye. "Hard-boiled" may help a bit for all that Chandler seems sometimes soft-boiled to the point of being underdone. (McGee, like Marlowe, seems to observe this without being able to alter his convictions.)

The private eye must be willing to assume the bop in the alley, the cop at his door at three o'clock in the morning, the shabby bungalow with a bleary and sullen drunk trying to catch him across the forehead with a wine bottle. He will have a wearily suspicious sense of the shallow lifting stairs to the elegant door of the elegant house on the other side of town.

His eyes will look narrowly at gaming tables and past them to the door in the wall that opens rarely during the evening. He may be the angrily ineffective shepherd of the dependent lamb at his side whose claws reach at money while her richly lipped mouth speaks a lie that has a muddling truth in it. He drives wearily but warily, doggedly wondering if there are still any orange groves in Arcata and then remembering that there aren't. He is wearily awake and if there is always, somewhere, the bed, he is never sure what will be in it. Meanwhile he drives down mean streets and, as the litany demands, Turk, Geary, Fillmore, Sepulveda, Wilshire, Lexington, Fifth and Mason, Beekman Place, Cay West, and Biscayne Boulevard, until they reach a glimpse and a gasp of the ocean or a brush of the thin air at Tahoe where they have slot machines on all four corners and another in the center of the street.

If the .38 is in his shoulder holster, he may find himself trying to remember whether or not it's loaded. He is pressed dully by the possibility that he might need to use it, but he is more aware of the hairpin curves that lead to the shabby cabin with the sagging porch always up the hill from the road.

Another bond between these disparate characters is a sense of imminent violence, of a lurking of evil often overlapping another such premonition and blurring the picture. There is also a promise (often more than a promise) of tired beds. Money is generally a factor, although the eye himself never has much of it and may indeed wonder how he'll pay the bills gathering dust above the drawer with the booze in it.

I am persuaded that the private eye who flourished from the twenties into the sixties is by now an endangered species (a sophomore sociologist could give us charts, graphs and tables to show why the aardvark is more active). Therefore, I have ventured to reprint the contents of a booklet which the late Arthur Lovell some years ago asked me to prepare as a sort of Christmas card for his friends. Barzun and Taylor (page 610) have thought well of it perhaps in part because it is as candidly personal as their judgments (with which it is often a fine game to disagree). On this occasion I have ventured to add some further notes and the sincere regret that many of the books cited are long out of print and difficult to come by.

First and last, I return with most admiration to Hammett, then warm to Chandler but wish that he didn't vitiate himself in part by self-doubts and a boyish excess of romanticism. Ross Macdonald is, after all, a synthetic and Archer an allegation. John D. MacDonald has, in spite of a formula he outwits very astutely, a vitality that will probably continue to be underestimated, because, like McGee, he is his own man. I remember as an ex-librarian, some years back, giving as nearly a full set of John D. MacDonald as I could assemble to our university library with the stipulation that, however uncomfortable for the system, the paperback originals should be catalogued as though they were in hardcover. I doubt that MacDonald himself worries much about preservation in university libraries which, twenty years ago, might have scrapped *Black Mask* if anyone had offered them a file of it. By now it has become a valuable research item.

Here with some titles and my assessments of them:

Adams, Cleve F(ranklin). *Sabotage* (1940). Adams' first book, by all odds his best and the only one I know to recommend with the exception of "John Spain's" *Dig Me a Grave*, q.v. Detective: Rex McBride.

Ard, William. *The Diary* (1952). Sex and sadism after the latter-day mode, but set forth with some sense of style. Detective: Timothy Dane.

Avery, A. A. *Anything for a Quiet Life* (1942). A thriller, derived in some degree from the McKesson/Robbins scandal of 1940; a long and involved chase rather remarkably sustained. Narrator: Donovan.

Ballard, W(illis) T(odhunter). *Dealing Out Death* (1948). About Bill Lennox, executive vice-president of General-Consolidated (films), who doesn't have to flex his biceps to prove that he's strong. A little corpse-heavy at the end.

Berkeley, Anthony, pseud. "The Policeman Only Taps Once" in *Six Against Scotland Yard* (1936). The happy consequence of Mr. Berkeley's reading of James M. Cain and his *faux naif* passes at fate.

Black, Thomas B. *The 3-13 Murders* (1946). Familiar and competent pre-Spillane pyrotechnicality with an avoidance of incidental cliches. Irritating habit of referring to women as "hairpins." Detective: Al Delaney.

Brackett, Leigh. *No Good From a Corpse* (1944). Chandleresque and a sound chase which bogs down somewhat in plot before it stops. It is worth adding that Chandler liked Brackett. Detective: Edmond Clive.

Cain, James M(allaham). *The Postman Always Rings Twice* (1934). It seems absurd to note Anthony Berkeley's "The Policeman Only Taps Once" without acknowledging its debt to Cain, who, in the original list, was one of the celebrated names left intentionally unmentioned. Mr. Cain's reputation has never seemed to me equalled by his prose.

Cain, Paul, pseud. (Peter Ruric). *Fast One* (1933). Leanly observed violence centering about one Kells, a fast man with a gun. Sheer narrative astonishingly maintained. Cain's *Seven Slayers* (Hollywood, Saint Enterprises, 1946) is a paperback collection of short stories in much the same mode.

Chandler, Raymond. *The High Window* (1942), *The Lady in the Lake* (1943), and *The Little Sister* (1949) with *The Simple Art of Murder* (1950) containing one essay, Chandler's apologia, and twelve short stories. Detective: Philip Marlowe (although in the short stories he is sometimes given other names). It is usual to cite Chandler's earlier novels, *The Big Sleep* (1939) and *Farewell, My Lovely* (1940). They are as clearly readable as they are apprentice pastiches through which Chandler was developing, past the pastiche and a nervous-tic of purple similitude, to the assurance of *The High Window*.

Because Chandler's writing has particular interest it may be useful to list the earlier paperback collections of his stories, all published by Avon: *Finger Man, and Other Stories* (1947: including "The Simple Art of Murder" and one fantasy "The Bronze Door"); *Five Murderers* (1944); *Five Sinister Characters* (1945); these last two were reshuffled and

"The Man Who Liked Dogs" (in Shaw, J. T., ed., *The Hard-boiled Omnibus*, 1946) was reworked in part for sequences in *Farewell, My Lovely* and *No Crime in the Mountains* in Anthony Boucher's *Great American Detective Stories* (1945) for parts of *The Lady in the Lake.*

Since this was written, much scholarship has been spilled upon Chandler, as upon Hammett. A discreet sampling of his letters, *Raymond Chandler Speaking,* edited by Dorothy Gardiner and Katherine Sorley Walker (Hamish Hamilton, 1962) omits much of their bite, including his candid judgment of Erle Stanley Gardner and his anger at naval pressure to alter the filmscript of *The Blue Dahlia,* as well as absorbing notes on the trial of Florence (Chandler) Maybrick.

It is worth noting that *The Big Sleep,* read yet again, is as good as anything he wrote, and embarrassing to note the awful cuteness of *Farewell, My Lovely,* which exhibits Marlowe clad mostly in smartypants. *Playback* (1958) is bitterly titled by the man absurdly anguished at "cannibalizing" his work.

Cheyney, Peter. *Dark Duet* (1943). Three related novelettes about Michael Kane and Ernest Guelvada, secret agents, and the only volume of Mr. Cheyney's many I've found any reason to keep. Chandler agreed, a harmony of opinion which may well account for the only British entry in this list.

Dent, Lester: see Shaw, Joseph T., ed., *The Hard-Boiled Omnibus.* There are probably more of Dent's tales worth rediscovery if only on the evidence of "Angelfish" in *Black Mask* for December 1936.

Dodge, David. *Death and Taxes* (1941), *Shear the Black Sheep* (1942), and *It Ain't Hay* (1946). Detective: James Whitney, CPA.

Finnegan, Robert, pseud. (Paul Ryan, alias "Mike Quin"). *The Bandaged Nude* (1947) and *Many a Monster* (1948). Detective: Dan Banion.

Gunn, James. *Deadlier than the Male* (1942). A story of murder rather than of detection.

Hammett, Dashiell. *The Maltese Falcon* (1930), preferably in the Modern Library edition which contains Hammett's introduction, and *The Glass Key* (1931). Detectives: Sam Spade and Ned Beaumont, respectively. These seem to me decidedly the best of his novels and choosing between them is impossible. Most readers will want to find the other novels and the volumes of short stories which Ellery Queen has collected (O blessed editor).

John Huston's brilliant screenplay of *The Maltese Falcon* was, in effect, ready for him in the text with its sharp camera eye, always as suggestive as it is ambiguous, observing events and (especially) observing expressions. Hammett seems always to have written as the detached observer, alert but uncommitted. It is worth note that Marlowe, Archer, and McGee all swim self-alertly through the narrative. The curious, especially those who feel unsteady at reading a mere "mystery story," might be induced to discovery of *The Glass Key* by the suggestion that they approach it as a study in aspects of loyalty and friendship. But some trout are not worth tickling.

NOVELS: *The Dain Curse* (1929), *Red Harvest* (1929), and *The Thin Man* (1934).

One of the most satisfactory evaluations of the hardboiled sort is Anthony Boucher's note in *The New York Times* of Sunday, August 10, 1952, marking the appearance of the latest of the collections of Hammett's short stories, *The Woman in the Dark* (q.v., below). We have his permission to quote it in part for its relevancy here:

"Both the admirers and the detractors of the current blood-bosoms-and-brandy [or, may I add, parenthetically, boom-lay-boom-lay-boom-lay-boom—J.S.] school of fictional detectives trace such capers back to Dashiell Hammett; and Mr. Hammett is alternately praised for recreating the detective story or damned for destroying it. Most of these critics seem completely unaware of what Mr. Hammett's work is really like.

"It is possible, it is true, to see some faint foreshadowing of the current private eye of books, screen and air in Sam Spade of *The Maltese Falcon;* but Spade appeared only in that novel and three short stories. The bulk of Mr. Hammett's detective writing was devoted to the anonymous Continental Op, who is the central character of three novels and at least twenty-five short stories and novelettes.

"In these Op stories Mr. Hammett did indeed revitalize the detective story, not only by the quality of his objective and realistic writing, but also by trying to depict believably the actual work of a private operative. And almost every characteristic of these stories has vanished completely from the work of the contemporaries who claim to be 'of the school of Hammett.'

"The Op is fortyish and a little heavier than he should be. He appears only in cases which might logically be brought to a private detective. He is on excellent terms with the police. He carefully avoids emotional involvements with the people in a case. He stays sober when working. He is no lone wolf, but a cog in a large and efficient organization. He is tough in self-defense, but completely devoid of sadism. Many of his cases involve no physical violence; in those which inevitably do, the violence is written with understatement. He describes one of his own most dangerous situations as 'a game that made up in tenseness what it lacked in action,' and the description fits most of his adventures."

NOVELETTE: *$106,000 Blood Money* (1943, reprinted from *Black Mask*, 1927, and since reprinted as *Blood Money* and *The Big Knockover*).

SHORT STORIES (with introductions by Ellery Queen): *The Adventures of Sam Spade, and Other Stories* (1945); "Too Many Have Lived," "They Can Only Hang You Once," "A Man Called Spade," "The Assistant Murderer," "Nightshade," "The Judge Laughed Last," "His Brother's Keeper." (Also issued as *They Can Only Hang You Once.*)

The Continental Op (1945); "Fly Paper," "Death on Pine Street," "Zigzags of Treachery," "The Farewell Murder."

The Creeping Siamese (1950); "The Creeping Siamese," "The Man Who Killed Dan Odams," "The Nails in Mr. Cayterer," "The Joke on Eloise Morey," "Tom, Dick, or Harry," "This King Business."

Dead Yellow Women (1947); "Dead Yellow Women," "The Golden Horseshoe," "House Dick," "Who Killed Bob Teal?" "The Green Elephant," "The Hairy One."

Hammett Homicides (1946); "The House on Turk Street," "The Girl with the Silver Eyes," "Night Shots," "The Main Death," "Two Sharp Knives," "Ruffian's Wife."

Nightmare Town; "Nightmare Town," "The Scorched Face," "Albert Pastor at Home," "Corkscrew."

The Return of the Continental Op (1945); "The Whosis Kid," "The Gutting of Couffignal," "Death and Company," "One Hour," "The Tenth Clue."

Woman in the Dark (1952); "Arson Plus," "Slippery Fingers," "The Black Hat that Wasn't There," "Woman in the Dark," "Afraid of a Gun," "Holiday," "The Man Who Stood in the Way."

A Man Named Thin (1962).

Hammett has suffered almost as much scholarly inquiry as Chandler in recent years and we have had telling glimpses of him from the remembrance of Lillian Hellman in *An Unfinished Woman* (1969) and *Pentimento* (1974). And that absorbing first draft of *The Thin Man* (from which he salvaged only the name Wynant) has been published in *City of San Francisco*, November 4, 1975, pages 32A–33 (pages 1–12 separately paged). It is sound, spare Hammett and teasing. Although less spare, Joe Gores's excellent novel, *Hammett* (Putnam, 1975) suggests that Gores one day might continue it to its conclusion without Nick, Nora, or Asta Charles.

Heberden, M(ary) V(iolet). *Murder of a Stuffed Shirt* (1944). Competent and relatively restrained among the Desmond Shannon tales as is *Subscription to Murder* (1940). See also Leonard, Charles L., pseud.

Herrington, Lee. *Carry My Coffin Slowly* (1951). Barney Moffatt, chief investigator for a Midwestern country attorney, investigates a very rapid set of incidents indeed. The rush of business is nicely plotted and sustained.

Homes, Geoffrey, pseud. (Daniel Mainwaring). *Build My Gallows High* (1946). The brief history of a wary if doomed cat's-paw.

Kane, Henry. *A Halo for Nobody* (1947) was Peter Chambers's first case and the only one in which I could discover any pleasure.

King, Sherwood. *If I Die Before I Wake* (1938).

Leonard, Charles L. (pseud. of M. V. Heberden, q.v.). *The Stolen Squadron* (1942). Wildly silly but so rapidly managed from little excitements to large-scale ones that you're sufficiently bound up with the personnel to gulp down the absurdities. The author wrote less-successful thrillers with her hard-boiled private eye (the despairing expedient of Military Intelligence) and she wrote much soberer and more probable pieces in which he was involved. (*Search for a Scientist*, 1947, or *Sinister Shelter*, 1949.)

Macdonald, John Ross, pseud. (Kenneth Millar). *The Way Some People Die* (1951) and *The Ivory Grin* (1952), with at least an agreeable nod at *The Moving Target* (1949) and *The Drowning Pool* (1950). Like Chandler, Mr. Macdonald began in pastiche and appeared for a time to grow into his own statement. Even Anthony Boucher was persuaded finally that Ross Macdonald had overtaken Chandler, and William Goldman, among others, has presented him as winner of the race. But rereading persuades me again that, after some promise, he is simply a clever master of pastiche. I am bewildered most of all by those perceptions able to meet Lew Archer as more than a name, a few attributes (almost bowdlerized from Marlowe in Chandler's tales), and a hiccup of similes which appear to be obligatory.

Masur, Harold Q. *Bury Me Deep* (1947). Fast and tough by rote, but played so effectively that it slips past the eyes. Detective: Scott Jordan.

Millar, Kenneth (see above, John Macdonald, pseud.). *The Three Roads* (1948). Not to be confused with anything Mr. Millar produced before it, least of all with a hard-boiled phoney called *Blue City*.

Miller, Wade, pseud. (Robert Wade and William Miller). Max Thursday's adventures in *Guilty Bystander* (1945), *Fatal Step* (1948), *Murder Charge* (1950), and *Shoot to Kill* (1951); synthetic but effective.

Morgan, Murray C. *The Viewless Winds* (1949). Violence in a coastal logging town, more thriller than mystery, but conceived and set down with bite.

Nielson, Helen. *Obit Delayed* (1952) which I found considerably more persuasive in its plot and management than its predecessors.

Perelman, S(idney) J(oseph). "Somewhere a Roscoe" in *Crazy Like a Fox* (1945) and "Farewell, My Lovely Appetizer" in *Keep It Crisp* (1946). Two devastatingly perceptive notes on the hard-boiled detective story, the first in its *Spicy Detective* version, the second discerning almost unbearable sentimentality beneath the brassy exterior of Hammett and (especially) Chandler. Two vital little exercises that no admirers of the hard-boiled school (nor any of its enemies) should miss.

Philips, James Atlee. *Pagoda* (1951). A fierce, abrupt, fragmentary little thriller set in Hong Kong and Rangoon, and probably one of its predecessors, *Suitable for Framing* (1949), which shares the same untidy ferocity.

Presnell, Frank G. *No Mourners Present* (1940). The best of the disorderly cases of John Webb, an unscrupulous attorney-at-law.

Quinn, E(leanor) Baker. *One Man's Muddle* (1937). Told by "James Strange," whose toughness of mind is compellingly evident and unexpectedly trans-Atlantic in flavor, and whose acrid observation is a curious anticipation of Chandler.

Reeves, Robert. *Dead and Done For* (1939). Celebrating Cellini Smith, detective, and a considerable improvement over his first case.

Shaw, Joseph T(hompson), ed. *The Hard-Boiled Omnibus* (1946). Stories selected from *Black Mask* by its most distinguished editor. The authors include J. J. des Ormeaux (Forrest Rosaire), Reuben Jennings Shaw, Dashiell Hammett, Ramon Decolta (and his alter ego, Raoul Whitfield), Raymond Chandler, Norbert Davis, George Harmon Coxe, Lester Dent (whose "Sail" is as exciting as anything in the volume), Charles G. Booth, Thomas Walsh, Roger Torrey, and Theodore Tinsley. Not all of the writers are represented at their best and a number of them have not since published novels or novels in the hard-boiled tradition.

Spain, John, pseud. (Cleve F. Adams). *Dig Me a Grave* (1942). Bill Rye, related to Hammett's Ned Beaumont, is the leg man in this. It is as fast, hard, and credible as its sequel *(Death Is Like That,* 1944) is not.

Spicer, Bart. Mr. Spicer seems one of the more considerable writers in the vein for a series of substantially sound tales about Carney Wilde, a detective with muscles and a conscience, a nice set of wits (a little too much given to spend themselves in the wisecrack), and no clear determination to stay within the boundaries of the hard-boiled sort although his first novel was sound and independent of allegiances in striking degree: *The Dark Light* (1949), *Blues for the Prince*

(1950), *The Golden Door* (1951), and *The Long Green* (1952) are all worth attention but the first and latest are perhaps most effective.

Stuart, William L. *The Dead Lie Still* (1945). A thriller compounded of but dashing successfully through its cliches, and *Night Cry* (1948) about an angry cop in grave difficulties.

Walsh, Thomas. *The Night Watch* (1952), about a cop's slip and fall. By the author of a good many *Black Mask* stories and a lot of softer ones in *The Saturday Evening Post,* as well as an admirable melodrama called *Nightmare in Manhattan* (1950).

Whitfield, Raoul. *Death in a Bowl* (1931). Try this one just after Chandler's *Farewell, My Lovely* and see if its toughness isn't more compelling. The bowl is Hollywood's and the death that of a motion-picture director. Whitfield, a prolific and vigorous contributor to the pulps, published two other novels, *Green Ice* (1930) and *The Virgin Kill* (1932), neither as satisfactory as this one.

These then are the hard-boiled tales which a couple of decades of reading and a dangerous number of years at reviewing have called into memory as worth the coursing. The writers and tales noted here are themselves of very unequal merit and it's quite possible that the quality which appeared to me to rescue an otherwise routine imitation from boredom will not affect another reader in the same way. Still the notes may be useful for simplifying the appalling process of rooting out the weeds and at the very least they provide a plump sitting duck for blasting.

I shall of course regret this omission or that other one as soon as the list is irretrievably beyond my care, just as I shall be dogged by the doubt that X or Y warranted admission after all. And this self-constituting torment may be some relief to the reader who finds himself particularly resentful of an omission or an inclusion.

MICHELE SLUNG

Michele Slung has made a career of reading and writing about mystery fiction. She also has gained international recognition as a specialist in the genre through her writings on women in detective fiction. Miss Slung's book on this subject, CRIME ON HER MIND, was published in England and America. Miss Slung has lived in the world of books since graduating from college, working in bookstores in Philadelphia and New York, reading for paperback publishers and book clubs, and writing book reviews, including those which appear in MS. MAGAZINE in a column titled "Mystery Tour."

WOMEN IN DETECTIVE FICTION

I wonder whether the Girls are mad,
And I wonder whether they mean to kill.
William Blake, "WILLIAM BOND"

Are women bloodthirsty? Would they just as soon concoct a cyanide cocktail as a cheese soufflé? Would most women cheerfully murder their husbands, their lovers, their rivals? Wouldn't most well-bred, sensitive, sensible, intelligent females hesitate before soiling their hands (*pace* Lady Macbeth) with blackmail, kidnapping, and other sordid crimes? Or are these criminal possibilities simply desires that are continually being repressed and sublimated? Certainly in the cases of many women whose names (and pseudonyms) are familiar to frequenters of lending libraries and bookshops, the sublimation, if it is that, has borne fruit. It was Kipling who gave us "the female of the species is more deadly than the male," but the protective coloration of "the weaker sex" causes us to forget this. Women *are* more lethal because of their historical camouflage, and when they put their minds to crime—as authors—the accomplishment has been enhanced by this surprise element.

In the field of mystery/detective/suspense fiction, a woman writer has never been bothered much by the question of equality, for the (poison?) pen is a great equalizer. Whether or not she might be handy with a heavy bludgeon matters little; the book is her blunt instrument. Entertainment is her motive and the *modus operandi* varies. And, though it may sound slightly sinister, her victims, albeit willing ones, are her readers. Her feminine intuition is not to be despised; rather, it is shaded with imagination, perception, sympathy, wit, and is wholly valuable. Add to this asset an eye for detail, a knowledge of human nature, and an ability to believe (as with the redoubtable Miss Marple) that almost anything is possible, including the worst, and one will think twice before asking of her: "What's a nice girl like you doing in a place like this?"

This is, of course, no simple, glib explanation for another question: "Why have there been so *many* women mystery writers?" It is a somewhat ridiculous query, for no one wonders why there are so many female novelists. Nevertheless, it is true that there are very few women writing in the two other similar sub-categories: westerns and science fiction (although some in the former and a growing number in the latter). I feel incapable of a complicated, analytic argument or explanation; instead I have attempted a lighthearted exposition that I hope will convey my respect and affection for those women whose work has given me so much pleasure over the years.

Certain critics to the contrary, I have few quarrels with the feminine sensibility as it manifests itself in the mystery genre. Moreover, for what it's worth, I sincerely believe that much of the great and classic detective literature would stand up to a commercial-type "blindfold" test: The magic of the stories and their moods transcend the sex of their authors. These women whom I am going to discuss (subjectively, with the usual apologies for arbitrariness, overlapping, omissions, and necessary brevity) have helped shape and popularize a grand tradition, one that may be said to be a fellowship of peers.

> There is no putting by that crown; queens you must always be . . . queens of higher mystery to the world beyond.
> John Ruskin, "OF QUEEN'S GARDENS"

PEERESSES AND LADIES-IN-WAITING. As I write this, it is with the knowledge that Agatha Christie has been dead only a short while. Her most famous sleuth, Hercule Poirot, is himself no longer with us, officially deceased with the publication of the 1975 Christie, *Curtain.* His demise rated an obituary on the front page of *The New York Times,* an unusual gesture to be accorded a fictional figure, but one appreciated by the members of the worldwide mystery-reading community. A similar fate, or at least a final adventure is in store for Miss Jane Marple, Dame Agatha's other major contribution to the pantheon of famous detectives. Then an era will come to a close—but not really. For just as there will always be an England, so will there always be detective stories, even though for vast numbers of people the name Agatha Christie is synonymous with the English detective story.

With the appearance on the scene of *The Mysterious Affair at Styles* in 1920 (a book that six publishers rejected and one that Christie had written more or less on a bet), the mystery book took on an aspect that has since been much maligned and redesigned, but that still represents and epitomizes the familiar formula of the Golden Age at its most cozily devious. She gave us tricks (*The Murder of Roger Ackroyd,* 1926; *Murder on the Orient Express,* 1934; *Ten Little Indians,* 1940), and treatises (the naive political diatribes of late works such as *Passenger to Frankfurt,* 1970), but she never abandoned her role as Girl Guide leading her readers up and down the garden path.

She gave us poisons and *pukka sahibs,* blackmailers and *blancmange,* vicious murder and vegetable marrows, red herrings, country vicarages, sinister conspiracies, and little gray cells. She gave us maxims, voiced through her detectives: "All good detective work is a mere matter of method" (Poirot); "One cannot expect very much from human nature," "Everyone is very much alike," and "There is a great deal of wickedness in small villages" (Miss Marple). We learn from Christie as she and other predecessors learned from Holmes. And in the quaint framework she provides, this is what we believe, just as we believe in the appearance of three corpses in succession in one medium-sized manor house in the course of a fortnight.

Once, when queried about the seeming ease of her prolificness, she replied aptly, "It's murder." But not even a Poirot or a Miss Marple could trace the full extent of her sales, her influence, or her fame. Sufficient to say, regarding her status as a national monument and a home industry, the 1975 film *Murder on the Orient Express* is to date the most successful British-made film of all time.

Dorothy L. Sayers shares honors with Dame Agatha as one of the best-known women in the mystery genre, but just as the quantity and the quality of their outputs differ, so does the nature of their appeals and the positions of their partisans. Sayers too wrote about a sort of fantasy England, but her efforts stemmed from an attempt at a more intense relationship with the upper order of things than did Christie's. Moreover, Sayers belonged to academia; she was a romantic bluestocking for whom the creation of Lord Peter Death Bredon Wimsey was an intellectual game. She once stated that her desire was to write a book that "was less like a conventional detective story and more like a novel." It is possible to revere her and still ask oneself, "Aren't *all* detective stories *novels?*" No matter, this and her other snobberies are irritating, beguiling, and perfectly acceptable. Her non-Wimsey writings in the field include the marvelous introduction to *The Omnibus of Crime* (1928), in which she shares with the reader her wide range of knowledge and incisive opinions concerning the then-existing body of mystery literature. From this essay it can be seen that her urge to innovation did not spring from a rigid desire for reform.

Sayers is highly adept at capturing the ambiance of closed, special-interest communities, whether of an advertising firm (*Murder Must Advertise*, 1933) or of a woman's college (*Gaudy Night*, 1936). With her naturally donnish proclivities, she exhibits a sometimes sly, often heavy-handed didacticism: Willy-nilly, one learns a lot about change ringing (*The Nine Tailors*, 1934), for example. (I remember, as a teenager, startling a secondhand bookseller whose cat was called Inky, short for incunabulum. How did I know what that meant? he wondered, when I nodded with approval and amusement. Why, from Lord Peter Wimsey, of course. Such was the nature of my introduction to bibliophily.)

Sayers was a limited writer, but a charming one, and clever. Her limitations reveal themselves most clearly in the depiction of the love affair between Lord Peter and the fiercely independent Harriet Vane, which is notable for its rarefied sexuality and well illustrates Sayer's involvement and uneasiness with these figures into whom she had breathed life. As a strict yet loving guardian whose wards had gotten out of hand, she handled it well enough but eventually threw up her hands and abandoned them for more "serious" pursuits, working on for twenty years after the publication of the last Peter Wimsey adventure.

Margery Allingham's first Albert Campion novel appeared in 1929, *The Crime at Black Dudley*, her last in 1965, *The Mind Readers*. (Her husband, Youngman Carter, finished one after her death and two others by himself.) The elusive Mr. Campion (related to the royal family, but happier in the role of "universal aunt") is notable for his shrewd playfulness and whimsical egalitarianism. The eccentric style of dialogue accounts for a good deal of the enchantment of an Allingham, but it takes patience to cope with the utterances of Campion's henchman, the lugubrious Mr. Magersfontein Lugg. Other distinguishing marks of an Allingham are her feeling for the mystical nature of British chauvinism, her odd warmth and drollery, and her leaping imagination.

Josephine Tey deserves mention here, if for no other reason than that she is quite often spoken of in the same hushed tones that many people reserve for Sayers. Her work is low-key and solid, and whether or not her most famous novel, *The Daughter of Time* (1951)—a painstaking vindication of Richard III through a bedridden policeman's research—is the masterpiece it is claimed to be, it is nonetheless a provocative *tour de force*.

Ngaio Marsh is someone I have chosen to include in this category without really knowing why. It is possible to be fond of her gentleman inspector, Roderick Alleyn, and to enjoy his cases without being able to remember much about them.

> *What shall I call thee when thou art a man?*
>
> Shakespeare, AS YOU LIKE IT

Lurking behind the masculine mask is an honorable enough tradition, from the Brontës through George Eliot and on. Furthermore, nowadays men often take female names in order to sell their romantic works. Recently an editor informed me that she was issuing an adventure-suspense novel with only the author's first initials given because, owing to the brutality and violence within the story, no one would believe a woman had written it. Anthony Gilbert (Lucy B. Malleson) has given us the cases of the slightly crooked lawyer, aptly named Arthur Crook. Mrs. Dorothy Tillet is still writing under the masculine byline of John Stephen Strange. David Frome was, of course, Leslie Ford, who in turn was actually Mrs. Zenith Jones; Frome wrote about Mr. Pinkerton, while it was Mary Roberts Rinehart who wrote about a *Miss* Pinkerton. Dell Shannon is also a woman, Elizabeth Linington. To list two of my favorites, as I am especially susceptible to the charms of the "screwball" mystery—Craig Rice (Georgiana Randolph) and Richard Shattuck (Dora Shattuck).

> *Curiouser and curiouser!*
> *Sentence first—verdict afterwards.*
>
> *Lewis Carroll,* ALICE IN WONDERLAND

CURIOSITIES, ECCENTRICS, AND ONE-BOOK FAME. ALSO TRUE CRIME. In the first category I place Lillian de la Torre and her *Dr. Sam: Johnson, Detector* (1946), in which that eighteenth-century notable investigates with the aid of Boswell in the role of Watson. There is an overlapping here, as de la Torre has also researched and written about actual historical felonies. I consider Gladys Mitchell to be a true eccentric in the field because almost all of her novels deal with some aspect of the darker and more dotty side of English rural life. Her heroine, Dame Beatrice Adela Lestrange Bradley, is an elderly, "lizardlike" practicing psychoanalyst whose interests include witchcraft, folklore, and related superstitions and who is somewhat of a witch herself. Another oddity worth mentioning is Margery

Lawrence, who produced a casebook of the psychic detective, Dr. Miles Pennoyer (*Number Seven Queer Street*, 1945).

I grant single-book celebrity to Helen Eustis (though she wrote another mystery a number of years later) for *The Horizontal Man* (1946), which uses the academic setting and surprise-murder gambit to low-key perfection. The same goes for Frances Noyes Hart whose *The Bellamy Trial* (1927) remains a classic of narrative revelation.

For exposition and analysis of true crime, I consider F. Tennyson Jesse, in such books as *Murder and Its Motives* (1924), to be the equal of Roughhead or Pearson. Besides her masterfully sympathetic fictional reworking of the Thompson-Bywaters case, *A Pin to See the Peepshow* (1934), she also created a most unusual female sleuth, the intuitive Solange Fontaine, in *The Solange Stories* (1931). Joseph Shearing (the *nom de plume* of Mrs. Gabrielle Long) also fictionalized true crime with a large measure of elegance and atmosphere, as did Mrs. Belloc Lowndes, who attempted explanations of both Lizzie Borden and Jack the Ripper, the latter in her celebrated *The Lodger* (1911).

> *It is charming to totter into vogue.*
>
> *Horace Walpole*

OF HISTORICAL INTEREST. Mrs. Ann Radcliffe was notorious in her day for her deliciously "horrid" romantic mysteries. The literary descendants of *The Mysteries of Udolpho* (1794) can be traced through the "sensation" novels of the nineteenth century to the extremely corrupted "Gothic" offerings of today. No greater compliment could be paid to any author than to be chosen as the subject of a lovingly malicious parody by Jane Austen, as Mrs. Radcliffe was in *Northanger Abbey*.

More specifically important in a historical sense is Anna Katherine Green, who has long been referred to as "the mother of the detective story," though many scholars now make this claim for one or another of the lesser-known women writers of the same period. Green wrote prodigiously and lived to the glorious age of eighty-nine. Singlehandedly she did more than almost any other writer of her time to further public acceptance of the detective genre, since her novels found many readers among the "respectable" classes. Her most famous book, *The Leavenworth Case* (1878), presents a plausible crime and an equally plausible detective, Ebenezer Gryce of the New York Metropolitan Police, and gives an insider's picture of Manhattan society life. Green also deserves credit for introducing the concept of the nosy-spinster sleuth, personified by Miss Amelia Butterworth, who snoops and aids the police in quite a few of Green's plots.

L. T. (Lillie Thomas) Meade deserves mention although she wrote her turn-of-the-century mystery stories with male collaborators. Writing alone she turned out innumerable schoolgirl novels. While the Baroness Orczy is best known for *The Scarlet Pimpernel* (1905), she wrote many detective tales, creating both the sedentary *The Man in the Corner* (1902) and the beauteous *Lady Molly of Scotland Yard* (1910). Carolyn Wells, a writer inspired by Anna K. Green, is someone I consider virtually unreadable today, yet her *oeuvre*

and her influence were equally large, and she contributed to the genre a groundbreaking work of criticism, *The Technique of the Mystery Story* (1913). Isabel
Ostrander is another author of this early period whose
works helped to build the foundations of detective
literature.

> *The H.I.B.K. being a device to which too*
> *many detective-story writers are prone;*
> *Namely, the Had I But Known.*
>
> *Ogden Nash,* "DON'T GUESS, LET ME TELL YOU"

There is simply too much controversy here, most of it
vituperative and all of it sexist. It is possible to deplore
a badly written, silly, and illogical mystery story without affixing the word "feminine" as the convenient pejorative. To my mind, this perpetuates rather
thoughtlessly a harmful linguistic stereotype. Besides,
there is much fun (with some necessary suspension of
disbelief, I admit) to be had from reading some of the
novels rejected and dismissed out-of-hand as H.I.B.K.
Ogden Nash had a point (and I refer you to the entire
poem), but his message has been carried to a cruel extreme. Mary Roberts Rinehart, Mignon G. Eberhart,
Mabel Seeley, and Leslie Ford are four women whose
works may be considered to fall in this category; but
each offers rewards along with the irritations. Their
books are all period pieces and, to some extent, novels
of manners. Seeley's are determinedly proletarian;
the others are set in the surroundings of the privi-
leged. In a fantasy world of genteel domestic murders
and beleaguered heroines, one should not expect to
find confusion wholly eliminated. Though many would

quickly disagree with me, I hold the genre to be richer for its (unwilling) flexibility to accommodate H.I.B.K.

The note I wanted; that of the strange and sinister embroidered on the very type of the normal and easy.

Henry James

SINISTER, SUSPENSEFUL, PSYCHOLOGICAL. For prime perpetrators of plots with psychological-suspense characteristics, one need look no further than the shelves occupied by the books of Margaret Millar and of Patricia Highsmith, the last-named having an extraordinary talent for illuminating the recesses of the criminal mind. She has also given the genre its most engaging amoral hero since Raffles in the character of *The Talented Mr. Ripley* (1955). Margaret Millar's notable ability to create situations that repel/attract a sensitive reader are typified in *The Beast in View* (1955). I also consider Charlotte Armstrong to belong on the edges of this mystery classification.

With suspense in mind, espionage and intrigue should also be considered. Helen MacInnes is still writing extremely successful books, although her earliest works *(Above Suspicion,* 1941, and *Assignment in Brittany,* 1942) are to be admired more. Martha Albrand and Ann Bridge are other women who have opted for international rather than domestic crime.

There is always room at the top.

Daniel Webster

As there always has been almost from the beginnings, there are now a large number of women writing in the mystery field. One wishes to give credit to all of them, in some way, and to encourage them. In this instance, however, I wish to single out only four by-lines, all of whom currently represent a high degree of style, ingenuity, and affection for the genre. Emma Lathen (actually two women) has perhaps the largest following of this group, with her stories of misdoings in the business world as encountered by the banker John Putnam Thatcher. Amanda Cross offers a humanist scholar's-eye view of the university life; her detective, Kate Fansler, shares with the readers the author's appreciation for *belles-lettres*. On the other side of the Atlantic, P. D. James and Ruth Rendell are capitalizing upon a strong heritage and adding to it, the former being particularly adroit at shaping a civilized milieu around an intricate plot. Her 1972 novel, *An Unsuitable Job for a Woman*, offers the most sympathetic and innovative portrayal of the woman detective yet to be done.

> *He who praises everybody praises nobody.*
>
> Samuel Johnson

MISCELLANEOUS NAME-DROPPING AND CONCLUSIONS. I would be the first to admit that this is an uneven survey; even a modest catalogue becomes a seemingly endless task. I have neglected such stalwarts as Christianna Brand, Doris Miles Disney, Dorothy Salisbury Davis, and Dolores Hitchens, also Helen McCloy, E. C. R. Lorac, Dorothy B. Hughes (one of the few women to attempt a hard-boiled ambiance), Vera Caspary, Lenore Offord, Theodora Du Bois, Josephine Bell, Joan Fleming, Dorothy Uhnak, Joyce Porter, Lillian

O'Donnell, Sara Woods, and Patricia Moyes. There are some whom I consider to be underrated: Hilda Lawrence, Helen Reilly, Patricia Wentworth, Phoebe Atwood Taylor (also writing as Alice Tilton), Elizabeth X. Ferrars, and Frances Crane. And one mustn't forget Georgette Heyer, who went on to greater commercial volume with her Regency novels, but who produced a dozen sublime set pieces of the Golden Age. Elizabeth Daly, too, merits attention for her Henry Gamadge stories; they have an otherworldly atmosphere that sets them quite apart. And I give a special nod to Ethel Lina White for having given us, besides some pleasant village mysteries, *The Wheel Spins* (1936), which in the hands of Alfred Hitchcock became that delightful and unforgettable movie *The Lady Vanishes*.

These are some of the women I consider to be important, interesting, and unusual, some of whose names we know and some we have forgotten. I have not attempted to compare them, really, to each other, nor have I tried to compare them to their male colleagues. Feeling such an occupation to be tedious and fruitless, I have simply tried to appreciate them, however glancingly, and to show their wide range of activities in the genre. My personal feelings, as a woman who has never looked back as she moved from Carolyn Keene to Agatha Christie quite a number of years ago, may be summed up appropriately by a woman whose name has become a meaningful one to feminists, Gertrude Stein. Having tried her hand at producing a mystery or two (of sorts) herself, she said, "Anyway I do like detective stories and will there please will there be more of them."

. . . the much-dreaded but little-known
people called Female Detectives . . .
Anonyma, THE EXPERIENCES OF A LADY DETECTIVE

PLANNED AFTERTHOUGHT. I make no extravagant claims for women detectives, just as I make none for women authors; however, they *do* exist—both in large numbers—and they are certainly to be valued. I think fondly of one of Agatha Christie's most endearing characters, Mrs. Ariadne Oliver, who is wont to declare, "Now if a *woman* were to be head of Scotland Yard!" Yet it is a mistake to believe that feminine intuition will *always* win out over scientific method, and the best women sleuths make the most of all opportunities and resources. Many of these fictional female investigators are worth knowing about and sampling if only for their historical interest, their quaint habits, and their ladylike preoccupations; others are more enduring. Unfortunately, the majority are second-class citizens only because of the general unavailability of the volumes detailing their cases. Almost everyone is familiar with the names of Nero Wolfe, Sam Spade, Ellery Queen, Sherlock Holmes, or Philo Vance, but who knows Madam Rosika Storey, Susan Dare, or Hildegarde Withers, to name a few that might be recalled by devoted buffs and longtime readers. Only Miss Marple, and perhaps Bertha Cool, have escaped obscurity. (Still, there are myriad forgotten male sleuths, also.) For me, just hearing of the existence of such figures as Violet Strange, Loveday Brooke, "Homicide Hannah" Van Doren, and Miss Van Snoop enriched my visceral sensations about the genre even before I was able to locate and know them for myself.

Oddly enough, or so it seems to interviewers I have encountered, a large percentage of the female sleuths were created by male authors. It's not too surprising, however, when one considers the number of women who created men detectives and contented themselves with being the women behind the men. Actually, the notion of the female detective got off the ground in the mid-nineteenth century more as a capitalization on the public's desire for new and novel kinds of sleuths than it did out of any real urge to give equal time to women and their intuitive talents. Now, in the 1970s, when heightened feminine consciousness is producing all manner of achievements, there has been a corresponding increase in the number of novels that feature women recognizable as full-blooded, intelligent, adult persons as sleuths. Almost all of these books have been written by women—making me doubly proud and involved, for not only can I enjoy them, but I can also respect them.

SEVEN   JOHN BALL

(A biographical sketch of Mr. Ball, who contributed two chapters to this book, appears opposite page 1.)

THE ETHNIC DETECTIVE

When detective stories be-
gan to find a whole new plateau of popularity in the
1920s, the economics of publishing were very different from what they are today. At that time a new book
could be produced in a hardcover format and sold at
retail for a dollar. Much less investment was involved
in giving a new author a chance to be read and the ap-
petite of the public for crime fiction was established.
Consequently a great many writers tried their hands
at the game and each one of them introduced, as the
genre demanded, a new detective to bid for the public's favor.

With so many new entries going to the post, there
was a lively search for unexploited types of characters
to play the central role. Well before the field of more or
less conventional individuals was fully explored, the
idea of the ethnic detective was tried out, occasionally
with disaster and sometimes with distinguished success.

A definition is perhaps in order here. A quick
description of an ethnic detective as "a minority individual" is visibly inadequate. To an American or a

European, a Chinese might appear to be an ethnic person despite the fact that one quarter of the entire human population is of Chinese origin. Add to the Chinese all of the other peoples described as being of Mongolian stock and the word "minority" no longer applies except in the strict mathematical sense.

An ethnic detective in literature might be more reasonably defined as someone who appears as a minority representative in the eyes of the reader. The fact that perceptions vary is illustrated by the incident of the Indian mother who was seated in front of the family wigwam telling a story to the children. With gifted skill she recreated a desperate battle being fought on the plains of the Old West. As the tale progressed her eyes brightened until the climax came. "And then," she recounted, "just when everything looked blackest, came the sound of many war whoops . . ."

Once in Ethiopia a little girl told me about the world's greatest detective (she was right) and showed me a picture of Basil Rathbone as proof. Very possibly she regarded him as a minority personage.

Since the majority of detective story readers live in Europe and North America, an ethnic detective may be assumed to be someone who would be a minority representative in this environment.

An early entry who became a household word is Charlie Chan of the Honolulu Police Department. Inspector Chan was already well experienced and the father of a notable family when he first appeared on the scene. (These two statements are, of course, to be taken separately.) The creation of Earl Derr Biggers, Charlie Chan appeared in six books of which *The Black Camel* is a good example.

He has also had a very long and durable career on the screen where he was most frequently played by Warner Oland or Sidney Toler, neither of whom claimed Chinese ancestry. A familiar part of the Charlie Chan image is his "number one son," a breezy, totally Americanized youth who never seems to have a first name. For the benefit of the curious, he is called Henry and Chan's eldest daughter, who distinguished herself in school, is named Rose.

Chan rose to great popularity through a familiar device, the outward image of a somewhat bumbling and inadequate individual who successfully conceals an exceptionally alert and astute mind. His imperfect command of English suggests a scholar's knowledge of Mandarin and Cantonese. In all of his recorded cases he untangles problems in the Caucasian community where his unique personality invariably stands out. He is now reported to be in retirement and making a study of ancient Chinese calligraphy.

Several centuries before Inspector Chan joined the Force he had a formidable forerunner in Judge Dee, an historical personage who held office as a magistrate during the Tang Dynasty (A.D. 618–907) in China. Judge Dee's cases have been fascinatingly told for the modern reader by the Dutch author, artist, and diplomat, Robert van Gulik who also provided illustrations in ancient Chinese style. Since throughout his brilliant career Judge Dee was on his home ground, ethnically speaking, he was not a minority representative to those who surrounded him during his lifetime, but he so appears to the contemporary reader in the Western world.

To this remarkable sleuth goes the credit for solving the most ingenious and baffling locked-room mystery this side of John Dickson Carr. The episode of the poisoned tea in *The Chinese Gold Murders* is a genuine tour de force, a problem wherein the solution is more fascinating than the puzzle. If there is such a thing as a jaded mystery reader, a good dose of Judge Dee is an almost guaranteed cure.

Despite the millions who populate the Japanese home islands, only one Japanese detective has so far won recognition in the big league—Mr. Moto. This is obviously not his true name, or perhaps it is only part of it, so his actual identity remains a mystery. Mr. Moto is a very different type of personality as compared to Charlie Chan. He was introduced to the mystery-reading public by John P. Marquand, the Pulitzer Prize winning novelist widely known for *The Late George Apley, H. M. Pulham, Esq.,* and other distinguished books. The author resided for some time in Peking where Mr. Moto has appeared on the scene. Since Moto is in actuality a secret service agent, not too much is known about him personally, but his recorded adventures make fascinating reading.

Another gentleman of the Eastern Hemisphere who merits attention is Inspector Ghote of the Bombay C.I.D. who makes up in tough-mindedness and devotion to duty whatever he may lack in instant perception and physical resources. The Inspector's exploits are being reported by H. R. F. Keating of London. Ghote (Go-tay) is married and the father of an adopted son. He seems destined to encounter a steady parade of the most insufferable and irritating persons imaginable, from street urchins to high-society snobs. He is impulsive, generous, sometimes even scatterbrained, but he is a hard customer to overcome when he is on a case. He is incorruptible, a definite point of distinction in most parts of the world, and a conscientious public servant destined for greater things. The accounts of his more interesting adventures are filled with colorful details of India; in particular, the water-walking scene in *Inspector Ghote Plays a Joker* is memorable.

Australia has contributed to the literature a unique personality whose stature seems likely to grow steadily despite the fact that his creator, Arthur W. Upfield, died in 1964. In all of detective and crime fiction it would be difficult to find anyone to compare to Detective-Inspector Napoleon Bonaparte. The literary level of the books about Inspector Bonaparte is distinguished and the composite canvas of Australia that emerges has won high praise.

Inspector Bonaparte is the offspring of a white father and an Australian aborigine mother. He was discovered as an abandoned infant and taken into an orphanage where his fanciful name was bestowed upon him. During his young manhood he combined a fine conventional education with a deep understanding of the culture and accomplishments of the Australian blacks. In particular, they taught him their phenomenal skills at tracking. He has been fully accepted by them and he bears on his body the scars of his initiation into one of the principal tribes. Blue-eyed and dark-skinned, Inspector Bonaparte is a man of two worlds fully welcomed by both.

Throughout his long reported career Bony, as he prefers to be called, has never failed to resolve a case to which he has been assigned. Much of his apparently endless patience springs from a great natural pride combined with a running undercurrent that requires him continually to prove himself.

A large part of this remarkable detective's work is done in the vast outback, a land of seemingly endless dimensions, rugged pioneering people, and the nomadic blacks who have only limited contact with the squatters and station owners who thinly populate so much of the continent. The cases are frequently fascinating, but as literature of Australia they are even more compelling. Certain of the books about Inspector Bonaparte have been used as assigned reading by several major universities for the sake of their anthropological content.

Quite obscure, but deserving of a better fate, is the Hawaiian plantation cop, Komako Koa. He appears in only three books written by Max Freedom Long and published within a two-year span just before the American involvement in World War II. After that he disappeared. Koa is a magnificent person—big, rugged, kindly, slow to anger, and deeply committed to his own heritage and culture. He far transcends the stories in which he appears, all of which are set in his native Hawaii in surroundings that are far from the Honolulu where Charlie Chan was in command of the situation.

Koa's narrator is given to introducing swarms of characters at one time who constantly bicker and infight throughout the case history. Also he is given to frequent had-I-but-knownism which will disturb some modern readers. Despite these drawbacks, Koa emerges as a man unique in the literature and one who would make a marvelous friend. By far the best of the three Komako Koa books is *The Lava Flow Murders*, which is written against the background of a major volcanic eruption actually witnessed by the author. The splendid setting and the personality of Koa overcome all obstacles and make this work well worth the reading, if a copy can be found.

A Turkish detective, and a very good one, is Nuri Iskirlak, whose efforts are being reported by the British novelist Joan Fleming. Nuri Bey is middle-aged, romantically inclined, a bibliophile, usually impoverished, and a fair linguist whose English is improving. As a detective he is an amateur who frequently finds himself up against the dope traffic that mars his beloved Istanbul. *When I Grow Rich,* in which Nuri Bey appears, won the Crime Writers' Award for the best crime novel of 1962, a highly coveted honor. The exploits of this honorable and sincere man have also won the praise of Anthony Boucher, which is a major distinction in itself.

Thanks to Robert L. Fish, Brazil is the home of Captain José Maria Carvalho Santos da Silva of the Federal Police. Big, rugged, pock-marked, and usually mustached, Captain da Silva is a total professional who knows his job and who performs it with conspicuous success. He is also part of the Interpol network. When not on duty Captain da Silva knows good liquor and frequently makes love with some of the most captivating girls in richly endowed Rio de Janeiro. Captain da Silva appears in at least ten books, notably *The Fugitive,* which received the celebrated Edgar Award of the Mystery Writers of America. In contrast to Hollywood's Oscar, the Edgar Allan Poe Award is given sparingly and obviously there can be only one best novel of the year.

Another Edgar winner is Lawrence G. Blochman, whose stories about the distinguished pathologist, Dr. Daniel Webster Coffee, are so scientifically accurate that the casebook *Clues for Dr. Coffee* is introduced by the Chief Medical Examiner of the City of New York and the Professor and Chairman of the Department of Forensic Medicine of the New York University School of Medicine, Dr. Milton Helpern, M.D. As his name clearly indicates, Dr. Coffee is an American, but his backup man, the resident pathologist of the Pasteur Hospital in the midwestern city of Northbank, is not.

Short, rotund, pink-turbaned Dr. Motilal Mookerji trained at Calcutta University. He has a vast knowledge of microbiology and biochemistry and is also well qualified in both histology and bacteriology. This quality of medical education is somewhat surprising for India, but Dr. Mookerji leaves no doubt as to his detective prowess with a microscope and the other paraphernalia of his profession. His use of English is clear and scientific if unique and picturesque.

This distinguished pair of physicians appeared in *Diagnosis: Homicide,* a collection of short stories that received the Edgar Award in 1950. The many mystery readers who have been entertained by the classic achievements of Dr. Thorndyke will find in Drs. Coffee and Mookerji a pair of worthy successors to that great man. Understandably, all of their reported cases deal with pathological matters and the degree of scientific detection displayed is very high indeed.

Probably the best known Israeli detective is Lt. Shomri Shomar of the Tel Aviv Police Department, who has solved a number of cases in New York City. Author Henry Klinger has explained that the lieutenant was in North America in order to broaden his base of experience. Empowered by the New York City Police Department to operate in its jurisdiction, and with his official rank, Lt. Shomar cuts a considerable swath. He is fortyish, dashing, fluent in four languages, and adorned by a Vandyke beard, which is frequently the subject of discussion. The lieutenant very often quotes the Bible (Old Testament) while he conducts his investigations and incidently charms the ladies. He does this so effectively that in at least one instance he spent the night with a lovely young woman who was also a definite suspect in the case at hand. He is in addition a dead shot with a rifle.

Lt. Shomar may be found in *The Three Cases of Shomri Shomar*, which should be read in order, as some back references in the later cases reveal the identity of the guilty persons in the earlier accounts.

Another Jewish detective who has attracted much favorable attention is "Mom," the creation of James Yaffe. This notable lady, whose origins and religious preference are never in doubt, has often enriched the pages of *Ellery Queen's Mystery Magazine,* a publication that serves effectively as a "Who's Who" in mystery literature.

In a spirit of true impartiality it is appropriate next to give attention to an Arab detective and there is a very good one, Inspector Chafik of the Baghdad police. In contrast to Madame L'Espanaye and her daughter, who lived—and died—on the unforgettable Rue Morgue, the inspector resides with his wife Leila on the Street of the Scatterer of Blessings. From this benevolent address he goes forth, frequently on summons from Sergeant Abdullah, to deal with homicide and other offenses against the Prophet. Charles B. Child records the inspector's cases, many of which have also appeared in *Ellery Queen's Mystery Magazine*. The good inspector has been known to make use of a swarm of elusive bazaar boys as unofficial assistants, a device for which there is an awesome precedent. The Army of Little Ears has been described by Mr. Queen as the Middle-Eastern auxiliary of the Baker Street Irregulars, and no wayward juvenile anywhere in the world could ask for more than that.

A gypsy detective of interest is Romano Gry, who changed his name from the Lovari original to Roman Grey when he set up shop in New York City as a dealer in antiques. A good example of his work will be found in Martin Smith's *Gypsy in Amber*.

The list of individuals who could be cited is beyond the limits of this chapter. There are several Caribbean detectives, such as Chief of Police Xavier Brooke of the island of St. Caro; his pursuit of a wanted criminal is reported in A. H. Z. Carr's *Finding Maubee*. Certainly the several ethnic members of Ed McBain's widely known 87th Precinct books should be noted. There are Mexican detectives, and others of different nationalities and backgrounds who appear in the literature. Perhaps the most distinctive in point of origin is the Tibetan detective Chin Kwang Khan, who appears in three paperback originals by Richard Foster

(Kendall Foster Crossen), *The Laughing Buddha Murders* being an example. Unfortunately, Chin is as unlikely a name for a Tibetan as Aloysius McGinty, a fact affirmed by my lovely ward, Miss Kesang Dolma Ngokhang of Lhasa, and the stories themselves are not notably distinguished.

In the special field of religious professionals who are also celebrated as detectives there are a number of entries, but two stand out with particular distinction. The first of these is Father Brown who appears in fifty-one short stories by G. K. Chesterton. From the moment that he first stepped onto the scene Father Brown has been established as one of the greats. He is included here only because he represents a religious minority in his native England. As would be expected from so distinguished an author, the Father Brown stories are beautifully written and can be expected to remain a permanent part of the literature. Many of the good priest's cases are well known, but the one which is perhaps most often cited is "The Invisible Man." The Father Brown stories have been collected in several volumes and all but one of them are included in the *Father Brown Omnibus*. Why one story was at first omitted from this otherwise definitive volume is perhaps the only mystery surrounding the little priest that he has not personally solved.

The second front-runner in the religious detective sweepstakes is Harry Kemelman's much-praised Rabbi David Small. The rabbi is constantly confronted with the need to keep peace among the members of his congregation, most of whom seem to be dedicated to various forms of infighting. As the new religious leader of the only temple in Barnard's Crossing, Massachusetts, he had his work cut out for him when he first appeared in *Friday the Rabbi Slept Late*. Rabbi Small is very much his own man; he refused to grow a beard simply to please certain members of his flock and he does not bow to expediency. A firm friend of Chief of Police Hugh Lanigan, he is also a detective of distinction.

Rabbi Small's cases are notable for penetrating characterizations and a keen insight into human behavior as he sees it in his daily work. He misses very little and does not permit either his youth or slight stature to detract from his dedication to his duties. While the rabbi was sleeping, Mr. Kemelman received the Edgar Award for the first book in this notable series.

Many other men of the cloth, and some women, have appeared in detective literature and with at least one valid reason: The practice of a religious profession outside of cloistered orders calls for an exceptional capability in human relations and psychology— which are also major ingredients in the makeup of a successful investigator.

Since much excellent work in the mystery field is the product of American authors, the noble red man has not been neglected. By training and heritage he is observant, skilled in hunting and tracking, and well equipped to make his way under adverse conditions in the vast out-of-doors. These conspicuous abilities have contributed to the success of several Indian detectives.

Bill S. Ballinger is the creator of Joaquin Hawks, an operative with the CIA. He is the son of a hereditary chief of the Nez Perce tribe who devoted forty years of his life to the U.S. Forest Service. His mother is a Mexican-American teacher. Thanks to a certain Asiatic cast to his features, Hawks is able to pass as an Asian despite his six-foot height and solid 190-pound body. He speaks English, Spanish, and Nez Perce with native fluency and he is also well qualified in Russian and Chinese (probably Mandarin).

Because of his appearance, he is frequently assigned to the Far East. His cases involve much action and high drama. Hawks appears in *The Chinese Mask* and other books laid in Thailand, Cambodia, and similar locales.

Two full-blooded Navajo Indians have made their mark on their home ground. Trooper Sam Watchman of the Arizona Highway Patrol has been described as the only Indian member of that service, a somewhat surprising status. To some extent he is what the *Diné* call an apple: red on the outside, white on the inside, but he is true to his heritage despite the fact that he works principally in a white man's world. *Diné*, incidentally, means "the people" and is the word the Navajo use to describe themselves.

Watchman is all cop and generally stays apart from the traditional differences that separate the Navajo from the Apaches (and perhaps even more so, from the Hopis). He works well with other police officers and is a respected member of his profession. A good introduction to Trooper Watchman is Brian Garfield's *The Threepersons Hunt.*

For thoroughly authentic Indian background, and an exceptional feeling for the vast open areas of the Southwest, the works of Tony Hillerman merit special attention. Lieutenant Joe Leaphorn, about whom he writes, is a Navajo and a member of that nation's Law and Order Division. Persons condemned to sojourn east of the Hudson River may not be aware that the Indian nations tend strongly to run their own affairs and have, in many instances, their own police forces. When some members of the Hopi Nation traveled to Europe, they did so on their own tribal passports, suitably decorated with feathers, and had their credentials accepted wherever they went.

Lt. Leaphorn is completely at home on the majestic Painted Desert, in the Four Corners area, and wherever his duties take him. He works efficiently with the authorities of other tribal agencies such as the Zunis. He takes genuine and justified pride in the fact that he represents the authority of the Tribal Council and not an outside agency.

This exceptional detective first appeared in *The Blessing Way* and scored an immediate success. If possible he was even better in the superbly titled *Dance Hall of the Dead*. A strong sense of presence pervades this work, which also gives a moving insight into the Shalako religion of the Zuni people. The motive for murder contained in this book, while not unique, is still worthy of note for the manner in which it is used. The knowledge and understanding of Indian cultures that Mr. Hillerman's books about Lt. Leaphorn reveal is distinguished and collectively they constitute an important addition to the literature. Also, they are first-rate literary entertainment.

Although individual short stories are largely outside the scope of this essay, attention must be given to

Manly Wade Wellman's "A Star for a Warrior," which introduced Indian detective David Return. This small masterpiece won first prize in the 1945 contest conducted by Ellery Queen in his mystery magazine. Since David Return has been compared with Uncle Abner as a totally American detective, he is traveling in impressive company. His tribe is fictitious, but he overcomes this handicap by having a grandfather, who is a senior lieutenant in the nation's police, with the significant name of Tough Feather. The story is not too easy to find, but it appears in Mr. Queen's anthology *The Golden Thirteen*.

Johnny Ortiz presents something of a problem in classification since he is part Apache, part Spanish, and part Anglo. Just to keep things interesting, he has a black girl friend. Johnny operates in a city recognizable as Santa Fe, New Mexico. He appears in *Murder in the Walls* and other books by Richard Martin Stern, a distinguished author who is even better known for having ignited *The Towering Inferno*.

In view of the population structure of the United States, it was inevitable that Negro detectives would appear on the scene. Frequently mentioned as one of the first is Octavus Roy Cohen's engaging Florian Slappey. Slappey made his initial appearance in the twenties when Harlem was a different environment from the one that exists today. Not distinguished by education, Slappey arrived in New York from Birmingham sporting what was then a substantial bankroll and was then promptly conned out of it. Bloodied but unbowed, he returned to the wars and before he was through he was known as a man to be reckoned with.

The atmosphere of the Florian Slappey stories reflects another day, but when read in the light of the period in which they are set, they are good fun as they were intended to be. Slappey is a definite character, the people who surround him are no more or less than they should be, and it is impossible to imagine that the author intended to give offense to anyone.

Other Negro detectives have appeared from time to time, such as Chief Brooke of St. Caro and George Baxt's Pharaoh Love, who appears in *A Queer Kind of Death*. Then a certain Virgil Tibbs of the Pasadena, California Police Department stepped into the picture.

In his mid-thirties, of normal stature, and substantially retiring in his manner, Tibbs is Pasadena's top homicide investigator. He was born in the Deep South where, during his early youth, he was subject to extreme racial hostility. Later he worked his way through the University of California doing largely menial work until his graduation with honors. Shortly thereafter he joined the Pasadena Police.

His first appearance was in a book called *In the Heat of the Night*. It attracted some attention by winning both the Edgar Award in the United States and the Golden Dagger in England, the latter for the best novel of the year by a non-British author. It was filmed by the Mirisch Corporation with Sidney Poitier portraying Mr. Tibbs and Rod Steiger as the southern small-town chief of police. The film received five Academy Awards including the one for the best picture of the year.

The Virgil Tibbs books are perhaps unique in that the various officers and civilian members of the Pasadena Police Department who appear in them with him are not fictitious, but the real men and women in their actual jobs. The Pasadena Police Department has extended extraordinary cooperation to the author at all levels and is largely responsible for whatever merit these works contain. [At the insistence of the Board, the author is identified as John Ball.]

Detailed examination of further ethnic detectives could go on at considerable length since the literature is extensive and there are many entries. Here are some of them:

Name	Creator	Ethnic origin
Jo Gar	Raoul Whitfield	Filipino
Hosteen Chuska	B and D Hitchens	Apache
Toussaint Moore	Ed Lacy	Black American
John Shaft	Ernest Tidyman	Black American
Dr. Quarshie	John Wyllie	Black African
Bolivar Manchenil	D. M. Douglass	Black Caribbean
Webster Flagg	Veronica Parker Johns	Black American
Sam Kelly	J. F. Burke	Black American
Gravedigger Johnson and Coffin Ed Jones	Chester Himes	Black Americans

Since it is always dangerous to read into any given set of circumstances more significance than they properly contain, it is most probable that the majority of the ethnic detectives who appear in the literature resulted from a search for novelty and/or specialized knowledge and background available to the authors who created them. It would probably be a mistake to assume that any large number of books featuring ethnic policemen or civilian investigators were written as social commentary or with the specific intention of underlining the plight of minorities. Most of the ethnic detectives, as a matter of fact, are quite happy in the work that they do and they are accepted very much on the basis of the way that they present themselves. No intelligent person questioned Charlie Chan's official status during his distinguished career, despite the fact that it began long before social consciousness as a phrase had been admitted into the working language.

Nevertheless, it is interesting to note that in the world of the detective story minority individuals made their appearances and were not only widely accepted, but also enjoyed considerable popularity almost half a century before housing-restriction covenants were struck down, equal opportunity employment became a national policy, and the winds of ethnic equality blew steadily across the whole of the nation.

This, perhaps, may offer some evidence in support of Philip Guedalia's famous comment, "The detective story is the normal recreation of noble minds."

Note: The author would like to express his appreciation to Phyllis A. Whitney, Aaron Marc Stein, James Sandoe, Allen Hubin, and Francis M. Nevins, Jr., for material assistance in the preparation of this chapter.

EIGHT

HILLARY WAUGH

*(A biographical sketch of
Mr. Waugh, who contributed two
chapters to this book,
appears on page 60.)*

THE POLICE PROCEDURAL

Let me, improperly, begin this article with a personal reminiscence. In early September of 1949, when I was a young writer with three private-eye-cute-young-couple novels behind me, I chanced upon a slim paperback entitled, *They All Died Young.** It was a collection of ten true murder cases in which the victims were young women.

I went through those stories, one by one, and was never the same thereafter. They had a vividness, a chilling horror to them that no fiction I had ever read or written could approach.

Immediately, I wanted to get the same kind of impact into my own books, and I pondered what made those stories hit the way that they did. The obvious answer was that these murders weren't make-believe, they had really happened. One of the victims, in fact, had been a nurse in my home city, who had had her throat cut and who had collapsed and died at the entrance of her hospital.

---

*Written by Charles Boswell

163

QUESTION: But how does one *know* they really happened, other than by the author's say-so?

ANSWER: Because they *sound* that way.

What I fixed upon as giving these stories their aura of horror was not the brutal ugliness of real murder, but the sense of authenticity of the reports. The stories shook me not because the author *said* they really happened, but because they *read* that way.

I thereupon determined to write a fictional murder mystery that would *sound* as if it had really happened. Since it is not private-eye-cute-young-couples who work the real homicides, but sheriffs, police chiefs, and police detectives, this meant a totally new approach—by me at least—to the whole art of mystery writing.

To finish this account, I did sit down and do such a book. The year was 1950 and the story was about the murder of a young college girl, solved, as in real life, through the efforts of those whose business it is—the professional policemen. So far as I knew, no one had ever done anything like that before then.

There was a lot going on, however, that I knew nothing about, including a ferment, of which I must have been a part, bubbling just below the surface and which burst into being between the time I wrote my book and the time it appeared in print, in late 1952. It was something that came to be known as the "police procedural."

Lawrence Treat is acknowledged as the first mystery writer to have professional policemen, shown in their natural habitat, solve a crime using authentic police methods. This was his book *V as in Victim,* published in 1945 and followed by *The Big Shot*, using the same characters.

While Larry was first, I doubt that it would be correct to call him the "father" of the police procedural, for this would suggest that a host of other writers were inspired to follow his lead. This did not happen; Larry was ahead of his time and a number of years passed before others began to follow suit. In fact, to quote Larry, "I didn't know I was writing procedurals until somebody invented the term and said that that was the kind of thing I was writing."

If there was a father of the procedural, I think it would have to be the radio program *Dragnet*. Perhaps its success was what created the field, or perhaps the *time* of the procedural, which Larry Treat's books foreshadowed, had finally arrived. In either case, I think the "father" title is deserved for while it is true that no procedural writer I have talked to points to *Dragnet* as a source of inspiration—most not having written their first procedurals until well after *Dragnet*'s demise—I would still regard it as inevitable that the potential of the police-station background was first brought to their attention by Joe Friday and company.

In any case, the police procedural, as yet still unnamed, came into being between the writing and publication of my own first procedural so that, when it appeared in print, it was reviewed as an attempt to translate *Dragnet* to novel form. Though erroneous, such critic reaction is, perhaps, further evidence for the "father" figure.

The police procedural represents the second major change in the nature of the mystery story since it achieved its present "whodunit" form with the advent of the classical detective story. The invention which established the classical period and the "whodunit" form was the shifting of the reader's role from that of observer—i.e., standing at Watson's side watching the great man operate—to that of participant—standing at the detective's side, trying to beat him at his own game.

As a result of this change of viewpoint, the classical detective stories became puzzle tales wherein a detective of outstanding intellect matched wits with a murderer, while the author matched wits with the reader.

The first change in this method of handling the mystery story occurred in the forties and early fifties with the establishment of the private-eye school. Tales in this new approach to the genre retained the puzzle form of the plot, but shifted the story emphasis from thought to action. Prowess took precedence over wits. The detectives in these adventures were for the most part loners, knights errant, fighting a desperate battle for Good against Evil. In the beginning days they were private detectives solving murders to save their clients or themselves. Later they became spies and their problems involved the safety of nations.*

Though the classical detective and the private-eye/ spy operated in radically different ways, both shared certain common traits. Both, for example, were virtually free of legal restraint; both were laws unto themselves; both operated alone and kept their own counsel.

---

*Technically speaking, the term "private-eye" is too limiting to embrace the whole field, and one is tempted to choose a broader title by terming it the "private-eye/spy" school or—heaven forbid—the "eye-spy" school.

The police procedural changes all that. The police procedural thrusts the detective into the middle of a working police force, full of rules and regulations. Instead of bypassing the police, as did its predecessors, the procedural takes the reader inside the department and shows how it operates.

These are stories, not just about policemen, but about the world of the policeman. Police Inspector Charlie Chan doesn't belong. (There're no police.) Nor does Inspector Maigret. (There are police, but Maigret, like Chan, remains his own man.)

When we speak of police procedurals, we are talking about the 87th Precinct books of Ed McBain, about the Elizabeth Linington–Dell Shannon–Lesley Egan, Glendale and Los Angeles police novels. There are John Creasey's Gideon and Roger West stories, there is the Martin Beck series by Maj Sjöwall and the late Per Wahlöö. These are tales about big-city police departments. In the small-town police procedural genre, there may be none other than my own Chief Fred Fellows.

This business of moving toward the police instead of away from the police is a radical shift in the character of the mystery story, and the nature of the procedural can best be understood by comparing it to the other two cited forms. Let us study them in this manner.

I. REALISM AND THE SUSPENSION OF DISBELIEF

"Suspension of disbelief" is one of those awkward phrases that is both hard to say and hard to understand. All it means is: How much *un*reality will the reader endure? How far can a writer go before the reader says, "This is ridiculous!"?

The degree of permissible unreality depends, quite obviously, upon the book. Readers will accept magic spells, witches, and gingerbread houses in fairy tales, but would reject, in disgust, machine guns and electric lights in Civil War novels. The same holds true in the mystery. A great deal more attention to realism is demanded in the police procedural than in the earlier forms. And with reason.

Consider the classical detective story. The moment the reader was brought in on the case and given a chance to solve it, the mystery became a game of wits between author and reader. Authors, therefore, devoted their attention to exploring the possibilities of the puzzle, of finding ways to fool the reader. The result was some of the most elaborately complex plots ever put on paper. Villains, to be worthy foes of the detective, became incredibly clever, incredibly painstaking and, upon occasion, incredibly lucky. The puzzles were exquisite pieces of intellectual architecture.

Such mysteries, naturally, could not pretend a resemblance to reality. Real life murders aren't that elaborately planned. Most actual killings, in fact, are spur-of-the-moment impulses with no more advance thought than will justify the term "premeditation." In real life, the hardest crime to solve is not the one in which every detail has been worked out months in advance, but the unwitnessed, spur-of-the-moment rape or robbery encounter wherein the victim was unknown to the villain.

Such real-life cases, however, would not fit the

puzzle mold of the classical mystery. Since puzzle was the aim, reality had to be sacrificed.

As a result, the classical detective story was structured in a language of its own. A large number of wholly artificial devices were accepted as proper baggage. Probably most notable was the traditional denouement wherein all suspects were gathered together and the detective pointed a finger at first one and then another, keeping suspense at its ultimate until, finally, he pointed to the villain and explained in detail how he had found him out. No matter that this is the last thing a real detective would do, the requisites of the puzzle story demanded this kind of approach.

Another was the detective's habit of keeping all the threads of the mystery in his own head, committing nothing to paper, confiding in no one. Keeping the reader in the dark made such behavior obligatory. It also customarily made the detective a tempting target for the murderer and the reader would forgive the lack of reality in favor of the puzzle and the suspense.

Certain artificialities in the form of clues also came to be accepted. These, however, were not born of necessity but stemmed from gross errors of ignorance due to the fact that the mystery writers of the era worked aloof from the police and did not bother to research that aspect of their novels.

One of the most notable was the gospel that fingerprints abound and are readily discoverable on guns. As an adjunct, it was also accepted that fingerprints would be protected rather than smudged if covered with a handkerchief. In point of fact, an identifiable fingerprint is very hard to come by, even on receptive surfaces like mirrors, and the chances of getting a print from a gun are, if not zero, very nearly so.

Other clues of misinformation which these stories circulated were that the expression on the victim's face revealed his emotion (surprise, fear, etc.) at the moment of death; that pathologists could tell almost to the minute how long the victim had been dead; and that headless corpses could readily be *mis*identified.

None of this is true, of course. The best description of the expression on a corpse's face is that there is none. As for times of death, so many variables affect the onset of postmortem changes that an accurate determination is a virtual impossibility without the help of additional evidence. And, of course, the means of identification of bodies by other than facial characteristics are amazingly many. However, for purposes of the puzzle, these gospels of ignorance helped the authors with their clue-planting and readers learned to accept them. The astute reader would, for instance, reflexively know that any body with the face damaged or the head missing belonged to someone else, and that the supposed victim was, in reality, the murderer.

Nor, finally, did murderers ever take the Fifth or deny the accusation, confident that they could never be convicted. Such a concession to realism would make for messy, inconclusive endings and that would not do. When the puzzle was solved, the book had to end.

Mysteries of the classical school might be summed up as follows: Realism is all right so long as it does not interfere with the puzzle.

The private-eye school of mystery fiction is generally accepted as coming to the fore as a revolt against the fantasyland of the puzzle story. It was as if a new breed of author were saying, "This is ridiculous! Let's bring reality to the mystery."

So the stories became more real. The corpses weren't so pretty and death was a matter taken seriously by all concerned, not merely by the detective.

The puzzle could not be as intricate, of course, but that was readily compensated for by having the plot line complicated by an overlay of action rather than one of intellectual obfuscation.

For all that, reality did not really come to the fore. Instead, it became subservient to action. The private-eye of these tales behaved in an extraordinarily unrealistic manner. He customarily arrived on the murder scene ahead of the police, tampered with evidence, pocketed clues, and broke laws with a recklessness that was only justified by the fact that the police in these stories were such bumbling idiots that, had the private-eye abided by the rules, the mystery would never have been solved. It was only because of his law-unto-himself behavior that the villains were ultimately caught.

As time went on, the stories got wilder, reaching the ultimate in the works of Mickey Spillane. Reality was as absent from the mystery as ever.

One might interpret the advent of the police procedural as if a new breed of author were saying, "This is ridiculous! Let's bring reality to the mystery." Except that one might now ask the ultimate question: How much reality can be brought to the mystery? Can it ever be total? And, if it can, is the police procedural the vehicle? Is the police procedural that ultimate form of the mystery that can combine puzzle, action, and total reality into one?

My personal guess is that total reality can never exist in mystery fiction and my definite conclusion is that it certainly can't exist in the procedural.

Consider, first, the narrow field of the small-town police procedural. There is no way total reality can be brought to a series of this kind. In certain areas the reader is obligated to suspend large amounts of disbelief.

Suppose, for example, an author can produce two small-town police procedurals a year—hardly a staggering output. In each there must be one or more confounding murders, problems that strain the resources of both the reader and the police department.

In reality, a town of, say, ten thousand inhabitants, insulated and self-contained, unassaulted by the outside world, would not have a real, honest-to-goodness murder once in a dozen years. That's eight murders a century.

Of these eight genuine murders per century, the chances are that seven of them would pose no problem at all. The police would know who did it ten minutes after they reached the scene and would have the case wrapped up in twenty-four hours.

Inasmuch as the author of the small-town procedural isn't going to write about easily solved mysteries, the stories he will tell are Crime of the Century tales. Except that, in the small-town he's writing about, they will take place twice a year.

If this seems against the odds, add in the fact that the small-town in question is fortunate enough to have a high-powered resident detective capable of cracking these seemingly insoluble mysteries, and we have to pay another homage to Dame Chance.

What about the other side of the coin? What about the big-city procedural? If we want to portray realism, is this not the locale that offers maximum opportunity? In 1966, there were 700 homicides in New York City. Ten years later, the number was almost 1500. A writer in this big city could not turn out books fast enough to cover the 1-in-8 hard-to-solve cases a single homicide detective might handle in a year.

That part of the story might be true to life. Accurate, also, might be the rules and regulations by which the police abide. The jargon can be learned, the difference between street-cops and book-cops can be understood. In time, an interested writer who has entrée can so familiarize himself with the world of real detectives that he will know their dangers and their territory, guffaw at their "in" jokes, understand the way they think and why. His books may be, therefore, rigorously accurate in all details, except . . .

The real-life detective does not do his detecting *a la* Sherlock Holmes. He may observe the way Holmes observed; he may well put the pieces of a puzzle together the way Holmes put them together, but this is not the way most real-life crimes are solved. The real-life murder is solved, not by ratiocination, not by the exercise of Hercule Poirot's little gray cells, but by the accumulation of information. Dozens of people are questioned—hundreds may be questioned—and, bit by bit, pieces of information are gathered which, ultimately, reveal what happened.

That's the hard way.

The easy way is to have the information brought in. Ask a chief of detectives how cases are solved and he won't answer, "clues," he'll answer, "informants."* There is an adage that a detective is only as good as his informants and it is, rest assured, true.

To the mystery writer, this poses certain problems. Consider the following (based upon a true case). There is a shooting in Harlem, one man dead in the hospital, a second man wounded. The wounded man, interviewed by police, tells the story that he and the victim were walking along the street when a man came out of a bar, gunned them down, and ran around the corner. He never saw the man before, he doesn't know why the man shot them. The family of the victim swears he had no enemies, the people in the bar saw nothing, witnesses to the actual shooting don't know who the man was. There is no gun, no clues, no anything.

To an outsider it sounds like a motiveless, unsolvable crime. Even Charlie Chan and Philo Vance would be up a tree.

The police, who are familiar with the local scene, will not be so confounded. They will speculate that it had to do with drugs, that the victim was either a pusher who sold bad junk, or he had robbed a pusher—either act being a killing offense. This gives them motive, but it does not tell them "who." They are not unduly distressed, however, for they anticipate that, later that night—maybe three o'clock in the morning—an informant will slip into headquarters, up to the squad room,

---

*The term informers carries ugly connotations and isn't used.

and tell the detectives who did it and why. The detectives would then check out the information and, a few days later, make an arrest.

That's the way it usually happens, but it makes for a very bad story. Certain adjustments would have to be imposed upon such a tale to put it into saleable form, to wit: the detective would have to solve the case without the aid of the informant.

But the moment we start doing this, we are moving away from reality again.

II. THE HERO

Let us now turn our attention to the heroes of these tales. What are they like and why are they that way?

The detectives of the classical period are all patterned after Sherlock Holmes. They are created as men of giant intellect, towering over their fellows. The only man, in fact, who can come close to matching the hero's intellect is the villain.

Generally speaking, the detective is also separated from the crowd in other ways. Father Brown wears a habit, Nero Wolfe is an obese gourmet, Poirot and Charlie Chan are foreigners, Vance a dilettante, Wimsey a Lord, the early Queen, effete. Every effort is undertaken to make these detectives memorable, to give them the kind of lasting identity that Holmes has. And the ones mentioned above have certainly achieved this distinction.

The homage paid to these detectives and their virtual freedom from the bothersome restrictions imposed on other mortals give them an enviable position. Not for them are there problems about money. They do not have to worry about their jobs, about wives and children. They, like Holmes, are free of all encumbrances, able to devote their great mental prowess exclusively to the murders at hand. It is not difficult for an author to establish reader identification with such a hero.

Let us move on to the hero of the private-eye school. This is a different species of being entirely. This man is a puzzle-solver too, but he is not content to sit and ponder. He is a man of energy and he solves the puzzles through action.

The Saint, James Bond, and Mike Hammer are extreme examples of the type, but they serve as illustrations. These private-eye heroes have more than a touch of Superman about them. They are tough, brave, resourceful, and—as we have noted before—a law unto themselves. They tend to be cavalier, even flamboyant. The qualities that separate them from the rest of the cast are their ability to operate in excess of everyone else, be it the alcohol they can absorb, the beatings they can take, the laws they can break, the women they can handle.

These men are heroes in the genuine sense of the word, meaning that they go out and battle for Right against Wrong, and WIN. They represent the Walter Mitty dream of the frustrated average man whose world has grown too large for an outcome to be affected by his own efforts. The hero's reckless disregard of authority and his success at overcoming obstacles are therapeutic to the reader. He identifies with such a man. He is eager to read more tales of his derring-do.

What happens, though, when an author seeks to create a hero for a police procedural? Immediately he's in trouble, for the attractive superman hero is denied him by the nature of the genre. Not only does realism require that the hero of procedurals be human rather than superhuman, but also the restrictions of his job and the society he is sworn to uphold.

Consider, first, the small-town procedural. Who can be the protagonist of such a story? Certainly not some handsome young cop who drinks a quart of Scotch for breakfast and has to fight his way past the blondes who camp outside his door—not even a handsome young cop who doesn't drink, smoke, or date —not a young cop at all, even if he's homely.

When it comes to solving serious crimes, the responsibility goes to the top men on the force, which means the chief of police, the detectives he's got, and the officer in charge of detectives. We're talking about older men, men who are probably married and raising families, men who wouldn't find a blonde in every bed, even if sleepy blondes abounded, because they have too little to offer. They are just struggling, balding, graying, unromantic, plain-looking, ordinary Joes.

It is much harder, obviously, for an author to create a memorable character, one the reader will want to keep reading about, if the character can't do or be anything memorable; —if he can't attain positions of authority until he is past his handsome, dashing youth; —if he can't dine on gourmet foods and know the right wines because he lives on a policeman's salary; —if he has to get to work on time, obey the law, go through all the red tape that real policemen do; —if he has to turn over significant parts of the investigation to others and stay in the good graces of the public and the board of police commissioners.

Such a man can't help being a rather gray, colorless character, leading a gray, colorless life. No single-handedly walking into the nest of thieves for him; —no sneaking into the bad guy's apartment to find crucial evidence; —no keeping to himself bits of vital information so that he can hog the limelight when he really socks it to them at the end.

In the small-town procedural, the solution of a case is not a one-man operation in any case. It can be accomplished by a team of two, but no fewer. Nor can the two be Mutt and Jeff, Johnson and Boswell, or Sherlock and Watson. The disparity must not appear too great. It cannot be me and my shadow, it must be a legitimate team of two.

What about a big-city procedural? In a big-city police force, the number of detectives in a squad will run between twenty and thirty. The problem of creating a hero is not multiplied, however. While many of the detectives may help in various phases of a serious crime—interviewing everybody in an apartment building, for example—and while lab technicians, pathologists, photo, emergency service, and other functionaries may be resorted to, these are information-gathering operations, which information will then be delivered to the detectives in charge, and these would probably again be a team of only two. In a New York

City homicide, for instance, the two would be the squad detective who "caught" the case and is therefore responsible for its disposition, and the member of the homicide squad—specialists in this kind of crime—who would be assigned to work with him.

This would appear to make the big-city procedural the same as a small-town procedural, with a pair of detectives carrying the ball. In fact, however, the author of a big-city procedural can go with an individual hero if he wants. If his hero is a member of a specialty squad, like homicide, the detective he'd be assigned to help would be different in each new case and he would remain as the sole, continuing character. In such handling, the rest of the detective squad and the other cases under investigation would be background.

Given this material to work with, what are the tactics for producing memorable detectives? It's not as easy a job as when a writer has the license to invent as he pleases, but the opportunities are still plentiful. The family life of the detectives can be explored—a possibility that was never entertained in the classic and private-eye forms. The relationships of the men with each other can play an important part in the story—an aspect of the mystery that didn't exist when detectives stood head, shoulders, and waist above their associates and communed only with themselves. In fact, the interior of the squad room can become the equivalent of a daytime serial setting—meaning that the readers get to know the people, their personalities and their problems so well that they look forward to the next book as a chance to rejoin old friends.

The hero aspect of the procedural is radically different from the other two forms, but it offers, probably, a much richer vein to mine.

III. BACKGROUND

Despite the difference in the hero form, it is in the area of background that the greatest distinction occurs between the police procedural and all other forms of the mystery. In the classical and private-eye forms, an author could get away with minimal research, or none at all. Some authors did do research and enhanced their books with information on special skills or backgrounds, giving their stories an added fillip. The research, however, was inevitably directed toward exotic subjects of intellectual interest. The one area that was not researched was the crass, mundane, very nonintellectual subject of how real detectives operated and what the business of solving murders was actually all about.

Of course, there was little incentive. The creators of the classical detectives did not need to know how the police operated, for the only function of the police was to take the murderer away at the end of the story.

Nor was there any particular reason why the writers of private-eye stories should do background research into the way real crimes were solved. If their heroes operated above the law, there was no need for the authors to know what the laws were. In fact, the only effect a knowledge of law would have upon an author would be to inhibit the freedom he was seeking to give his character.

With the police procedural, of course, the situation is totally reversed. Since it sets itself to show realistic-appearing policemen encountering realistic crimes and solving them in a realistic manner, a knowledge of how police forces are actually structured (they vary greatly from city to city) becomes essential. Not only must procedures be known and understood, but also the law. Even a rookie cop has been drilled in criminal law and knows what he can and cannot do, as well as the requirements he must satisfy. The writer, therefore, had better give himself a similar background and know such things as the rules of evidence and how to cope with the Miranda decision.

The writer of a procedural must be true to life in other ways. Since his readership will grant him scant suspension of disbelief, he cannot have his hero over-drink without getting drunk or sick. His hero can't get bashed unconscious without going to the hospital for observation. Everything must be true to life. All kinds of little bits and pieces of annoying trivia will have to be checked and verified, lest readers start complaining.

The problem, then, for the procedural writer is not merely to come up with a compelling story. He has the added obligation and chore of researching.

IV. PUZZLE AND FAIR PLAY

Lastly, we come to the story that takes place against this procedural background. Here one encounters a situation which poses interesting questions.

In both the classical and private-eye type mysteries, there was a puzzle to be solved, a villain to be caught and, since the reader was engaged as a participant, an element of fair play to be included. The reader had to know everything the detective knew. The reader went through the case at the detective's side.

The puzzle was in greatest evidence in the classical tale. It was the whole point of the story. In the private-eye genre the puzzle played second fiddle to the action, but it was still there.

Does it exist in the procedural?

The answer is, of course, yes. But, depending upon the type of procedural, it can be foremost, as is likely in the small-town procedural where nothing else is happening, or as low as third fiddle in the big-city type of tale, coming in behind both action and background.

It still, however, must be there. The problem cannot solve itself nor, as mentioned earlier, be solved via the unsolicited arrival of an informant. The detectives must work at a solution and the solution must result from their work. And, of course, the reader again is taken along with the detective—at least on the major case—and is apprised of all the information that the detective is privy to.

These qualities, the solving of a puzzle with the reader given all the clues, are the hallmarks of the mystery story and must be present. Omit them and the tale, no matter how mysterious, how murderous, how police-oriented, is not a proper mystery.

Now comes an aspect of the police-procedural tale which, while it has been a matter of moment to me, does not seem to concern anyone else, with the exception, perhaps, of Ed McBain. (See his deaf man, El

Sordo, in such as "Let's Hear It for the Deaf Man.")
This is the element of the "Fair Fight."

Sherlock Holmes had his Moriarty, a man whose talents were a match for his own. In like manner, the mighty-minded detectives of the classical age had to be similarly tested. In order to don the mantle of super-genius, they had to best the best. This is why the puzzles they had to unravel were so elaborate, why the murderers were so clever, why all the odds had to be stacked in their opponent's favor. Chance could not solve the case for the detective. It could only operate on behalf of the villain, making the detective's problem ever more difficult. The detective, to earn his victory, had to prove his supremacy over both the foe and the odds. There could be no sere leaf on the laurel.

In like manner, the private-eye had to outsmart the gangleader, the nightclub owner or, in the case of the spy, the arrayed forces of the enemy country. The odds always had to be on the side of the opposition, to be overcome along with the foe.

Now we come to the police procedural and we find there is a change in the battle line-up.

Given: One murderer.

And what is there against him?

We can count on at least two detectives devoting full time to his apprehension while, behind them, at beck and call, lie the total resources of the police, medical, and legal systems of the community. Let the villain hole up in an abandoned warehouse and the hero will not go in and shoot it out with him in a one-to-one showdown. There will be dozens of men, all more heavily armed and protected than their quarry. They will have tear gas, searchlights, walkie-talkies, helicopters—an awesome array of tools—creating a maximum mismatch (quite properly) in order to reduce the element of danger to the "good guys" to a minimum.

The disparity is even greater than that. The police detective will be as observant as a Sherlock Holmes by virtue of his training and years of conditioning. If he cannot match Holmes's brilliant mind, he has learned, through long experience, what to look for and where to look, which is almost as good. And the available laboratory facilities can produce, from clues, information the like of which Conan Doyle would never have dreamed.

Meanwhile, against this super-Sherlock stands no Moriarty. The average murderer in real life is below average in mentality. He is motivated by emotion rather than brains. His responses are less planned, his motives less well thought-out. As a physical specimen he would rarely be capable of holding his own against a detective in an even fight. He is more than likely to be one of life's losers. He is outgunned, outmaneuvered, and outwitted every step of the way. The fight is anything but fair.

Does anybody care?

Interestingly enough, I sought, in my own small-town police procedurals, to cope with the problem as follows: The murderers were of better than average intelligence—middle- and upper-middle-class in background (not unreasonable in the small-town genre). Then, due partly to their cleverness, the rest to the luck that fell their way, the whole police apparatus would fail to uncover them. An impasse would be reached, at which point the battle became a one-to-one fight between the chief-of-police hero and the villain. The chief would have to come up, on his own, with the one move or idea that would break the case.

This may well have been a wasted concern on my part, however, for nowhere does there seem to be anyone—reader, critic, or other procedural writer—who has given the matter a thought. Do readers feel a certain sympathy for the outgunned and outnumbered murderer? Do they root for the underdog?

Apparently not. In these realistic days where bodies smell and victims spill blood instead of ketchup, perhaps the readers' desire for justice (or is it vengeance?) is such that they don't care how the killer is brought to bay. Perhaps, as another author suggests, the interest in the police procedural lies not in story but in the fascination of this strange world of the policeman and what it is that sets him apart from the rest of mankind; that makes him advance where others retreat, that makes him the helper instead of the helpless.

Or, perhaps what counts is the satisfaction we feel at seeing a great power for Good overthrow the forces of Evil. Perhaps the police procedural excites that emotion within man that is so evident in war: The desire to annihilate the enemy, and the more overwhelming the victory, the more satisfying it is.

V. CONCLUSIONS

A comparison of the police-procedural mystery with its predecessors produces eye-opening results. What comes through most strongly is the close relationship between the classical and private-eye forms, and the separateness of the police procedural. This is evident in the areas we have discussed, but the very difference creates a message of its own.

The classical detective story and the private-eye novel were inevitably described as "light reading." One picked up the former for the puzzle, the latter for the action and the accent was on fun. (The lack of reality helped. Who can take the unreal seriously?)

Reviewers of police procedurals, however, don't talk in terms of "light reading." "Social message" is more commonly the measure of evaluation. The police procedural, by showing policemen as they are, shows, by definition, the social ills they contend against as *they* are. Sometimes the social commentaries revealed by procedural authors are deliberately intended, sometimes the revelations are unconsciously done. In either case, the very nature of the procedural provokes a type of story totally beyond the aim of the other forms.

The puzzle—all-important to the classical story— can sink to the depths of being nothing more than the glue that holds a procedural in the genre. There is little else the new form has in common with the old.

One can only ponder the meaning of the changes in the mystery genre. Perhaps the switch from classical to private-eye seemed, at the time, as enormous as the new switch from them to the procedural. Perhaps we should, therefore, pay more attention to the common ground the procedural shares with its predecessors than the differences.

Where does the mystery go from here? Can it go anywhere? Do the changes in the mystery point a direction? The future will produce answers to these questions but as to what they will be, this writer does not feel equipped to venture an opinion.

*Donald A. Yates traces his
beginnings as a mystery buff to
the early 1940s when, as a boy, he
read Ellery Queen's* CHINESE
ORANGE MYSTERY *and knew that
his life would never again be
the same. He wrote his first
detective story—a locked-room
tale—at the age of 13 (it is still
unpublished), and many more
thereafter (published). Dr. Yates,
who is professor of Spanish
American literature at Michigan
State University, has translated
numerous detective stories
and novels from Spanish into
English. He has written detective
dramas for the stage and
television, has been a mystery/
crime fiction reviewer for many
years, and has published several
critical essays on the genre.
Dr. Yates translated and edited*
LATIN BLOOD: THE BEST CRIME
STORIES OF SPANISH AMERICA.

LOCKED ROOMS AND PUZZLES:
A CRITICAL MEMOIR

In his most extravagant daydreams, Edgar Allan Poe surely could never have imagined what he had started when, in 1841, in "The Murders in the Rue Morgue," he wrote the mutilated body of a young woman into a locked and apparently inaccessible room and then proceeded to fashion a rational explanation for that horrible and perplexing discovery. Poe's tale was the first crime puzzle elaborated for examination by a "detective" and, quite obviously, by an alert and aware reader as well. (Who today can deny that with his first tale of ratiocination Poe created not only a new kind of story, but also a distinctly new kind of reader?)

For the creator of C. Auguste Dupin, this story embodied a longing that he himself most likely experienced—a hopeful yearning for the eventual triumph of intellect and order over distressingly pathetic circumstances. Yet historical judgment has come to regard his narrative in a different light. Here was not only the first "detective story" but also a special type of fictional puzzle—a "locked-room problem"—that by rights stands as the begetter of the incalculable number of puzzle stories that have since been composed to satisfy a quickly established reader predilection for a tale that 1) posed a problem in crime, 2) methodically sifted through pertinent evidence and testimony, and 3) evolved a solution compatible with the facts as they had been presented. Such was the beginning.

I

Essentially, the detective story is a puzzle story. Characteristically, in no other type of fiction does the author so deliberately anticipate and prepare his encounter with his reader. That reader knows in advance what he wants and, within the limits of his ingenuity and the conventions of the genre, the author dutifully provides what is expected. (Precisely because of such "predictables," detective fiction has been excluded—justly or not—from serious critical consideration alongside works of "mainline" fiction.)

As we have observed, of all puzzle-type stories, the "locked room" problem is the oldest. It seems also to be the most perennially appealing, representing as it does the ideal expression of the popular "impossible crime" type of puzzle. The reason for its popularity is not entirely clear. I can offer my own explanation, but first consider the observation of a celebrated author and critic of detective fiction, Dorothy Sayers. She pointed out that man has long delighted in perplexing himself with puzzles, riddles, conundrums, and the like, apparently for the purpose of experiencing the anticipated and curiously reassuring pleasure of discovering their answer or solution.[1] While this is, admittedly, a form of torment, it is also a form of entertainment. Hence it might be appropriate to state that, generally speaking, within this classification most detective fiction can be included: it is, in essence, "entertainment fiction."

Looking back, I can see that from an early age I have responded enthusiastically to the appeal of the puzzle. Not everybody is fond of this sort of writing, but it seems that if chance leads certain persons to detective fiction, something in their character and fundamental view of things—depending, too, perhaps on their capacity for wonder—first arouses interest and then produces keen satisfaction. In my own case, life was pleasant and uneventful until my thirteenth year, when I read Ellery Queen's *The Chinese Orange Mystery*, perched in a tree in a gully behind my house in Ann Arbor. Nothing has been quite the same since. The bizarre attraction of the scene of that crime was nearly more than my mind could accept. What a challenge! And what a solution! Suddenly, I couldn't get enough. I began to read incessantly. My head was soon filled with other ingenious challenges and solutions. Then new plots began to take shape in my imagination. I read all of Queen, then Christie, Gardner, Carr and Dickson, Conan Doyle . . .

There are passive mystery readers who come along for the ride and others who actively try to match wits with the author. I was in the latter category. At times I figured out the solution; other times I came up with a solution that seemed correct and inevitable, given the facts of the problem, and then the author found his way to *another* explanation! I decided not to waste these other, perfectly creditable solutions, so I wrote them down and in a year or so I was writing my own detective stories.

I invented a brilliant amateur detective—Kingsley Quentin—and sent him out on his first case, "The Adventure of the Wounded Tyrolean." Youth is confident if not cocksure. My title came from a footnote on page 31 of Ellery Queen's *The Spanish Cape Mystery* (1934) where, clarifying a reference in the text to a "most baffling murder-case," you will read as follows:

> One of the most extraordinary cases Ellery has ever investigated. The newspapers called it "The Case of the Wounded Tyrolean"; more specific identification may not be given here. It is one of the few problems, to my knowledge, which stalemated Ellery; and it is still an unsolved crime.

If Ellery Queen hadn't cracked it, it must have been a tough case. Surely a locked-room puzzle. What else? So I gave Kingsley Quentin a classic problem to solve. The plot idea came from a solution I foresaw to a John Dickson Carr novel. I was sure it was the right one. But Carr had something else in mind and the ingenious solution belonged to me. I remember plotting out the puzzle, delighting in the utter simplicity of it all. A man is found stabbed in the back in a locked room. The coroner pronounces him dead and Quentin arrives. He takes careful note of the position of the body, the location of the furniture, the testimony of the person who discovered the scene, and other such details. Later he examines the autopsy report. And he reasons. There are four ways in which a person can die: 1) natural death, 2) accidental death, 3) murder, and 4) suicide. Quentin goes on to prove conclusively that the victim did not die from any of the four causes. Impossible?

Right. An impossible crime in impossible circumstances. But Quentin arrives logically at the solution, and the whole scheme is revealed.

I wrote it up and sent it to *Ellery Queen's Mystery Magazine*. Ellery Queen did not publish it. I still have the manuscript among some old papers. And no one, so far as I know, has ever used that solution.

II

My own love affair with detective puzzles did not end with that rejection. I went right on reading—and writing. It has been said that we do our most impressionable reading before we reach eighteen. After that, though we continue to read, books do not impress us in the same way. Another way of stating this is to point out that the most memorable books and the most vivid reading experiences are those of our early years. So it was with me. I can be thankful that I was reading detective stories. They train one to be a careful and observant reader—no small benefit. And through their stress on order and the dramatic they provide a stimulating counterpoint or contrast to our everyday surroundings.

John Dickson Carr was quoted back in the mid-thirties as saying: "I have prowled around Limehouse, Shepheard's at Cairo, and the gummiest sections of Paris, but I have never yet seen a really choice murder in a locked room; a mysterious master mind, or a really good-looking adventuress with slant eyes. This is discouraging."[2] Carr, more than anyone else, has made a fine art of conceiving "impossible" crimes and then demonstrating how they could indeed be carried out. In his highly entertaining novels (some of which he signed with the pseudonym of Carter Dickson) he has offered his readers generous doses of the exotic and mystifying elements that have come to characterize the best in puzzle fiction. He may not have stumbled onto an authentic "locked-room" murder in his own lifetime, but he has given the world so many "locked-room" mysteries to ponder over that his name is today irrevocably linked to that special kind of "impossible" crime.

Between Poe and Carr-Dickson the puzzle story enjoyed more than a century of varied and lively cultivation. Some time ago in an article entitled "The Locked House: An Essay on Locked Rooms," I examined that most classic of impossible crime traditions and briefly sketched its history. Other specialists have written on the subject in recent years. English critic and book collector Robert Adey has prepared an anthology of locked-room short stories dating from the period 1838–1918, and has also published in the *Antiquarian Book Monthly Review* a short essay entitled "A Brief History of the Early Years of the Locked Room,"[3] wherein he reviews the development of the locked-room gambit during the eighty-year period encompassed by his proposed anthology. (I hope he eventually finds a publisher for it.)

Over the years I've put together the contents of my own ideal anthology of locked-room tales. If some day I publish it, there will be fifteen pieces gathered under the title of (what else?) *The Locked House*. I note that among my favorites there is no duplication of stories included in the Adey selection. This is surely proof that the locked-room tradition—not to mention that of the more freewheeling impossible-crime category—

is anything but a narrative dead-end despite detective-fiction critic and historian Howard Haycraft's advice, given back in 1941 to would-be mystery writers: "Avoid the Locked-Room puzzle. Only a genius can invest it with novelty or interest to-day."[4]

That was some thirty-five years ago. If more arguments were needed to show that the locked-room/impossible-crime convention is a vigorous and dynamic form with vitality to spare, we need only examine the contents of the only existing collection of "impossible crimes and escapes" —*The Locked Room Reader* (Random House, 1968), edited by the late Hans Stefan Santesson. Of the sixteen pieces included, *thirteen* were first published after Haycraft's judgment was offered!

I note, too, that between my list of favorites and the contents of Santesson's anthology, there is only one duplication—Melville Davisson Post's superb "The Doomdorf Mystery." Santesson's main achievement in the volume was to bring back into print and prominence Israel Zangwill's classic *The Big Bow Mystery* (1892). In my earlier essay on the locked-room tradition, I wrote the following about this ingenious story:

> The year 1895 saw the publication of a tremendously popular, though virtually forgotten detective novel by Israel Zangwill. It was titled *The Big Bow Mystery*. The author, a successful journalist of the time, first wrote the tale in serial form for a daily newspaper. His original and imaginative resolution of the locked-room problems made of the story a brilliant *tour de force*.
>
> So appealing, in fact, was his solution to the problem of a man apparently murdered in an inaccessible room that it has been employed with considerable success in numerous detective tales

since—by John Dickson Carr, G. K. Chesterton, and James Yaffe, to mention only those that come immediately to mind.

Following the appearance of *The Big Bow Mystery*, Zangwill, in a coy mood, made a public statement to the effect that when he began to write the commissioned story he had no idea who the murderer might be, but that as the readers of the serial began to send in their unsolicited, premature solutions identifying the killer, he automatically began to eliminate from possible guilt every character the readers named. When the time came for the denouement to be written, Zangwill claimed, he had only one unsuspected character left. Therefore, he made *that* person the murderer.

It was a charming hoax, but we know better. The plot, its solution, and its culprit were firmly fixed in Zangwill's mind long before he wrote the final scene. We have his own words on the truth of the matter: "Long before *The Big Bow Mystery* was written, I said to myself one night that no mystery monger had ever murdered a man in a room to which there was no possible access. The puzzle was scarcely propounded ere the solution flew up.[5]

Looking back now on these words, I can see that I could well have been mistaken. Zangwill *could* indeed have conceived of the locked-room *idea* as he said (without committing himself to any specific individual as the criminal) and then played along with his readers the game he has described. Technically, Zangwill was wrong about being the first person ever to have "murdered a man in a room to which there was no access." That, of course, was the trick that Poe accomplished. (Robert Adey wonders if Zangwill had possibly read the Irishman Joseph Sheridan Le Fanu's early tale—which had no solution—and decided to do the job up right.)

The Big Bow Mystery was composed during 1891. Had Zangwill dawdled a few months longer, he might well have been twice wrong in thinking that he was the first person to bring off a locked-room murder. For in the February 1892 issue of the *Strand Magazine,* Sir Arthur Conan Doyle offered to an eager public one of his most memorable Sherlock Holmes exploits, "The Adventure of the Speckled Band," wherein a deadly swamp adder dutifully collaborates with a "locked-room murderer."

Few people seem to realize the great debt that Doyle owed to Poe and his Dupin. The truth of the matter is that the man who gave Sherlock Holmes to the world was indebted to the American for many of the characteristics of his detective as well as for numerous plot ideas which he developed into Holmes stories. In no instance is this latter debt more apparent than in "The Speckled Band." To be sure, the atmosphere of the story was completely Doyle's. (Atmosphere, with him, was a strong point; consider, for example, *The Hound of the Baskervilles.*) However, the type of problem—a genuine locked-room puzzle—as Doyle knew (and Zangwill ought to have known) was of Poe's design. But after "The Murders in the Rue Morgue" the concept belonged to the world.

To his credit, Doyle described the fatal circumstances with model economy. (Helen Stoner speaks):

> [The coroner] investigated the case with great care . . . but he was unable to find any satisfactory causes of death. My evidence showed that the

door had been fastened upon the inner side, and the windows were blocked by old-fashioned shutters with broad iron bars, which were carefully sounded and were shown to be quite solid all around, and the flooring was also thoroughly examined, with the same result. The chimney is wide, but is barred up by four large staples. It is certain, therefore, that my sister was quite alone when she met her end.[6]

Where have we heard that before?

III

Well, we have heard it many times since 1892. In our century the locked-room impossible crime has been brilliantly developed and elaborated on. In 1907 Gaston Leroux's *The Mystery of the Yellow Room* gives the problem a *new* twist in one of the most ingenious detective novels ever written. An *accident* occurs behind that locked door. But nonetheless . . . In 1918, in "The Doomdorf Mystery," Melville Davisson Post created a memorable locked-room parable of good versus evil for the shrewd talents of his rural West Virginia squire/detective, Uncle Abner. It is one of the best and most appropriate locked-room solutions ever devised, given the Old Testament flavor of the story. A religious tone infused into a locked-room mystery? Why not? In the realm of the impossible-crime concept, anything it would seem, is possible.

In the twenties and thirties gimmicks and gadgets for locking the critical door or window *from the outside* enjoyed a vogue of sorts. S. S. Van Dine's *The "Canary" Murder Case* (1927) proposed one method. And Ellery

Queen, who in a sense descended from Van Dine as Doyle did from Poe, gave us in 1934 his intricate *The Chinese Orange Mystery.* The Queen novel included his customary "Challenge to the Reader," a moment toward the end of the novel where the author inserts a page stating that the reader now possesses all the facts that detective Ellery Queen has assembled—and the latter has just announced that he knows the identity of the murderer. Can the reader reach the same solution on his own? This was surely the single most important contribution of "the Queens" (the writing partnership of Frederic Dannay and Manfred B. Lee) to the development of the detective novel—the ultimate refinement of the concept of "fair play" with the reader. Their timing was inspired: At the moment when the Queens were plotting their first novel (*The Roman Hat Mystery,* 1929), Dorothy Sayers was publishing the judgment that "the tendency is for the modern educated public to demand fair play from the writer."[7]

For those critics who feel that the highly complex machinations involved in getting a door locked from the outside strains credulity beyond the breaking point, I can suggest that true life circumstances have on occasion reproduced the classic terms of the locked room. Again I quote from my earlier piece:

> Should [such gimmicks] strike you as being an absurd and perhaps exaggerated expression of the locked-room puzzle, I would like to recommend to you a report on a real-life murder case in which a Chinese laundryman was murdered in his New York shop, under authentic locked-room circumstances. Alan Hynd has given a good account of the baffling crime in the January 1933

issue of *Mystery* magazine. And in *Actor's Blood*
(1936) writer-journalist Ben Hecht gives his colorful fictionization of the same incident in the story
"The Mystery of the Fabulous Laundryman." In
Hecht's bizarre case, the murderer, as if to stress
the beauty of his crime and eliminate the suspicion of a suicide, lopped off the unfortunate laundryman's hands and carried them off. (p. 279)

At almost the same time, John Dickson Carr was can-
onizing the locked-room puzzle in his fine novel *The
Three Coffins* (1935) by giving the seventeenth chapter
over to a "Locked Room Lecture" by his greatly admired detective, Dr. Fell. The exposition covers some
fifteen pages and is pure intellectual delight. (The surprise selection in my projected locked-room anthology
was to be this chapter from the Carr novel.)

There is an amusing byplay involving the usual
distinctions made between literature and reality in
the opening paragraphs of this celebrated chapter.

"But, if you're going to analyze impossible situations," interrupted Pettis, "why discuss detective fiction?"

"Because," said the doctor, frankly, "we're in
a detective story, and we don't fool the reader by
pretending we're not. Let's not invent elaborate
excuses to drag in a discussion of detective stories. Let's candidly glory in the noblest pursuits
possible to characters in a book."[8]

Later on in the thirties—probably the most glorious
decade for the impossible-crime story on both sides of
the Atlantic—the mystifying and resourceful Clayton
Rawson playfully undertook to restore real-life substance to Dr. Fell when he wrote in his locked-room
puzzler, *Death from a Top Hat* (1938):

"Ever heard of Dr. Fell, Inspector?"

Gavin's grunt was negative.

"Harte?"

"I'm way ahead of you. You're thinking of his 'Locked Room Lecture' in *The Three Coffins*. Right?"

Merlini nodded, his eyes twinkling. "Yes, Dr. Fell, Inspector, is an English detective of considerable ability, whose cases have been recorded by John Dickson Carr."[9]

Rawson then proceeds to give a resumé of Carr's categorization of the locked-room conventions—all included, of course, within the pages of another locked-room mystery.

Carr's well-deserved reputation is not based solely on his long series of locked-room puzzles, for his more general ambition has been to give all sorts of impossible situations and phenomena perfectly logical (if highly imaginative) explanations. He delights, for example, in having a victim walk out into the middle of a tennis court, leaving distinct footprints, and there vanish into thin air. He takes similar enjoyment from having a man dive into an ordinary backyard swimming pool and disappear from sight.

IV

At some idle moment in the future, it would be interesting to compile a list of representative impossible-crime novels and short stories. It would be an attractive guide, and would extend, without diminishing either in resourcefulness or versatility, up into our own day. In these pages we have touched only on titles published up to the late 1930s. The past four decades— four decades since the *Chinese Orange!*—have been rich ones, characterized generally by a higher level of literateness of style.

Such a list would have to include multiple entries by, among others, Anthony Boucher (under his own name as well as his H. H. Holmes pseudonym), Herbert Brean, John Dickson Carr/Carter Dickson, Ellery Queen, Helen McCloy, and Clayton Rawson. There would be at least one book each by Agatha Christie, Freeman Wills Crofts, Michael Gilbert, Harry Stephen Keeler, John Rhode, Hake Talbot, S. S. Van Dine, Edgar Wallace, and Anthony Wynne. The short-story list would add to these names those of G. K. Chesterton, Jacques Futrelle, Thomas Hanshew, Edward Hoch, C. Daly King, Melville Davisson Post, and Dorothy Sayers.

What an enormous appeal this type of puzzle story has had for detective-fiction writers for more than a century! Surely the tale of the impossible made plausible will always be with us. And it seems safe to say that the locked-room puzzle is here to stay. Commenting on Poe's original tale of ratiocination, Robert Adey has written:

> The locked room motif was to prove a popular one in the years that followed. Perhaps because it is a capsulation of all that is good and easily comprehensible in detective fiction. A problem simple to state and with a bewildering and ingenious variety of solutions.[10]

I'll second that.

One last word, in case your curiosity was snagged. In my first and now distant and secret debut as a mystery writer, I posed the problem of a victim found in a genuine (no gimmicks) locked room. Of the four ways of dying it was proved that he did not die 1) a natural death; 2) an accidental death; 3) he did not commit suicide; and 4) he was not murdered. What was the solution?

Wasn't it Sherlock Holmes who said: "When you have eliminated the impossible, whatever remains, however improbable, must be the truth"?

Happy hunting!

NOTES

[1] Introduction to *The Omnibus of Crime*, New York: Payson and Clark Ltd, 1929, p. 9.

[2] Quoted on the dust jacket of his *The Three Coffins*, New York: Harper & Bros., 1935.

[3] The title given here is actually the subtitle. The author's intended title, "Behind a Victorian Locked Door," was lost at the printer's. The sharp-eyed reader will have noted that the earliest date given for Adey's locked-room collection is 1838—some three years before Poe's "Murders in the Rue Morgue." The explanation is that although there is a description of an unsolved locked-room murder in J. Sheridan Le Fanu's "Passage in the Secret History of an Irish Countess" (1838), the author "employs no detective and there is no denouement as such."

[4] Howard Haycraft, *Murder for Pleasure: The Life and Times of the Detective Story*, New York: D. Appleton-Century, 1941, p. 250.

[5] In *The Mystery Writer's Art*, edited by Francis M. Nevins, Jr., Bowling Green: Bowling Green University Popular Press, 1970, pp. 276–277.

[6] *The Complete Sherlock Holmes*, Garden City: Garden City Publishing Company, 1938, pp. 297–298.

[7] Sayers, *op. cit.*, p. 21.

[8] *Death from a Top Hat*, New York: G. P. Putnam's Sons, 1938.

[9] John Dickson Carr, *op. cit.*

[10] Robert Adey, *op. cit.*, p. 15.

TEN

MICHAEL GILBERT

Michael Gilbert, British solicitor, makes a career of upholding the law of the land. Michael Gilbert, author, makes yet another career of writing about those who transgress the law and those who pursue the transgressors. Acknowledged as one of the more accomplished detective-story writers of the post-World War II generation, Mr. Gilbert has produced innumerable short stories, many of them while commuting from his home in Kent to his offices in Lincoln's Inn, London. Eulogized by Ellery Queen as "the compleat professional" storyteller, Mr. Gilbert is equally at home with the play, the novel, or the short-story form. Among his detective novels are CLOSE QUARTERS *(his first, in 1947),* SMALLBONE DECEASED, *and* DEATH HAS DEEP ROOTS.

THE SPY IN FACT AND FICTION

There was a game, which was popular in my childhood, but which seems to have given way now to more sophisticated entertainments. It was called *L'Attaque*. Each player arranged his pieces on a board, which was roughly the size of a chess board. They represented officers in the army, and ranged in rank from humble second lieutenants to lieutenant generals, generals and field marshals, all in correct and gorgeous military uniform. There may have been non-commissioned officers, but at that class-conscious period I doubt it. Your opponent could see only the backs of your pieces. From his viewpoint there was no method of distinguishing their rank.

The game proceeded by a series of challenges. You would move a figure of yours forward until he could "challenge" a figure belonging to your opponent. If the rank of your challenger was higher than that of the challengee, then you had won, and your opponent's piece was removed. It was a question of tactics and of memory.

There was one exception to the strict military ranking and precedence of the pieces. One figure was not in uniform at all. He was a sinister character wearing a cloak and a dark hat. Before him, even the exalted field marshal bit the dust. He was the joker in the pack, disturbing, unpredictable, and omnipotent. He was the spy.

"Unfair," my sisters used to say when the spy felled a major general in epaulettes and cocked hat, with a sword and five rows of campaign medals.

"Unfair," generations before and since have proclaimed.

In his definitive introduction to the history of the spy, which he wrote as preface to a collection of short stories, Eric Ambler says: "Admirable though he may be in terms of character and probity, the fact remains that, in his professional capacity, the spy is *ipso facto* a liar and a thief. He may be worse. It may be his business to suborn and corrupt, calculatedly to play upon the weaknesses of other men in order to make them traitors. He may have to use blackmail and extortion to get results. The fact that his motives are not those of a common criminal is beside the point. The motives of the public hangman are not those of a common murderer but that makes it no more agreeable to shake hands with the fellow."

This seems a hard verdict on a man who goes abroad, often for inadequate pay, with no kudos for his work and the possibility of an unpleasant and ignominious death. And what about the attitudes of the people who send him?

"The result," says Ambler, "is a conspiracy of silence and a myth. 'We know it has to be done, but we will not talk about it. We will give the orders if we must—though it is better if those who are to do the work will write their own orders—but we cannot participate. And we do not want to know how the results are obtained. Our hands must be clean.'"

Faced with this quandary—honorable gentlemen asked to do a dishonorable job—there was a tendency to compromise. The remarkable Colonel Colquhoun Grant of Lingieston, Wellington's chief intelligence officer, spent much of his time behind enemy lines, but was careful to do so dressed in full regimental uniform and mounted on a fast horse. Benedict Arnold, says Ambler, when faced with the same difficulty, attempted to get out of it by wearing a civilian coat but clinging to his military boots and britches. In the same style General Ironside, when, as a young intelligence officer, he joined the German Expeditionary Force against the Hereros, disguised himself as a Boer waggoner, but retained his self-respect by keeping his fox terrier with him and addressing it in English (the only language which the animal understood).

The First World War changed all this, as it changed so many things. In a struggle of unexampled brutality, evenly balanced, and fought à l'outrance, there was no scope for nice notions of morality and gentlemanly conduct. As soon as the contending generals realized that "a spy in the right place was worth more than a division in the wrong place" they began, with enthusiasm, to play the game which has never ceased, in war or in peace, up to the present moment, and which shows little sign of ceasing until the millennium arrives and peace falls at last on this troubled world.

As the game proceeded, fact quickly outstripped fiction.

"In the higher ranges of Secret Service work," wrote Winston Churchill, "the actual facts, in many cases, were in every respect equal to the most fantastic inventions of romance or melodrama. Tangle within tangle, plot and counterplot, ruse and treachery, cross and double-cross, true agent, false agent, double agent, gold and steel, the bomb, the dagger and the firing party were interwoven in a texture incredible and yet true. The Chief and the high officers of the Service revelled in these subterranean labyrinths and amid the crash of war pursued their task with cold and silent passion."

Before taking this matter further, we must widen and define the canvas.

Modern states recognize two broad divisions of intelligence operations. On the one hand there is the spy, or agent as he prefers to call himself, who goes abroad to gather information. He is controlled by the Foreign Office (or whatever limb of government corresponds to the Foreign Office in the state concerned). He will usually operate from the diplomatic enclave in the place he is investigating, and may have a minor diplomatic post, and the immunity which goes with it.

Quite distinct from this there is the Security Force, which operates at home, under the Home Office, in close cooperation with the appropriate arm of the police. Broadly speaking, in England, the first of these functions is carried out by M.I.6 (also called D.I.6, or the Secret Intelligence Service, or Passport Control—all secret organizations proliferate in nomenclature). The second function is carried out by M.I.5, with the help of the Special Branch.

The same broad division exists in other countries. In the United States it is the Federal Bureau of Investigation which looks after home security and the Central Intelligence Agency which operates abroad. (To confuse matters further, the "Secret Service" is a branch of the U.S. Treasury dealing with counterfeiting.) In France the Deuxième Bureau, beloved of novelists, no longer exists. The S.D.E.C.E. looks after foreign intelligence and the DST watches home security. In Russia the complications defy brief analysis. Different directorates of the KGB deal with home and foreign intelligence, but there is also the GRU which duplicates many KGB functions abroad. One sometimes wonders whether these confusions are created deliberately.

Naturally, none of these organizations grew, as it were, in the public eye. Nevertheless, between the two World Wars, as the knowledgeable learned something about them, and made up even more, a sort of national image became discernible. This is important in the present context, because what appears in fiction, on any esoteric subject, will be a reflection of popular opinions about that subject. It may be a myth, but it will be a myth founded on what the French would call an *idée reçue*, or accepted ideology. (A further, most intriguing development may take place. Truth may actually accept, and take over, the myth; it is a matter we shall be considering later.)

The foremost intelligence apparatus affecting the

public imagination at that time in England was, naturally, that of Nazi Germany. The Germans were viewed, in the thirties, as inevitable opponents in the return match which was to be played sooner or later; and just as their army, navy, and air force were magnified (though perhaps not unduly so) into menaces of the first order, so were their secret services regarded as the last word in efficiency.

Facts which have since come to light have cast some doubts on this, but it is true that the German passion for meticulous order, cross-indexing, and analysis of detail was capable of producing startling results in this field.

One example, which typifies the system, was recorded by Wilhelm Höttl. During both World Wars trade continued between Sweden and Germany and a great number of Swedish business men traveled between the two countries. The German Secret Service filed photocopies of *all* Swedish passports and indexed *every* mark and variation in the stamping. An official then noticed that, in a small number of passports, the stamp of the issuing authority was pushed slightly to the left. Inquiries led to the conclusion that the Swedish Secret Service had adopted this simple and unobtrusive method of making their agents known to their own frontier officials. As soon as the Germans realized this, not only were they able to identify, at sight, those apparently innocent travelers as secret agents; they were also able to provide their own agents with passports on which the stamp had been similarly displaced; and they were then able to travel to Stockholm with perfect security and freedom from interference.

The French Secret Service was respected, like their artillery, for its professionalism, but it did not enjoy the reputation for ruthlessness which attached, justly we may judge from subsequent events, to the corresponding Russian service, usually referred to by writers at this period as the OGPU. Their long arm and their patience were exemplified in the public eye by the assassination of Trotsky in Mexico City many years after he had quitted the USSR.

The reputation of the British Secret Service at this time was high. It was resting on the laurels it had won during the First World War. "It is probable," says Churchill, "that on the whole, during that war, the British Secret Service was more efficient and gained greater triumphs, both in the detection of spies and in the collection of information from the enemy than that of any country, hostile, allied or neutral."

This was the dawn of day, when the dew was on the grass, the era before Fuchs and Philby arrived and the spy came in from the cold. It was an era of comparative innocence. Spying was a game, "The Great Game," as Kipling was the first to call it.

> "It is necessary, from time to time, to send unarmed men into No Man's Land and the Back of Beyond across the Khudajanta-Khan (the Lord-Knows-Where) Mountains, just to find out what is going on there among people who some day or other may become dangerous enemies. The understanding is that if the men return with their reports so much the better for them. They may receive some sort of decoration, given, so far as the public can make out, for no real reason. If they do not come back—and people disappear very mys-

teriously at the Back of Beyond—that is their own concern, and no questions will be asked and no enquiries made."

The game involved serious risks, like big-game hunting or climbing on Everest, and it was a game played by gentlemen.

"We have had our agents working in Persia and Mesopotamia for years—mostly young officers in the Indian Army. They carry their lives in their hands, and now and then one disappears, and the cellars of Bagdad might tell a tale. But they find out many things, and they count the game worth the candle. They could give us no details. All but one—the best of them—he had been working between Mosul and the Persian frontier as a mule-teer and had been south into the Bakhtiari Hills. He found out something, but his enemies knew that he knew and he was pursued. Three months ago, just before Kut, he staggered into Delamain's camp with ten bullet holes in him and a knife slash on his forehead. He died in ten minutes."

"What a great fellow! What was his name?" I asked.

Sir Walter did not answer at once. He was looking out of the window. "His name," he said at last, "was Harry Bullivant. He was my son. God rest his brave soul."

That, as you will hardly need to be told, is John Buchan and the book is *Greenmantle*. For a boy who first read that passage half a century or more ago it set a standard of chivalrous espionage which has been a long time dying. But dying it is, as we shall shortly see.

As we are tracing the history of the spy story, we move from peak to peak. The next great writer in the genre, the one who dominated the thirties, and is still happily with us in the seventies, was Eric Ambler.

He developed and expanded one of Buchan's themes. Richard Hannay was accustomed to describe himself as an amateur or a "lucky muddler." At the beginning of "The Three Hostages" he says:

> It's quite true that in the War I had some queer jobs and was lucky enough to bring some of them off. But don't you see, I was a soldier then, under orders. . . . That's all done with. I'm in a different mood now. My mind is weedy and grass grown. I've settled so deep in the country that I'm just an ordinary hay-seed farmer.

Ambler took this idea a good deal further. The principal figure in his prewar books was neither a professional soldier nor a professional agent. He was that well-known prototype, the English business man traveling abroad in search of orders for his firm. His journeys might take him, logically enough, to France, Italy, Central or Eastern Europe (no Iron Curtain in those days), or even to Turkey. In the course of such business, he becomes involved, as a business man might, in local politics; perhaps bribes are offered which, being English, he indignantly rejects. Odd things begin to happen. His subordinates appear curiously unreliable. The scene darkens. The mist deepens. It is all damnably plausible.

Readership identification is complete. Just so has many an Englishman traveling in foreign parts found himself, innocently but terrifyingly, involved in the red tape of Continental bureaucracy. His visa is not entirely in order. Would he mind stepping this way for a moment? Only a formality. The door of the office closes on him. The nightmare of entanglement begins.

It was Eric Ambler's *forte* to show that what John Buchan used to describe as the "thin veneer of civilization" has hidden cracks in it, secret crevasses into which an innocent traveler might slip, never to be heard of again.

> On the rare occasions—when matters concerned with insurance had been under consideration—on which Graham had thought about his own death it had been to reaffirm the conviction that he would die of natural causes and in bed. Accidents did happen, of course; but he was a careful driver, an imaginative pedestrian and a strong swimmer; he neither rode horses nor climbed mountains; he was not subject to attacks of dizziness; he did not hunt big game and he had never had even the smallest desire to jump in front of an approaching train.

That is the new character: hero and victim in one. Ambler had the perception to see that when difficulties and dangers come the way of a man like that they are twice as convincing, and therefore twice as alarming as anything which could befall your case-hardened professional agent.

In the post-war period Ambler was still writing, but the field was empty of big names for a few years. This may have been because the market was glutted with war stories.

Then, in 1953:

> The scent and smoke and sweat of a casino are nauseating at three in the morning. Then the

soul-erosion produced by high gambling—a compost of greed and fear and nervous tension—becomes unbearable, and the senses awake and revolt from it.

James Bond was born.

Ian Fleming's books are difficult to criticize. It is easy to be facetious about them. Their author was often facetious about them himself. There is no question that they deserved the enormous success which they attained. They are excellent reading, cunningly constructed and beautifully upholstered. They go down like a drink of iced lager on a hot day.

What are the reservations one has about them, then? Partly it is the upholstery. The endless repetition of details which look like the advertising pages of a magazine for men-about-town. The impeccable footwear and headwear; the pigskin suitcases; the lightweight tropical suits and the aftershave lotion. And the meals! And the drinks! Maybe these were more attractive in the austerity of the early fifties than they are now. There is, also, an inevitability about the development of the stories which is, at the same time, a strength and a weakness. Just as, with your favorite chocolates, you know that you will get at least two nut-crunchies and two strawberry creams in each quarter-pound box, so in each book about James Bond you could rely on a fair measure of torture and a fair measure of lovemaking. It was this reliability, no doubt, which added to the sales.

If this sounds disparaging, you must take it with a pinch of salt. I have read every book Ian Fleming has written. So, to judge from the tattered paperbacks in their rooms, have all my children. The difference between Ian Fleming and most of the other writers I mention here is that I have not found myself wanting to read any of his books twice.

For my money, there have been two really great postwar writers in this field: The first of these is John Le Carré. Here I have to express what is almost certainly a minority opinion. I think he wrote two superlative books in this field and two only. They were *Call for the Dead* and *The Spy Who Came in from the Cold*. Of these I thought the first was, marginally, the better. It certainly made a better film.

Both books were so far above the average that it seemed as if a powerful luminary had appeared, who was going to light up the spy-book firmament for blessed years to come. Unfortunately something seems to have gone wrong. After the disappointment of *The Looking Glass War* I have found Le Carré increasingly difficult to read with any real enjoyment.

I did warn you that this was a minority judgment.

This brings us to Len Deighton, the latest and greatest of the postwar spy-story writers. He has qualities which, for me, set him apart. The first is an ability to write in the Raymond Chandler style of light but taut first-person narration, a style which thousands have tried to copy without, I suspect, realizing the pitfalls it contains for the less expert. The second is an ability to bring people and places, vividly and precisely, before the eyes of the reader.

In *Billion Dollar Brain*, the fourth, and in some ways the best of his six spy books, he whisks us from London to Helsinki, to Leningrad, to Riga, to the deep south of Texas, and back to Manhattan.

Five o'clock is the top dead center of the Manhattan night. Just for one hour the city is inert. The hearses have been brought up to the doors of the city hospitals, but they haven't yet begun to load. The last cinema on Forty-second Street has closed and even the billiard rooms have racked the cues and shut down. The City's seventy thousand wild cats have pounced upon pigeons in Riverside Park or on Norwegian wharf rats in Washington Market and now they too are asleep under the long lines of still cars. The only movement is compressed steam roaring along at three hundred miles an hour under the roadways, escaping now and again with a spectral puff, and the shuffle of wet newspapers as far as the eye can see down the long, long streets to the bloodshot dawn.

A man who can write like that has no need of subtle plots; and indeed some of Deighton's plots are hard to follow and even harder to believe in.

A third, and devastating, weapon in his professional armory is his mastery of technical detail. In the first books this was apt to be tacked on arbitrarily in the shape of long and sometimes tiresome appendices. In later books the information is inserted, most subtly, into the text itself. It must represent a great deal of very specialized research. "I had a sneaking feeling," said one critic, "that I was breaking the Official Secrets Act every time I opened the book."

It raises an intriguing question: To what extent does a writer about spies need to know anything about intelligence operations?

This is different from the problem that arises in other fields of what might be called background expertise.

If you are writing about lawyers, witch-doctors, cabinet-makers, or collectors of seventeenth-century coffeepots there are a number of sources of information readily available to you. Public libraries are stocked with books about them. The Encyclopaedia Britannica is a very present help. If the printed word fails it is not difficult, after a little inquiry, to find a friendly expert. All experts, including policemen, like to talk about their own subject. They will be endlessly patient and helpful, and will usually feel adequately rewarded by a signed copy of your book when it appears.

In intelligence matters none of these aids exists. Anyone who knows anything worth telling is fast bound by the Official Secrets Act. And anyway, who *does* know anything? There is, unfortunately, no Official Directory of Spies and Counter Espionage Agents. The only reliable rule is that if a man tells you he is in the Secret Service he is almost certainly lying.

To what extent, if at all, has this inhibited writers? John Buchan had a job during the First World War with intelligence contacts (albeit an office job) just as Ian Fleming had in World War Two. Other writers had closer and more active connections with the subject matter of their books. Erskine Childers sailed his small boat through the waterways which were the *locale* of *The Riddle of the Sands;* Somerset Maugham undertook intelligence missions in Switzerland as did Compton MacKenzie among the islands of the Aegean.

This may have been useful for background purposes, but did not always result in greater accuracy of detail. Len Deighton who (so far as I know) has never been personally involved in such matters would never have made the mistake, which Ian Fleming made, of referring in a postwar novel to the Deuxième Bureau, which ceased to exist in 1940.

There is a corresponding advantage here. Since the general public knows nothing at all of what goes on in those discreet offices in Whitehall and St. James, the writer with a facile pen and a vivid imagination can devise any ploys and tricks which happen to suit his narrative, without the danger of readers telling him that he is talking nonsense. His freedom of invention is absolute.

An American, writing recently in one of the Sunday papers, implied, though he did not actually state, that he himself had had firsthand experience of working for the CIA, and went on to discuss which particular writers the "spooks" (expressive Americanism for agents) found most interesting and useful. He had compiled a short list of six names: Gerald Browne, Brian Freemantle, Brian Garfield, Nicholas Luard, Owen Sela, and Alan Williams. All of these authors' books, he said, were worthy of close study by spooks, since they were realistically written, and contained a number of useful and practical hints.

Thus does the wheel come full circle. Fiction starts by following after fact. Fact now follows after fiction.

But indeed, times have changed. Spying is not what it used to be. The Bruce-Partington plans gather dust on the shelves of the Admiralty, staff officers are no longer in danger of seduction by glamorous courtesans. It is enough to make Mata Hari turn in her dishonored grave.

The emphasis now is on propaganda on the one

hand and activism on the other. The lead here has been taken by the Russians and Americans, followed by the embattled countries of the Middle East.

"To say that the CIA does assassinations all the time," complained their ex-Director William E. Colby in a recent interview, "is unfair. There were a few occasions on which we tried. None of them worked."

Shades of Kipling and Buchan!

The whole scene is changing. In the same interview Mr. Colby explained: "In the old image, intelligence used to be spying, Mata Hari and so on. Today intelligence is an intellectual process of assembling information from press, radio, books and speeches. Which is why we're called the Central Intelligence Agency. All this information is centralized and studied by experts. And then there are electronics, computers, technology."

To which the interviewer replied: "Mr. Colby, CIA may be partly that. But it is also something worse. Something dirtier. I mean a political force that secretly organizes *coups d'etat* and plots assassinations. A second government, that punishes whoever is against the interests of the United States."

This is the field in which the writer of spy stories today and tomorrow will have to find his material.

I started with the old-fashioned game of *L'Attaque*. The other day I happened to see, in a toy-shop window, a new game. It is called the "Game of Nations."

On the box was a quotation, not from a spy story, but from a serious work by Miles Copeland with the same title.

"Skill and nerve," it said, "are the principal requirements in this amoral and cynical game, in which there are neither winners nor losers—only survivors. The first object of any player is to keep himself in the game."

Turn that into fiction, and you will have written the great spy story of today.

ELEVEN

PHYLLIS A. WHITNEY

Phyllis A. Whitney began writing mysteries for young people before she wrote Gothics for adult readers. She has won two Edgars and several scrolls from the Mystery Writers of America for her juvenile mysteries. Of her fifty-five books to date, thirty-nine are mysteries. Miss Whitney has been a children's book editor, reviewing for the CHICAGO SUN *and the* PHILADELPHIA INQUIRER. *For eleven years she taught writing at New York University, and her book,* WRITING JUVENILE FICTION, *is a standard text in the field. Miss Whitney now alternates between adult and juvenile novels, producing two books a year. Her works have been published in nineteen countries around the world. Miss Whitney was chosen president of the Mystery Writers of America in 1975.*

GOTHIC MYSTERIES

As we know it today, the Gothic, or romantic-suspense novel, is a phenomenon that has swept around the world, particularly during the second half of this century. It has become even more popular than its forebears. Although most such stories were originally written in English, they have been translated into the languages of many countries where they are finding a large readership.

The Gothic is one of the earliest members of the mystery family, and its heritage is fairly illustrious. It antedates the detective story and has existed almost as long as the novel itself.

Perhaps a definition is in order for the uninitiated. *The American Heritage Dictionary* puts it this way: "Of or pertaining to a literary style of fiction prevalent in the late eighteenth and early nineteenth centuries which emphasizes the grotesque, mysterious, and desolate."

Horace Walpole probably started it all when he built his monstrosity of a pseudo-Gothic castle at Strawberry Hill, adding numerous rooms to the original cottage, as well as a round tower, a cloister, and a gallery, and filling it all with period pieces and oddities that he regarded as suitable to the mood. Then having created his charming folderol, he became obsessed by it and put it into his most famous novel, *The Castle of Otranto* (1765). The novel became so popular that it was followed by many imitators. Among the better-known contributors to the genre were Mary Shelley (*Frankenstein*, 1818) and Lord Byron's physician Polidori *(Vampyre)*, who added their own touches of monster and vampire.

From the books that resulted, certain common ingredients began to emerge: a castle, groans in the night, flitting ghosts, skeletons, skulls, and midnight murders—with, of course, the beautiful damsel-in-distress, and always a brooding sense of mystery. The earliest examples were on the florid and sensational side, elaborate in their language, and given to a less-than-subtle building of terror in characters and reader. The genre did not descend to earth and take on a more reasonable and realistic form until the advent of the Brontës many decades later. All modern Gothic writers must pay their respects to *Jane Eyre* and *Wuthering Heights*. Equivalents of Heathcliff's lonely moors and Jane's formidable Mr. Rochester still haunt present-day Gothics.

However, the Gothic novel lay fallow for many years after the Brontës were gone, with only occasional isolated gestures in that direction. It wasn't until Daphne du Maurier wrote *Rebecca* and added her own Maxim de Winter to the list of somber heroes that lightning struck again. That book is one of the best-loved romantic suspense novels of this century; it has never been out of print since its publication in 1938. The motion picture made from it, starring Laurence Olivier, Joan Fontaine, and Judith Anderson, has become a classic.

Yet the stroke of lightning was still only that—an individual stroke. Daphne du Maurier had paid her own respects in print to *Jane Eyre;* now and then other writers followed her into this same mysterious and romantic landscape to tell their own tales of suspense. Mary Stewart and Victoria Holt became best-selling novelists in the genre, one using the modern scene, the other a nineteenth-century period background. Readers were there, eager for more, and certain editors already had their ears to the ground, but the real storm had not yet swept the country.

Then, in 1963 an editor of paperbacks, noting that his mother's favorite novel was *Rebecca,* cast about for similar books to start a new series. The obvious name that presented itself was "Gothic." The first book in the series, published tentatively, sold well. The name caught on, and the entire book trade picked up the label. We now have a full tide of so-called Gothics published every year with that maiden-in-distress fleeing across millions of book jackets toward an audience of readers that is apparently insatiable.

For a long while English women writers topped the field, but today more and more Americans are writing Gothic novels and doing it well.

For the most part, such novels are written by women for women, yet men read them too. A few men are now writing them—sometimes bravely under their own names, more often under feminine pseudonyms. Fortunately, those published first in hardcover are usually well written, with sound characterization and a special descriptive magic that strongly appeals to women. Because of the flood of popularity, however, some new books being published as paperback originals do not measure up to the best of the Gothics, and there is the danger that shoddy examples may even cause a lessening of the Gothic's popularity.

Letters from readers still express satisfaction in finding mystery novels in these times that are not too bloody and are not filled with explicit sex. Perhaps the sort of sex that smoulders in *Jane Eyre* is of a more potent variety than that which is detailed and leaves the imagination with nothing to work on. Of course there is some violence, but it is usually offstage, and it is more likely to be a *threat* of violence that keeps the reader hanging on every page. The always-fleeing girl is there, but she is a much more liberated woman than her earlier counterparts. True, she may tumble gladly into the hero's arms in a last-minute rescue, but she is quite capable of doing something about her dire situation on her own and falls into a faint only when someone bops her on the head.

Backgrounds are still tremendously important. The ancient castle may still be there if the tale takes place in Spain or in Germany, but in any case there is nearly always a large and brooding house to haunt the scene and to lend an atmosphere of rising terror to the story. Outdoors there can be pounding seas or storm-ridden mountains; the heroine can find herself running in fear through damp fogs or facing the noon-time demons abroad in bright sunlight.

Not only the immediate setting of the story is important, but so too is the general background. The exotic is welcome in these stories, and consequently we have our heroines traveling to Greece and Turkey and Spain, or even to Africa or Scandinavia. Anywhere at all, in fact, providing the writer can depict the foreign scene with authenticity and plausibility. Or, if a foreign scene is not possible, then the writer seeks out interesting localities in his or her own country. This usually means settings in the British Isles or in America. Writers bring their own sensitivity of background to each scene they want to write about and let it create in them the mood they will later transfer to paper. Mood and emotion are very important.

Nearly all of these novels begin with the heroine arriving on the scene—either returning to a place she has not seen for many years or coming to one totally new to her. Devising a way of getting her to that place is one of the first problems a writer has to solve. What unusual but logical reason causes her to go there? And how does one get her there without resorting to that worn-to-shreds landing by plane in the opening chapter?

Interiors are also important. Most women readers like to know about furniture and bric-a-brac and will even stand for some holding up of the story while such fascinating details are sketched in. Often in conventional mystery novels we never know how anyone is dressed or how a room is furnished, but in a Gothic there are fashion touches all the way through and the antiques are nicely labeled. Women readers often feel that better visualization is possible if it is clear that the heroine is wearing a lime green pantsuit and open-toed sandals, or whatever. So far none of these pant-suits has made its way to the Gothic jacket where long, flowing skirts are still favored by the artists.

A word should be said about these book jackets, since they are a distinguishing part of the whole. Women editors who recognized the market fought for years to get that damsel-in-distress, those brooding colors and stormy skies, that old house with a lighted window onto all jackets of Gothics. They realized that it was necessary to use a signature to attract the reader and to tell her at once that this was the book for which she was looking. The paperbacks came across with quite stunning cover paintings that often surpassed what was being done in the hardcover field, and there is no doubt that those jackets sold books.

Always in these stories there is the ancient strug-gle of good and evil, something that should take place in every mystery story worthy of the name. The strug-gle here is often more psychological than physical. Where men readers want fast action and outward com-bat, the female reader is often more fascinated by the psychological clash with all its ramifications. A seem-ingly quiet scene in a drawing room (there are always drawing rooms!) can be fraught with suspense when the outcome is a matter of future happiness. Dialogue counts and there are often word clashes, but all talk must be to a purpose and must move the story ahead.

This is not to say that physical clash and action are not also present. Periodically through the story the heroine must be threatened by danger, and writers are sometimes hard put to get in those required scenes without resorting to the overdone whack on the head. Skillful plotting is necessary and a skillful fooling of the reader: We must fool and be fooled, or there is disappointment at the end of the story.

Since these are escape novels, and valued as such, one isn't apt to meet garbage cans and dirty sinks in their pages. The realistic humdrum of everyday living that is always under the reader's nose isn't wanted here. Characters are apt to be successful and well-to-do; they can wear couturier clothes and live in old mansions. Only the vulnerable and appealing young heroine may feel uneasy amid wealth and luxury and preserve something of a conscience. She is the tie-in with a reality the reader knows. Often both hero and heroine have an admirable concern for the state of the world and are trying to do something about it, but probably not right now with that step echoing in a supposedly empty corridor and the tower shutters banging in the wind.

Another more down-to-earth though still glamorous aspect in these novels (and one they have in common with many other mysteries) is some specialty of knowledge that may be displayed by some of the characters. The story-people may know all about the illumination of medieval manuscripts, or about the making of china. Or perhaps be expert on ancient armor, the painting of eggshells, or the history of clipper ships.

Whatever it is, the writer is in for a good deal of re-search, since she must know even more than her fic-tional people or her ignorance will show.

This aspect of the story may be valuable in several ways. It connects the real world without being grubby, lends more interesting background touches, and pos-sibly provides plot twists to further the action.

When we approach the climax there must, of course, be a chase scene, as is often the case in other mysteries as well. All the promised threats and dangers will have come to a head, and now there must be a life-or-death struggle. Trying to figure out new ways of accomplishing this has caused many a Gothic writer to develop new gray hairs. Yet it is done over and over, and if the characterization has been good and the writ-ing skilled, the reader will be involved in the desperate struggle and will be caught up once more in that de-lightful suspension of disbelief that is more common to the mystery novel than to almost any other type of fiction.

Still another familiar ingredient, ever since the Brontës, is that dark-browed hero (he may be blond, but he still has a dark and brooding nature), and here it is sometimes difficult to play variations. The reader isn't happy when he turns out to be the villain instead of the hero. The stamp of Heathcliff, Mr. Rochester, and Maxim de Winter is as much a signature in today's Gothic as was the bloodstained dagger of the past. He is likely to be a dominating, chauvinistic figure who, nevertheless, succumbs to our liberated heroine's charms—though, of course, *she* has succumbed to his early in the story and has been suffering all along.

While all this is fun to write about objectively, as I am doing now, and can be talked about tongue-in-cheek in one's sane and waking hours, these novels are written with love and solemn belief while the writer is at the typewriter. They cannot be successful otherwise. Phoniness always shows. There is feeling and emotion in these stories, and they *must* be real and convincing.

One important distinction between the mystery novel for men and the romantic suspense novel for women is the absence of police on the scene. In the Gothic it is felt that police clutter the action and hold up the story. If any detecting is to be done, it is entirely of an amateur nature, and there is little time spent in sitting around examining clues. If there is an onstage crime and the police must be called in, the author gets rid of them as quickly as possible. Often the murder is for a time considered suicide or an accident in order to avoid police procedure. Sometimes it is even a murder in the past, which the heroine finds she must investigate for her own happiness. After that the *threat* of new violence will work for a time to keep the story going without police interference. But that threat had better be real, not faked.

Stupidity on the heroine's part must, of course, be avoided. Something that ought to be told to the police had better be told, unless there is a sound reason to keep silent. The down-to-the-docks-at-midnight syndrome had better be given very good motivation. Heroes of men's mystery novels are permitted to involve themselves in all sorts of ridiculous and dangerous action and no one complains. But let a Gothic heroine step foolishly into danger and the critics scream. She must be *forced* into that necessary danger.

Within the confines of the Gothic pattern, a great deal of variation appears to be possible. The author, in dealing with depths of human nature and human emotions, has a vein to mine that is not likely to be exhausted. Her rewards come in the applause of readers both here and abroad, as well as in the quite astonishing sales that usually eclipse those of most mystery novels. The elements may shift and change somewhat as the years pass, yet the basic appeal of these tales of romantic suspense and mystery lasts from century to century. The ultimate threat of vicarious danger seems to have an endless appeal to human nature.

TWELVE   ROBERT E. BRINEY

Robert E. Briney grew up
surrounded by books. From an
early enthusiasm for Zane Grey
and the Hardy Boys he graduated
to Perry Mason, The Saint, and
an occasional Ellery Queeen.
But the attraction of more eldritch
fare was even stronger when he
discovered Fu Manchu and the
horror tales of H. P. Lovecraft.
His major interest now lies in the
exotic story of mystery and
suspense. Since 1970 he has
edited THE ROHMER REVIEW, *a*
journal devoted to the life
and works of Sax Rohmer. He
annotated MASTER OF VILLANY:
A BIOGRAPHY OF SAX ROHMER,
by Cay Van Ash and
Elizabeth Sax Rohmer.
Dr. Briney has contributed
frequently to journals of the
genre, and was a
contributing editor of the
ENCYCLOPEDIA OF MYSTERY
& DETECTION.

DEATH RAYS, DEMONS, AND WORMS
UNKNOWN TO SCIENCE

The Fantastic Element in Mystery Fiction

I

From the earliest days mystery fiction has exhibited a
thread—and often more than a thread—of the fanciful and fantastic. The early Gothic novels, such as
Horace Walpole's *The Castle of Otranto* (1764) or Mrs.
Radcliffe's *The Mysteries of Udolpho* (1794), had their
ghostly manifestations, either real or spurious. The
"penny dreadfuls," interminable serials issued in
weekly installments priced at a penny each, offered
enthusiastic accounts of the grisly crimes of *Varney the
Vampyre* (1847) and *Wagner, the Wehr-Wolf* (1846–7).
Coming closer to the center-line of the *genre*, we find
the "father of the detective story," Edgar Allan Poe,
indulging his taste for the *outré* in those same stories
that would later be recognized as the *fontes et origines*
of the basic elements in modern detective fiction: witness the antics of a homicidal orangutan unmasked

and explained by formal ratiocination. In *The Moon-stone* (1867) by Wilkie Collins, generally regarded as the first full-length detective novel in English, the police detective Sergeant Cuff had to deal with an accursed jewel and a band of mysterious Orientals.

Even that most rational of beings, the world's first consulting detective, had his extravagant encounters. At the end of a breathless chase across the fog-shrouded moor, Holmes and Watson came face-to-face with the embodiment of the Baskerville legend:

> . . . an enormous coal-black hound, but not such a hound as mortal eyes have ever seen. Fire burst from its open mouth, its eyes glowed with a smouldering glare, its muzzle and hackles and dewlap were outlined in flickering flame.[1]

The hound, however, succumbed to an ordinary bullet, and the mystery was dispelled by inexorable logic. Holmes was not tolerant of fantasy. In another connection, he somewhat snappishly remarked, "The idea of a vampire was to me absurd. Such things do not happen in criminal practice in England."[2] Nevertheless, the uncanny element could not entirely be avoided. Some of Holmes's cases seem to have involved aspects too fantastic for publication. We have, for example, only a single tantalizing reference to the affair of

> . . . Isadora Persano, the well-known journalist and duellist, who was found stark staring mad with a matchbox in front of him which contained a remarkable worm, said to be unknown to science.[3]

Such further information as may once have existed, in that famous tin dispatch-box in the vaults of Cox &

Company, Charing Cross, is now presumably lost, a casualty of the bombing of London in World War II.

Just what do we mean by a "fantastic" element in mystery fiction? Not merely something eccentric, grotesque or irrational, though those qualities are often present. Something more substantial is intended, some touch of strangeness, from the supernatural to the science-fictional: a real or apparent departure from natural law or current knowledge.

This breach of the ordinary may be only an incidental part of the main plot, such as the ghost story related in Chapter 5 of Edmund Crispin's *The Case of the Gilded Fly* (1944) or the farcical science-fiction story, "John Jones' Dollar," which Harry Stephen Keeler inserted into his novel *The Face of the Man from Saturn* (1933). Even when the fantasy is a more crucial part of the story, it may have been introduced only to be explained away at the end. This is a dangerous practice, for the more convincingly inexplicable the phenomena, the more persuasive and ingenious the author must be in his explanations in order not to leave the reader feeling cheated. John Dickson Carr is the acknowledged master among the "explainers of miracles," having worked more variations on the theme than any other author. Clayton Rawson, in his stories of the Great Merlini, displayed enviable skill at this game. Helen McCloy's "The Singing Diamonds," involving unidentified flying objects and the chain of mysterious deaths that followed their sighting, is also a distinguished accomplishment. But perhaps the single most satisfying example of this specialized form of the detective story is the novel *Rim of the Pit* by Hake

Talbot (Henning Nelms), first published in 1944. There is no better brief description of this story than that in Anthony Boucher's introduction to the 1965 reprint:[4]

> a tale of the North Woods in the noble old tradition of the isolated and snowbound houseparty, with a séance which seems to produce genuine results against the will of the medium, and with a spirit-possessed murderer who seems able to fly. It offers, indeed, not one miracle but a whole basket of them, piling impossibility upon impossibility until one feels all but convinced that this is no detective story but a genuine post-Gothic tale of terror [. . .].

In many cases, of course, the fantastic elements are not explained away, but remain intact at the end of the story. There is generally no equivocation involved. However, in those stories characterized by what Frank D. McSherry has called "the Janus Resolution,"[5] the natural and the supernatural explanations are developed in parallel and are left on an equal footing at the end of the story, so that it is up to the reader to decide which to believe. Several of the novels discussed later, such as *Through a Glass, Darkly* by Helen McCloy or *The Reluctant Medium* by L. P. Davies, are of this type.

Before proceeding, let us dispose of some of the items which will not be discussed further in our survey, even though they fall within the general boundaries of the topic. We exclude "straight" ghost stories or supernatural tales, such as the works of M. R. James or H. P. Lovecraft and novels such as *The Exorcist, Rosemary's Baby,* or *The Mephisto Waltz.*[6] Stories whose only claim to inclusion is the presence of spiritualistic phenomena—mediums and their messages—are left out. The numerous books featuring pulp-magazine heroes—*The Shadow, Doc Savage, The Avenger, The Phantom Detective,* and others—are omitted, along with the lengthy series of paperback novels based on television programs such as *Dark Shadows* and *The Man from U.N.C.L.E.* Finally, we deal only with material which originated in English and (with one or two exceptions) which has appeared in book form, either hardcover or paperback.

Even granting these somewhat arbitrary exclusions, the body of material which remains is too extensive for comprehensive treatment. It is inevitable that some readers will find that their favorite authors or books have been left out. May all such omissions, whether due to space limitations, personal taste, lapse of memory, or simple ignorance, be viewed with charity.

II

One of the most successful purveyors of the exotic and fantastic in mystery fiction was the British writer who called himself Sax Rohmer (1883–1959). In a succession of mystery thrillers produced over a span of more than fifty-five years he regaled his readers with almost every variety of bizarre setting, event, and character. But it was one particular character who brought him widespread fame and made him, at the height of his popularity, one of the most widely read and highly paid writers of popular fiction in the world. This character was the durable Oriental mastermind, Dr. Fu Manchu.

Sax Rohmer's real name, in spite of what several reputable reference works will tell you, was Arthur Henry Ward. During his teens he discarded the "Henry" and began calling himself Arthur Sarsfield Ward, in response to a claim by his mother that her family was descended from the famous seventeenth-century Irish hero, Patrick Sarsfield. Several short stories of various types—mystery, fantasy, humor, historical adventure—were published under the by-line A. Sarsfield Ward in 1903–06; the first two of these were in print before the author's twenty-first birthday. But sales were uncertain. Becoming convinced that he would not find a steady audience for his fiction, Ward turned to the composition of comedy songs and sketches for the music-hall stage. At this endeavor he was both skillful and successful. He devised the striking name Sax Rohmer, which he used not only as a by-line on his songs, but in private life as well. It was under this name that he introduced himself to his future wife, and to this day his widow uses the name Rohmer rather than Ward. After his marriage in 1909 he returned to fiction writing, first as A. Sarsfield Ward and then as Sax Rohmer.[7]

Rohmer proved himself an expert practitioner of a fictional form much in favor with editors and readers of magazine fiction—the series of individual stories, each complete in itself but nevertheless forming part of a larger narrative. It was by means of such a series, in the British fiction magazine *The Story-Teller* in the fall of 1912, that Dr. Fu Manchu was introduced:

> Imagine a person, tall, lean and feline, high-shouldered, with a brow like Shakespeare and a

face like Satan, a close-shaven skull, and long, magnetic eyes of the true cat-green. Invest him with all the cruel cunning of an entire Eastern race, accumulated in one giant intellect, with all the resources of science past and present, with all the resources, if you will, of a wealthy government—which, however, already has denied all knowledge of his existence. Imagine that awful being, and you have a mental picture of Dr. Fu-Manchu, the yellow peril incarnate in one man.[8]

This personage, whom *The New Yorker* characterized as "sinister, puissant, and altogether terrifying,"[9] was the head of a world-wide organization, the Si-Fan, dedicated to the dominance of the Orient and the downfall of Occidental civilization.

The Fu Manchu series was picked up by the American weekly magazine *Collier's*, which provided a ready-made mass audience. (*Collier's* was to be the single most receptive and most influential market for Rohmer's fiction. From 1913 to 1949 over two hundred separate issues of the magazine contained material by Rohmer, including serializations of seventeen books.) The stories were an immediate success, and were quickly collected in book form as *The Insidious Dr. Fu-Manchu* (1913; British title, *The Mystery of Dr. Fu-Manchu*). The first book was followed by two others of similar structure. These three books form a single unit, an extended narrative in thirty episodes, ending with the break-up of the Si-Fan and the apparent death of Fu Manchu. The folly of taking anything for granted where "the devil doctor" is concerned is shown by the fact that the series then continued through eleven subsequent novels. The final novel, *Emperor Fu Manchu,* was published only weeks before the author's death in 1959. The series was completed when four short stories were resurrected from Sunday-supplement magazines and included in the posthumous collection, *The Wrath of Fu Manchu and Other Stories* (1972). As the series progressed, the relationship between Fu Manchu and the Si-Fan kept shifting. At times he was the master of this organization, at others merely its agent; sometimes he worked for its aims, while on other occasions he was concerned only with his own personal power. And his own goals continued to change as well. Whereas he had begun as an unqualified menace to the West, the passing years found him working for world peace (in his own unique way) by assassinating the fascist leaders of Europe *(The Drums of Fu Manchu,* 1939) and combatting Communism *(Shadow of Fu Manchu,* 1948). There were inevitable relapses, such as his attempt to gain control of the Panama Canal in *The Island of Fu Manchu* (1941); among the tools employed in this endeavor were voodoo ceremonies and an invisibility machine.

Through all the philosophical changes, certain features in the stories remain constant. One can count on the bizarre agents of death, both animate and inanimate: the Zayat Kiss, the Green Mist, the Coughing Horror, the Flower of Silence, the Tûlun-Nûr Chest, the Ericksen Ray, the Scarlet Brides, and numerous other "worms unknown to science," as well as:

> "My scorpions—have you met my scorpions? No? My pythons and hamadryads? Then there are my fungi and my tiny allies, the bacilli. [. . .] And we must not forget my black spiders, with

their diamond eyes—my spiders, that sit in the dark and watch—then leap!"[10]

There are always the luxurious apartments and laboratories hidden within waterfront tenements or behind the façades of modern office buildings, furnished with exotic appointments from both Near and Far East. There is the pet marmoset Peko, the only creature for whom Fu Manchu displays affection. There are the catalepsy-inducing serum, *F. katalepsis,* and the longevity elixir which keeps Fu Manchu alert and active far beyond a normal life-span. There are Fu Manchu's human agents, drawn from almost every secret sect in the world: dacoits from Burma, Thugs from India, *Hashishîn* from Syria and Persia, zombies from Haiti—and sober lawyers, surgeons, scientists, and inventors from almost every civilized nation. And there is the beautiful and headstrong Fah Lo Suee, Fu Manchu's daughter, who proves to be a two-edged weapon.

Through the years the Fu Manchu books have been issued in literally hundreds of reprint editions, and have seldom been out of print for long at a time. At intervals, the entire series is still being made available in paperback editions. In addition to their incarnations in print, the stories have formed the basis for several successful radio adaptations, a string of films of uneven quality (of which the prize is undoubtedly *The Mask of Fu Manchu* [1932], with Boris Karloff in a virtuoso performance as the insidious doctor), panel art ("comic strip") versions (one of which ran for more than ten years in the French paper *Le Parisien Libéré*), and a forgettable television series.

Sax Rohmer did not invent the idea of the "sinister Oriental" or its collective manifestation as the "Yellow Peril." The latter was the brain-child of sensational journalism in the late nineteenth century. It had been nurtured in popular magazines and newspapers, and was put to fictional use by a number of writers, including M. P. Shiel (*The Yellow Danger*, 1898). In fixing upon Orientals as objects of suspicion and perpetrators of nameless crimes, Rohmer was reflecting attitudes already firmly implanted in the public mind. It was never the specific ethnic nature of his characters that was of primary interest to Rohmer, but rather their exoticism when viewed by Western eyes. He employed Chinese (and Arab and Indian) villains rather than Mafia dons or Russian anarchists because he could ascribe to them customs and backgrounds that would seem strange and wonderful to his readers, and could surround them with jade and lacquer-work, *mushra-bîyeh* screens and perforated brass lamps, Bokhara carpets, ancient Egyptian artifacts, silken robes, incense. . . . Nevertheless, one cannot gloss over the ethnic aspersions and jingoist sentiments in the early books. They are neither so frequent nor so deep-rooted as some critics have charged, but they are there, and a modern reader must come to terms with them. (In just such fashion one must deal with the somewhat old-fashioned prose and the occasional peculiarities of syntax. Some modern readers find both the attitudes and the prose style easy to accommodate, while for others they are insuperable barriers to enjoyment of the stories.) In later books the attitudes (and the prose style) become more modern, and Fu Manchu is seldom treated as a specifically Chinese villain.

There were certainly times when Rohmer would have liked to lay Fu Manchu permanently to rest. An indication of this is the fact that fourteen years elapsed between the third and fourth books in the series. But Rohmer found, as had Conan Doyle somewhat earlier, that he had wrought too well. His creation had so taken root in the popular imagination that each time he tried to break away and devote himself to other writing, he was drawn back inevitably to his most famous (and most profitable) character. Fu Manchu has long had the same mythic status as Sherlock Holmes and Tarzan; the name is used in popular speech and writing, and is readily recognized by people who have never read the original stories or heard of their author.

In addition to the chronicles of Dr. Fu Manchu, Rohmer wrote some three dozen other books. Some of these, such as *The Yellow Claw* (1915) and *The Golden Scorpion* (1918), adhere closely to the Fu Manchu model. In fact, Fu Manchu makes a brief anonymous appearance in the latter book, in which the chief villain dispatches his enemies with a disintegration ray. Both books feature one of Rohmer's series detectives, Gaston Max of the Paris Sûreté. In *The Day the World Ended* (1930), Max encounters Anubis, a rather Baroque version of the supertechnological mastermind who would later appear so frequently in Ian Fleming's James Bond novels. (Indeed, Fleming owed much to the patterns established by Rohmer, as is particularly evident in his own treatment of the "sinister Oriental," *Dr. No.*)

Rohmer's most interesting detective appears in only one book. The title character of *The Dream Detective* (1920) is Moris Klaw, proprietor of a very odd curio shop (guarded by a parrot who reacts to visitors with the cry, "Moris Klaw! Moris Klaw! The Devil's come for you!"). Klaw is a psychic detective. He investigates cases of haunting, possession, and plain ordinary murder by visiting the scene of the crime and sleeping upon an "odically sterilized" pillow which he carries with him. When he awakes, he finds that his sleeping mind has "photographed" past events which enable him to unravel the mystery. Ten of his cases are included in the book, ranging from an amusing crime story about a man who beheads mummies (for an entirely rational reason, as it turns out) to an eerily effective fantasy concerning an experiment in Egyptian magic.

Toward the end of his writing career Rohmer descended all too frequently into self-parody, as in the five novels about Sumuru, a carefully de-ethnicized female version of Fu Manchu. But his late years also produced one of his best fantastic detective stories, *The Moon Is Red,* published in England in 1954. The focus of this novel is a series of mysterious murders all of which occur on nights when the moon is full. All of the victims are young women with red hair, who have been strangled and savagely beaten. All are found in rooms locked from the inside and having windows accessible only to some abnormally acrobatic creature. Around the bodies are strewn shreds of paper and cloth, torn by strong teeth. . . .

III

Sax Rohmer added exotic paraphernalia and touches of outright fantasy to stories which were fundamentally crime thrillers. In the work of other authors both the fantasy element and the strict detective-story plotting are more evident.

One such author is John Dickson Carr. Carr was born in Uniontown, Pennsylvania, in 1905. His father was a lawyer and U.S. Congressman, and later served as Postmaster of Uniontown. By the age of fourteen Carr was writing sports columns and reporting on murder trials for the local newspaper. He attended several schools, and was scheduled to enroll in the University of Pennsylvania Law School. Instead, he went to Paris, and wrote his first detective novel, *It Walks by Night,* which was published in 1930. He settled in England, where he made his home until after the Second World War. Most of his novels of the 1930s and 1940s have an English setting.

Carr has made a specialty of the story of impossible crime, particularly locked-room murders. His ingenious plots and his skill at flummoxing the reader are legendary. Of equal importance is his mastery of bizarre incident and eerie atmosphere. A prime example is *Hag's Nook* (1933), the first of the Gideon Fell novels, set in and near a long-abandoned prison, the subject of unsavory legends. An apparently supernatural vengeance in the past, described with grisly effectiveness in the form of an ancient diary, is made to serve as the model for a coldly rational modern murder. A somewhat similar device is used in the first Sir Henry Merrivale story, *The Plague Court Murders* (1934), published under the Carter Dickson pseudonym.

In *The Burning Court* (1937), the past once again rises to haunt the present. Edward Stevens, editor with a New York publishing house, is reading the manuscript of the latest book of murder-trials by author Gaudan Cross. One of the trials reported is that ,of a certain Marie D'Aubray, guillotined in 1861 for murder by poison. The name of the murderess, and the portrait included with the manuscript, are those of Stevens's own wife. . . . The nightmare grows when a recent death near their cottage in rural Pennsylvania turns out to be murder—by poison. Each new fact that comes to light seems to draw the net more tightly about Stevens's wife. Is she indeed one of the "non-dead"— a woman who, convicted and executed for murder by poisoning, is able to return from the dead and assume corporeal form in a later generation? Since this is Carr at his trickiest, there are not one but two complete solutions to the mystery.

Even when such touches were not essential to the plot, Carr could not resist inserting hints of the supernormal. Family curses, precognition, intimations of vampirism, ghosts, and witchcraft are scattered through his novels, keeping the characters (and the reader) in a continual state of pleasurable unease. In almost every case these references are red herrings, and are explained away at the denouement. But there are three novels in which the fantastic element remains solidly and inarguably present.

These books are expressions of Carr's fascination with the past and his passion for historical reconstruction. One might consider them a trio of variations on the theme of the famous play *Berkeley Square* by John Balderston (based in turn on Henry James's unfinished novel *The Sense of the Past* [1917]). In *The Devil in Velvet* (1951) Nicholas Fenton, professor of history at Cambridge University in the year 1925, makes a bargain with the Devil in order to be sent back in time to the seventeenth century. His purpose is to prevent a murder which he has read about in an old manuscript and which, over a period of years, has come to obsess him. The Devil keeps his word, and Nicholas finds himself inhabiting the body of another Nicholas Fenton in the year 1675. He is unsuccessful in preventing the murder, and very soon finds himself faced with the problem of solving it—and of outwitting the Devil in order to save his own life and that of the woman he loves. A rousing historical adventure, full of swordplay and beautiful women—a meticulously plotted formal detective puzzle—a story of the supernatural: three *genres* blended in one novel.

Modern personalities alive in the past are also at the heart of *Fear Is the Same* (1956) by Carter Dickson, and *Fire, Burn!* (1957). In the former novel, Philip Clavering and Jennifer Baird, living in the year 1795, gradually begin to "remember" events from future existences in 1955—and to realize that identical webs of murder are tightening around them in both eras. In the latter novel, John Cheviot, a detective Superintendent at present-day Scotland Yard, enters a London taxi for a short trip, and steps out into the year 1829. Here he becomes involved in the turbulent early history of Scotland Yard, and with the solution of an "impossible" crime. Only the sketchiest explanation is offered for the journey backward in time, and all of the events in 1829 are presented realistically and with careful attention to historical accuracy.

Detectives whose normal habitat is the "straight" mystery have sometimes been permitted to stray into fantasy. In Margery Allingham's *The Mind Readers*

(1965), Albert Campion and Charley Luke get involved with extrasensory perception and supernormally intelligent children, in a naive and unconvincing narrative. Fergus O'Breen, the jaunty Irish detective in four novels by Anthony Boucher, encounters various manifestations of the preternatural in three short stories: a werewolf in "The Compleat Werewolf," time travel in "Elsewhen," and witchcraft in "The Pink Caterpillar." And Martin Lamb, the narrator of Boucher's first novel, *The Case of the Seven of Calvary* (1937), returns in "The Anomaly of the Empty Man" to hear Dr. Horace Verner, the cousin of a certain well-known consulting detective, explain how a man can vanish from inside a full set of clothes, leaving them in their natural arrangement: socks inside shoes, underwear inside trousers, belt fastened, etc.[11]

Two British writers who have specialized in the fantastic side of mystery fiction are L. P. Davies and John Blackburn. Some of Davies's novels are science fiction, and labeled as such, but the majority have been published as crime fiction. The most common theme in these books is the problem of confused or hidden identity. A man of unknown or mysterious background is introduced, and his origin must be discovered (either by himself or by others) before the plot can be resolved. One of the fascinations of reading a typical Davies novel is the question of whether the author can possibly devise a natural explanation for his extraordinary premises. In *Who Is Lewis Pinder?* (1965), for example, the title character is an amnesiac found unconscious in a country lane. Attempts to identify him pay off all

250   THE MYSTERY STORY

too prodigally, in the form of incontrovertible evidence (fingerprints and medical records) proving him to be not one but four separate individuals, all of whom have been dead for more than twenty years! In this case the author's remarkable ingenuity is equal to the task of supplying a rational (if necessarily far-fetched) explanation. In other Davies novels, the inexplicable is not so easily disposed of.

The Paper Dolls (1964) begins with the death of a schoolboy who had, without reason or warning, thrown himself off the roof of the school. In trying to understand the background of this useless death, teacher Gordon Seacombe discovers other twelve-year-olds with very strange characteristics; one of them is a boy who suffers pain and bruises without any injuries to cause them, a right-handed boy who suddenly becomes left-handed and executes a technically expert sketch of a location that he has never visited or heard of. Seacombe gradually realizes that the odd boys are linked together, and that they are using their extraordinary mental powers to warn him off and confuse his investigation. But he cannot stop, for he also realizes that the boys are growing more powerful, and are working toward some monstrous event that must not be allowed to happen.

In *The Lampton Dreamers* (1966), several inhabitants of the village of Lampton are visited with the same disturbing dream. Thereafter the village is plagued with poison-pen letters, vandalism, and violent death. What could cause a number of people all to have the same dream, and to act in ways contrary to their natures?

Many years before the opening of *The Reluctant Medium* (1966), a man named Walter Hudd, convicted of a crime he did not commit, killed himself in prison. Years later, his accuser receives a note reading, "I have come back from the dead, Matthew Rawson, to seek retribution." The note, which a medium claims was produced by automatic writing, is in Hudd's handwriting. From then on, Rawson's household is terrorized by ghostly voices, glimpses of the supposedly dead man, sounds of his limping footsteps, and the scent of verbena (characteristic of Hudd's shaving lotion). Then, one by one, people of importance in Hudd's life begin to turn up dead. . . .

John Blackburn's specialty is the story of large-scale menace, of either superscientific or supernatural origin. The menace is never treated impersonally, but always poses direct and immediate threat to the main characters. No current writer does better than Blackburn with scenes of individuals at the mercy of malevolent and seemingly unstoppable forces. In his first novel, *A Scent of New-Mown Hay* (1958), a survivor of a Nazi concentration camp unleashes a mutant strain of fungus which does widespread damage. In common with several later novels, the story has an espionage framework, with General Kirk and other agents of the British Foreign Office Intelligence tracking down the culprit. In *A Sour-Apple Tree* (1959) the search for a traitorous scientist is punctuated by a series of inexplicable murders. *Broken Boy* (1959) opens with what seems to be a straightforward murder, as the mutilated body of a woman is fished out of a river. As her identity is sought, the picture widens to include Communist agents and hints of espionage. Further investigation uncovers a cult of revenge-seeking women, the survival of an ancient and unholy religion, and ritual sacrifices in underground chapels. General Kirk and his agents are once more involved. In *Nothing but the Night* (1968) an occultist helps to unravel a pattern of bizarre murders. In *Bury Him Darkly* (1969) the menace originates in the tomb of Sir Martin Railstone, an unorthodox eighteenth-century scientist and prophet. A modern-day disciple of Railstone breaks into the tomb, and shortly thereafter dies in agony, screaming "Something's alive in there!" The "something alive" is soon on the loose, threatening the entire country.

In other Blackburn novels, such as *Children of the Night* (1966) and *Devil Daddy* (1972), fantasy and espionage are no longer on an equal footing; the investigative element is played down and the fantastic element takes center stage.

The fantastic menace combatted by secret-service agents is also the common theme of John Creasey's novels of Dr. Stanislaus Alexander Palfrey and the international organization known as Z5. Of the nearly six hundred books produced by Creasey in the course of a long and fecund career, some thirty-four belong to the Palfrey/Z5 series.

The organization began (in *Traitor's Doom*, 1942) as a fairly traditional spy-and-counterspy group. It was later given formal status as the "inter-Allied Intelligence Branch" and awarded the cryptic designation "Z5." The chief agents were "Sap" Palfrey and Drusilla Blair (later Mrs. Palfrey), representing England; Stefan Andromovitch, an outsize Russian; and

Cornelius Bruton, an American. The early adventures are well-plotted and fast-paced war stories, still quite readable today. The original editions, which are not too hard to find in England, offer the bonus of authentic "period" atmosphere; some of this has been excised in later reprints, in a lamentable effort to streamline and update the stories.

Rather than being disbanded at the end of World War II, Z5 metamorphosed into a very special kind of international peace-keeping organization, affiliated in a loose and unspecified way with the budding United Nations and drawing manpower and support from all nations. It was completely non-political in nature. Its main duties were to uncover and counteract threats to world peace or welfare stemming from private individuals or groups rather than from international frictions. With uncanny foresight, Z5's planners were preparing for the lengthy parade of unhinged and power-hungry villains who were lurking in the wings with their fantastic weapons and wild plans for conquest.

The first of the new global menaces appears on the scene in *Dark Harvest* (1947), the ninth book in the series. The villain is a madman named Karen, an American racist and ultra-isolationist whose slogan is "America for the Americans, and let the rest of the world rot." To reduce the rest of the world to savagery or slavery, he unleashes *bitua,* a sort of radioactive coal-dust which kills all plant life and sterilizes the land. Several large-scale disasters ensue before the agents of Z5 are eventually triumphant.

The secret weapons in the Palfrey stories generally have italicized pseudo-scientific names: *bitua, heligite, fatalis,* and so on. Another feature of *Dark Harvest* which is repeated often in the later books is the cavalier fashion in which Creasey disposes of large segments of the earth's population. There is almost always a miraculous regeneration before the next book begins.

The villain in *Sons of Satan* (1948) is *Abba* (yes, in italics), leader of a worldwide conspiracy to set up devil-worship as a new religion, using it as a cover for seizing political power. In *The Man Who Shook the World* (1950), a series of underground explosions generates earthquakes and tidal waves that cause widespread panic and destruction. The eponymous villain is a man who is able to exert mental control over his agents at a distance, from his headquarters in the "Land of No Return" in the Matto Grosso.

The Children of Hate (1952; later reprinted as *The Killers of Innocence,* 1971) is one of the best books in the series. From early reports of kidnapped children—some of whom are never seen again, while others return to their homes oddly changed—through sightings of midget jet aircraft in the vicinity of mysterious explosions, the suspense and tension build nicely, up to the final confrontation of Palfrey with Madame Theresa, the Queen of the Children of Hate. One disappointment connected with the book is visible only in retrospect: the most interesting and complex character in the book is apparently recruited into Z5 at the end of the story, and yet he never reappears in later adventures.

In *The Touch of Death* (1954) we encounter another mystery substance, *fatalis,* derived from uranium ore.

People properly treated with *fatalis* become carriers, spreading death at a mere touch of their hands. The mastermind who sends them on their errands is another madman bent on world domination. The villain in *The Mists of Fear* (1955) may or may not be a madman, but he is one of Z5's most formidable antagonists. He is Botticelli, a self-styled Supreme Being, invulnerable to human foes. ("I can control matter. I can also teach others to do so.") He is attended by twelve "angels," to whom he has taught some of his own powers, and controls the *elementa,* artificially created sentient beings whose natural state is a vapor or mist. The *elementa* kill on command, and also gather in large clouds and cause violent meteorological disturbances. Botticelli's aim is to supplant all the world's religions with a single religion, with himself as God. Up until three pages from the end, the book is fast-paced and suspenseful, if more than slightly silly. But Creasey has done his job too well in building Botticelli's invulnerability. He must resort to an unexplained accident and an even more unexplained and unsatisfying miracle to bring on the happy ending.

Beginning in the 1960s the tone of the Palfrey novels changed. Creasey himself began referring to them as "allegorical fantasies dealing with the major problems of our times." Such concerns as flood, famine, drought, environmental pollution, noise pollution, and overpopulation served as hooks on which to hang stories that were generally too weak to sustain the extra didactic weight. *The Sleep* (1964), *The Famine* (1967), *The Smog* (1970), and similar books are fast-paced and slickly done, with pseudo-scientific trappings thicker than ever, but the vitality and spontaneity of the earlier books just isn't there.

Returning to less world-shaking affairs, let us look at a handful of novels and short stories illustrating various uses of fantasy in mystery fiction.

Leslie H. Whitten was for several years an associate of political columnist Jack Anderson. His first novel, *Progeny of the Adder* (1965), is set in Washington, D.C., and concerns a police search for the killer of several women whose bodies were found floating in the Potomac River, drained of blood. This story is told with careful attention to details of police procedure, which make it all the more convincing when the very odd and sinister nature of the culprit is gradually uncovered. (Almost the same plot idea was later used, not by Whitten, for a television film called *The Night Stalker*. Successful as this film was, Whitten's novelistic treatment is superior in every way.)

Whitten's second novel, *Moon of the Wolf* (1967), is set in the small Mississippi delta town of Stanley in 1938. Sheriff's deputy Aaron Whitaker is called to investigate the killing of a young Negro nurse, Ellie Burrifous, found in the fields outside of town with her throat ripped open and one arm torn completely from her body. Ellie's brother Lawrence is arrested and jailed, though only the county's redneck farmers even pretend to believe that he is guilty. But the killings continue, each more savage than the last, and accompanied by the baleful howling of a wolf—in country where no wolves have been seen for over twenty years. Old Hugh Burrifous, Ellie's dying father, mutters about "the loukerouk, the loukerouk," and sees the invisible mark of the pentagram on each new victim's palm. . . . The climactic scene, as the killer stalks his final prey through the halls and classrooms of a deserted school building at night, is enough to raise a permanent set of goose-bumps on any susceptible reader.

Goose-bumps are also a stock-in-trade of Robert Bloch, an author one instinctively feels must have a place in any discussion of fantasy in mystery fiction. His credentials for inclusion, however, come not from his famous suspense novels (*The Scarf, Psycho, American Gothic,* and others) but from his short stories. "Yours Truly, Jack the Ripper" was first published in the pulp magazine *Weird Tales* in 1943, and was included in the short story collection *The Opener of the Way* (1945). It is the story of the quest of Sir Guy Hollis, convinced that Jack the Ripper was able to preserve his youth by supernatural means and is still alive in modern Chicago. The story was dramatized on radio more than twenty times, and has been reprinted almost as often. Other interesting Bloch stories are his posthumous collaboration with Poe, "The Lighthouse," and the chilling "The Man Who Collected Poe," both included in Sam Moskowitz's anthology *The Man Who Called Himself Poe* (1969).

Flush as May (1963) was the first novel by former *Punch* humorist P. M. Hubbard. It is a curious mixture of the light-hearted and the sinister. Margaret Canting, an Oxford undergraduate on holiday, discovers the body of a man in the fields near the village of Lodstone. When she returns with the local constable, the body has disappeared, and no one appears to believe it ever existed. Margaret is stubborn as well as intelligent, and is determined to unravel the mystery. It is not long before she begins to realize the significance of the body being found on May Morning, and of the growing interest shown in her quest by Sir James Utley, an anthropologist specializing in the folkways of the ancient Britons. The present-day mystery merges with secrets more than a thousand years old, leading up to a final confrontation in the churchyard on Lodstone Hill.

A later Hubbard novel, *The Dancing Man* (1971), also involves influences out of Britain's pre-Christian past, though in more covert form.

In Helen McCloy's *Through a Glass, Darkly* (1949), psychiatrist-detective Basil Willing investigates the case of a teacher at an exclusive girls' school who may (or may not) be able to send forth an astral double to kill on command. There are seemingly reliable reports of the teacher being seen in two places simultaneously, and the evidence linking her to murder is very persuasive. Is she being framed by an exceptionally clever killer, or is she—through her *Doppelgänger*—the guilty party?

L. Ron Hubbard, in the decade and a half before he invented Dianetics and became the founder of the Church of Scientology, was a prolific and popular writer of pulp magazine fiction: Westerns (on which he once used the pen-name Winchester Remington Colt), adventure stories, true romances, fantasy, and science fiction. (Dianetics was introduced to the world in the pages of *Astounding Science Fiction* magazine.)

He also worked as a script-writer in Hollywood. According to his son,[12] he was a two-finger typist who could reach ninety words per minute and could turn out complete saleable manuscripts in first draft. In spite of this speed, much of his writing was of respectable quality. For the magazine *Unknown* (July 1940) he wrote one of his best stories, the short novel entitled *Fear*. James Lowry, ethnologist and professor at Atworthy College, has just published an article in a tabloid newspaper expressing disbelief in demons and spirits. As a result of this article, and the narrow-mindedness of the college president, he is dismissed from his teaching job. Some time later he suffers a blackout, and when he returns to consciousness of his surroundings he realizes that four hours are missing from his life. He has lost his hat, and he knows, without being able to explain why, that it is a vital clue to what happened to him during those lost hours. He sets out on his search, beset by dreams and hallucinations, often unable to distinguish between reality and delirium. The story is punctuated by the comments of watching spirits, which may exist only in Lowry's increasingly disorganized mind. And when he has finally found his hat and filled in the four missing hours—

> Somewhere high above, there seemed to hang a tinkle of laughter, high, amused laughter, gloating and mocking and evil.
> *"Who ever heard of demons, my sister?"*
> *"No one at all, my brother."*
> Of course, though, it was probably just the sigh of wind whining below the cellar door.

Whether read as a fantasy of demonic vengeance or as a novel of psychological suspense, *Fear* is a work of remarkable power.

Frank M. Robinson's first short story appeared in *Astounding Science Fiction* in June 1950, just one month after Hubbard's initial Dianetics article. Over the next five years Robinson contributed well-crafted and suspenseful stories to more than a dozen of the science fiction and fantasy magazines then being published. His first novel, *The Power* (1956), was not science fiction, though it borrowed a science-fictional idea: the hunt for a mutant superman. The book's hardcover publishers billed it quite accurately as "a novel of menace." *The Power* was written while the author was pursuing an advanced journalism degree at Northwestern University, and was submitted, chapter by chapter, to fulfill written assignments in a graduate course—surely one of the oddest term papers ever seen at the Medill School of Journalism! The story concerns a navy-subsidized research team studying human endurance and survival characteristics. Results of an anonymous questionnaire suggest that one of the team members is a mental and physical superman; the questionnaire could have been dismissed as a hoax or accident, except that the one team member who takes it seriously promptly dies under mysterious circumstances. He leaves an uncompleted letter to team chairman William Tanner: "I want to tell you about Adam Hart. . . ." Tanner's investigation immediately takes a personal turn when there is an attempt on his life and it becomes clear that he is the focus of the mysterious superman's attentions:

No mail since Monday. Because his name had somehow disappeared from all the lists? Because all the files that mentioned him had been yanked? And there was the case of the records in Wisconsin and the disappearance of his thesis from the library. And then the bank book and his appointment with the dentist . . .

He was being isolated, he thought. Anything in print that mentioned his name was disappearing. People were being conditioned to forget that he had ever existed. One by one his connections with people were being severed. It was like a dental surgeon blocking off the nerves with shots of novocain.

Just before the tooth was pulled.[13]

Tanner's nightmare battle against Adam Hart is hair-raising and compulsively readable.

Robinson's recent writing has been done in collaboration with another science-fiction writer, Thomas N. Scortia. The team has written *The Glass Inferno* (1974), one of the two novels on which the motion picture *The Towering Inferno* was based, and *The Prometheus Crisis* (1975), a minutely detailed, circumstantial, and unremittingly chilling account of the blowup of a nuclear power plant.

In H. F. Heard's *A Taste for Honey* (1941) a bee-keeper's wife is stung to death by bees. A neighbor in the small English village who exhibits undue curiosity about the unusual cause of death finds himself pursued across the countryside and into his own home by a swarm of the deadly insects. He is saved, and the mystery unravelled, by a newcomer to the district: an elderly gentleman, a certain Mr. Mycroft, with some experience of beekeeping and a strong bent for deductive reasoning.

The Witching Night (1952) by C. S. Cody is a tense, edge-of-the-chair tale of murder by witchcraft, set in the windswept dune area at the southern tip of Lake Michigan. Individuals who enquire too closely about a mysterious group known as the Dune-Dwellers suddenly develop a persistent headache, untreatable by any medicine or pain-killer, and accompanied by a gradual wasting away of the body. After watching a friend die in just this fashion, Dr. Joe Loomis is determined to track down the cause. He realizes that he is close to an answer when his own headache begins. . . . A somewhat similar novel, with its own attractions in the way of suspense, is *The Dreamers* (1958) by British film historian Roger Manvell.

To Walk the Night (1937) by William Sloane has been variously described as a detective novel, a ghost story, a novel of terror, and a science-fiction story. Under any heading it is a remarkable book, one of the most thoughtful as well as one of the most frightening of mysteries. It begins with a father's attempt to find out, from his son Jerry's best friend, Bark Jones, why his son has shot himself. The bulk of the book consists of Bark's answer, as he tries to sort out in his own mind the events that led to the tragedy. It started with the inexplicable and terrible death of astronomer Walter LeNormand, one of Jerry's teachers at college. Seated at his work-table, in full view of Jerry and Bark, he burned to death—while the chair in which he was seated remained virtually unmarked. After LeNormand's death, Bark and Jerry met his enigmatic widow, Selena. While Bark became ever more convinced of her strangeness, he could only watch helplessly as Jerry fell in love with her. Soon Jerry and Selena married. But Jerry's alert mind and inquisitive nature would not let any mystery lie unsolved, and he continued to investigate LeNormand's death. What he discovered, and what Bark and Jerry's father reconstruct after his death, lie at the heart of this fascinating and ambiguous novel.

A later novel by the same author, *The Edge of Running Water* (1939), deals with the mysterious events accompanying a scientific investigation of survival after death. Here there is less of the detective novel and more of the story of terror, leading up to an apocalyptic climax.

Cornell Woolrich's *Night Has a Thousand Eyes* (1945) began as a magazine story called "Speak to Me of Death" (*Argosy*, 1937). The book edition was first published under the name George Hopley, and was reprinted in paperback as by William Irish. Now, after thirty years, the book is finally being issued under the Woolrich by-line. The story is set in Woolrich's dark and hopeless universe, on the borderline between reality and fantasy. Jeremiah Thompkins, an unwilling seer, seems able to foretell future events. Time after time his reluctant prophecies come true, until even such a skeptic as wealthy industrialist Harlan Reid is convinced. And then Thompkins foretells Reid's own death, at midnight on a specific date, "by the jaws of a lion." Police detective Shawm, in love with Reid's daughter, tries to prove the prophecy a hoax, but one by one all the loopholes are closed . . . and the fatal midnight creeps inexorably closer.[14]

No survey of the fantastic in mystery fiction could be complete without mention of the work of Harry Stephen Keeler, perhaps the oddest oddball ever to bemuse a reader. It is no exaggeration to say that Keeler created his own alternate universe and filled it with people and events which, while having their own zany internal consistency, do not necessarily bear any relation to the "real" world. As merely one example, whenever Keeler needed to tie up a handful of loose ends, he had no hesitation in inventing "facts" out of whole cloth; witness the confident assertion on page 737 of *The Matilda Hunter Murder* (1931) that "people who are the offspring of polydactylics are invariably violet blind." In other words, if your mother had six fingers on one hand, you cannot distinguish between violet and black. The reference to page 737 is not a typographical error, either. One of Keeler's characteristics was a penchant for enormously long novels, some of them so long that he had to chop them into two or even three parts in order to have them accepted by a publisher. Another Keeler touch was his fertile use of coincidence, carrying this plot device far beyond any bounds envisioned by other writers. Bizarre plots, stories-within-stories (he filled out many of his books by reprinting his own and his wife's pulp-magazine stories), miraculous inventions and their consequences (several of his stories have future settings), characters with incredible names, and barbed satiric shafts directed at all available targets—these are only some of the ingredients of Keeler's private cosmos. Unfortunately for his continued success, his prose was as idiosyncratic as his ideas. He made heavy use of bizarre dialects, and seldom made a simple, direct statement if there was an involuted way of saying the same thing. This prolixity did not prevent his books from being extremely popular in the 1920s and 1930s, but by the late 1940s no American publisher was willing to handle his work. British publishers carried on for a few years longer, but in time even they gave up. Keeler's last novels were published only in Portuguese or Spanish translations, and at his death he left several manuscripts that had not been published in any form.

IV

Stories of psychic or occult detectives have always formed a popular if highly specialized sub-category of mystery fiction. Typically, the psychic detective is an investigator who, in addition to or in place of standard investigative techniques, makes use of specialized knowledge of psychic or occult phenomena, ceremonial magic, supernatural forces, or related arcana. The cases investigated must, of course, be ones for which these nontraditional methods are appropriate: they must have at least the appearance of supernatural or occult events, even if this element is explained away at the denouement.

One of the earliest psychic detectives on record is Joseph Sheridan Le Fanu's Dr. Martin Hesselius, who appears in "Green Tea" and other stories collected in the volume *In a Glass Darkly* (1872). Dr. Hesselius is untypical in one way, however: in most of the stories he serves as an outside commentator and explicator rather than as a direct participant in the action. Closer to the norm for psychic investigators is his spiritual descendant, Dr. Abraham Van Helsing, in Bram Stoker's *Dracula* (1897). And the norm itself is virtually defined by the stories in *John Silence: Physician Extraordinary* (1908) by Algernon Blackwood. The opening paragraphs of "A Psychical Invasion" inform us that

> the cases that especially appealed to him were of no ordinary kind, but rather of that intangible, elusive, and difficult nature best described as psychical affliction. [. . .]
> In order to grapple with cases of this peculiar kind, he had submitted himself to a long and severe training, at once physical, mental, and spiritual.

Even Dr. Silence was not always the active investigator. In "Ancient Sorceries" he reverted to the role of outside commentator, and in "Secret Worship" he was absent from the bulk of the story and merely stepped in at the climax to save an individual beset by dark forces.

Shortly after the publication of the John Silence stories, the great weird story writer William Hope Hodgson introduced Carnacki, the Ghost Finder. Six stories were collected under this title in 1913. Although Hodgson's books were very popular in England prior to his death in World War I, his work remained virtually unknown elsewhere for more than thirty years. It was not until 1947 that *Carnacki, the Ghost-Finder* saw print in the United States. If we had only this book by which to judge Hodgson, his work would hardly have gained the high standing which it now enjoys among enthusiasts of the weird and fantastic. Despite occasional inventive touches, the stories are largely routine and the explanations so off-hand that it is hard to believe the author intended them to be taken seriously.

The dullness of Carnacki was very soon counterbalanced by the eccentricity of Sax Rohmer's "dream detective," Moris Klaw, whom we have already mentioned. And within a few years, an interesting variation on the pattern was produced by Ella Scrymsour, with the creation of what was probably the first female occult detective. Five stories of "Sheila Crerar, psychic investigator" appeared in 1920 in *The Blue Magazine,* a British fiction periodical. Unfortunately, these seem not to have been preserved in book form.

In *The Secrets of Dr. Taverner* (1926) the medical profession once more contributed a psychic detective. The author, Dion Fortune (pseudonym of Violet M. Firth), was an occultist, a writer on mysticism, and founder of the Society of Inner Light. Her stories treat occult phenomena in an entirely matter-of-fact manner, which often serves to enhance their effect. Her earnest and somewhat humorless narrative style produced at least one memorable line. The story "Blood-Lust" ends with this exchange:

"Then that German we all saw—?"
"Was merely a corpse who was insufficiently dead."

All of the occult detectives so far mentioned have been British, but the most extensively chronicled figure in this category was a Frenchman, and his exploits were recorded by an American. Seabury Quinn's detective Jules de Grandin was introduced in 1925 in the pages of the legendary pulp fiction magazine *Weird Tales.* Over the next quarter of a century, Quinn produced a total of ninety-three de Grandin stories, including one full-length novel. Ten of the stories, drawn from the first five years, were issued in book form in 1966 under the title *The Phantom Fighter*. Six more collections, containing a total of thirty-three stories, have been prepared for paperback publication in 1976 under the Popular Library imprint.

Seabury Quinn's first story was published in 1919 in the short-lived magazine, *The Thrill Book*. When *Weird Tales* was founded in 1923, Quinn began to write for that market, and remained a prolific and steady contributor throughout the magazine's more than thirty year life-span. Of his more than five hundred short stories, roughly one hundred and eighty appeared in *Weird Tales*. For much of his career, writing was only a part-time occupation. For eighteen years Quinn was editor of *Casket and Sunnyside,* a leading trade journal for morticians. He was also a lawyer and a specialist in medical jurisprudence.

In the de Grandin stories, Quinn began by sticking fairly closely to well-chosen models. The first story, "Terror on the Links," was a variation on Poe's "Murders in the Rue Morgue," and the characters of de Grandin and his companion Dr. Trowbridge were obviously suggested by the Holmes-and-Watson and Poirot-and-Hastings combinations. As the series developed, Quinn became progressively more fond of his creation and gradually endowed him with almost every talent that he could think of. In a letter to magazine illustrator Virgil Finlay in 1936, Quinn described de Grandin as

> quick of movement, wonderfully strong without being heavily muscled, an expert fencer, skilled in

jiu-jitsu and the French science of foot-boxing (la savate), equally expert with either rifle or pistol, and [. . .] at once a trained soldier, surgeon and physician in addition to being a deeply learned occultist and student of all branches of the supernatural.[15]

In addition, de Grandin is the author of that widely known text, *Accelerated Evolution,* and may be the only man who ever succeeded in electrocuting a ghost. To offset this catalogue of marvels, he has an "utterly insatiable thirst" for any sort of alcoholic beverage, an almost equally insatiable gluttony, an intense admiration for himself, an inclination toward foppishness in dress, and a stock of very peculiar French exclamations with which he enlivens his conversation. *("Par le barbe d'un bouc vert!")*

All in all, de Grandin's peculiarities are little more obtrusive than those of Agatha Christie's Poirot, and the author's well-developed story-telling skill and sure touch with the macabre make the series well worth investigating. Many of the stories are particularly notable for their mixture of the *outré* with strict detective story plotting, a feature not common in other authors' essays in this sub-genre. To give one example out of the ninety-three: the case of "The Silver Countess" begins as de Grandin is called in by a friend of Trowbridge's to investigate the disappearance of an odd assortment of minor religious articles (a prayer book, a set of cheap beads, a book of devotional verse, a painting of the Virgin) and certain vampire-like attacks upon a young house-guest. Following clues such as the inscription on a funerary sculpture, the curious story told by a young rabbi, and a chance glimpse of a six-toed foot, de Grandin is led to discover a medieval legend and its deadly modern manifestation.

The psychic detective has continued to flourish on both sides of the Atlantic. In 1945 the British writer Margery Lawrence offered the cases of Dr. Miles Pennoyer of *Number Seven, Queer Street*. The book was reprinted in the United States in 1969 by Mycroft & Moran, the mystery fiction affiliate of August Derleth's Arkham House. The prolific American writer of mystery short stories, Edward D. Hoch, created the character of Simon Ark, who functioned sometimes as a detective but more often as a crusader against occult evil. Two paperback collections, *The Judges of Hades* and *City of Brass* (both 1971), contain eight stories out of a much longer series. Joseph Payne Brennan, poet, short-story writer and librarian (at Yale University), wrote about Lucius Leffing, an occult detective in the classic pattern. Seventeen of his cases, recorded over a ten-year period, were collected in *The Casebook of Lucius Leffing* (1972).

Investigators of the occult have also appeared in formats other than the short story series. Such characters play supporting roles in the novels *The Haunting of Hill House* (1959) by Shirley Jackson and *Hell House* (1971) by Richard Matheson, among others.

Related to psychic detectives are the individuals or groups who do not so much investigate the occult or supernatural as combat its manifestations (invariably evil). John Silence, Jules de Grandin, and Simon Ark, in some of their cases, fit this description, as do such individuals as Manly Wade Wellman's John

Thunstone (in *Weird Tales*) and John the ballad-singer (*Who Fears the Devil?*, 1963), or Dennis Wheatley's Gregory Sallust (*Black August*, 1934) and Duke de Richleau (*The Devil Rides Out*, 1934).

Of the groups battling supernatural evil, among the most interesting is The Guardians, in a series of novels published under the by-line Peter Saxon. Both the concept and the by-line were the creation of British publisher and fiction entrepreneur W. Howard Baker, who wrote three or four of the books himself and commissioned the others. Baker is the man behind the modern revival of Sexton Blake, and a prolific author of mysteries and war novels. The six novels in the series were published as paperbacks in the United States, the first two by Lancer Books and the last four by Berkley Medallion Books. The leader of The Guardians is the mysterious Gideon Cross, and his chief assistant is a beautiful young woman named Anne Ashby. These characters' names, their relationship with each other, and the veiled hints of their past history all provide clear evidence that Baker/Saxon was familiar with John Dickson Carr's *The Burning Court*. In the first novel, *Through the Dark Curtain* (1968), The Guardians battle the Sons of Anglia, a society devoted to reviving the power of the ancient Druids. The focus shifts to Scottish witchcraft survivals in *The Curse of Rathlaw* (1968). Australian aboriginal magic is the source of *The Killing Bone* (1969); in *Dark Ways to Death* (1969) the problem is voodoo and Devil worship, and in *The Haunting of Alan Mais* (1969) it is demonic possession. In the final novel, *The Vampires of Finistère* (1970), with inspiration from A. Merritt's *Creep, Shadow Creep!*, a village on the coast of Brittany is menaced by creatures from a sunken city offshore.

More recently, in the series of paperback novels about Kitty Telefair by Florence Stevenson, we have a less solemn variation on the Guardian theme. The Telefairs and the Caswells are families of hereditary occultists. Kitty and her fiancé, Colin Caswell, are also television personalities, moving in the modern world of literary and show-business celebrities and society people. Kitty's sensitivity to the presence of occult forces continually gets her into trouble, from which she escapes sometimes by her own efforts, sometimes with the aid of her fiancé and family. In *The Witching Hour* (1971) mysterious disappearances of young opera singers lead Kitty to investigate the remarkable longevity of diva Gilda Gianini. In *Where Satan Dwells* (1971) it is Ailsa Ware, a fading film star, who is the focus of unnatural forces. *Altar of Evil* (1973) concerns a modern girl possessed by monsters out of Greek mythology. In *Mistress of Devil's Manor* (1973) Kitty is menaced by unquiet spirits in a Western ghost town. In *The Sorcerer of the Castle* (1974) and *The Silent Watcher* (1975) she meets vampires and were-animals. All of the books have a light and good-humored tone, unlike the ponderous solemnity usually found in stories of supernatural menace. But the horrors are vividly imagined and compellingly described.

The Kitty Telefair books are labeled and marketed as Gothics, which is only partly accurate. But the "Gothic" designation is appropriate, and then some, for one of Florence Stevenson's other novels. *The Curse of the Concullens* (1970) is probably the funniest Gothic ever published. Among its characters are a revenant of a drowned girl, who always appears sopping wet and sniffling; an Irish vampire with nationalist convictions, who only attacks English victims; and a baby werewolf who is discovered at inopportune moments gnawing on the furniture. The book is not only a send-up of almost every Gothic cliché, but a strong and interesting story in its own right, and a delight from beginning to end. It is also one of the more successful Gothics, with paperback sales of close to 100,000 copies and a new printing scheduled for late 1976.

Not all detectives involved in supernatural cases are themselves possessed of abnormal talents or arcane knowledge. A prime example is Gregory George Gordon Green, known as "Gees," the creation of British writer E. Charles Vivian under his pen-name Jack Mann. Gees is a former policeman who quit the force after two years, being unable to stand the strict discipline any longer. He set up in business for himself, and offended his rich and dignified father by placing advertisements in newspapers inviting the public to "Consult Gees' Confidential Agency for everything from mumps to murder." The Agency is overseen by Miss Brandon, in love with her boss and frustrated by his evident inability to see her as more than an efficient secretary. She screens all inquiries and advises callers as to whether "our Mr. Green" will be able to see them. *Gees' First Case* (1937), involving murder by Communist plotters in England, is not fantastic. It does, however, establish one convention of the series: Gees' romantic entanglement with one of the female principals in the case, usually a woman of mysterious antecedents. In later books, such involvements almost invariably have tragic consequences.

In *Grey Shapes* (1937) Gees is called to investigate the mysterious slaughter of flocks of sheep in Cumberland; obvious clues, which the experienced reader recognizes before anyone in the book does, lead to the discovery and destruction of a family of werewolves. *Nightmare Farm* (1937) involves haunting and ghostly vengeance by a former owner of the title property. *Maker of Shadows* (1938) evokes more echoes of A. Merritt's *Creep, Shadow Creep!*, with its story of a modern sorcerer who enslaves people and turns them into shadows. In *The Ninth Life* (1939) Gees is hired to break up an "unsuitable" engagement, and encounters an avatar of an ancient Egyptian goddess.

The original editions of the Gees novels were issued primarily for the lending-library trade in England, and are extreme rarities today. Fortunately, the peculiarly named American publisher, Bookfinger, has rescued them from obscurity and has published limited editions of five out of the eight titles in the series.

Of the modern Gothics in which the supernatural plays a dominant role, among the most consistently enjoyable are the well-crafted novels of Barbara Michaels. (This is the byline which Barbara Mertz uses on her fiction. Mrs. Mertz is the holder of a Ph.D. from the Oriental Institute of the University of Chicago and is the author of *Temples, Tombs and Heiroglyphs: The Story of Egyptology* [1964].)

In *Ammie, Come Home* (1968) attention is centered on a Georgetown house in which unquiet spirits from the Revolutionary War period are active. Two of the spirits invade the personalities of a young woman and one of her college teachers. It gradually becomes apparent that one of the ghosts is attempting to reveal a two-hundred-year-old crime, while the other is fighting to conceal it. In the end it is modern detective work rather than exorcism which uncovers the long-buried secrets and puts the ghosts to rest.

Prince of Darkness (1969) is set in the wealthy Maryland town of Middleburg. Investigating a series of odd events in the town, British writer Peter Stewart and folklore scholar Dr. Katherine More become aware that Middleburg, beneath its surface of unobtrusive luxury, is the headquarters for a particularly nasty modern witchcraft group, and that the malevolent attentions of that group are now focused upon them.

In *The Dark on the Other Side* (1970) Michael Collins, a magazine writer commissioned to write a biographical article on author Gordon Randolph, becomes a guest in Randolph's isolated country home. From the first evening, he is aware of something very wrong in the household. Randolph's wife Linda seems to be deeply frightened, and hides the fear by drinking herself into fits of sharp-tongued virulence, while Randolph himself is apparently the forbearing and anguished husband. Which behavior is the façade behind which the darkness is stirring? To reveal the precise nature of that darkness and to disperse it (after a couple of mysterious deaths) require detective work and the peculiar Van Helsing-like talents of Collins's friend, Dr. Galen Rosenberg.

The Crying Child (1971) returns to the theme of *Ammie, Come Home.* This time it is King's Island in Casco Bay, off the coast of Maine, which is haunted by the spectre of a crying child, and in which ghosts from a century ago return to possess the modern inhabitants. Once more it is the systematic uncovering of the facts which plays the main role in quieting the spirits.

In later novels the supernatural is much less central to the plot. In *House of Many Shadows* (1974) the ghosts from the past are never really integrated into the present action, and seem to be present mainly to provide a convenient come-uppance for the villain, while in *Witch* (1973) the supernatural touch is so light that only one character ever notices it.

V

There was a time when almost every commentator on science fiction felt obliged to make the observation that "science fiction and detective stories don't mix." This was generally taken to mean that there was a fundamental incompatibility between two specialized genres: the "hard science" sf story on the one hand and the fair-to-the-reader detective puzzle on the other. This view was set forth with accustomed firmness by John W. Campbell, Jr., editor of *Astounding Science Fiction* (later known as *Analog*) and one of the most influential men in the development of modern sf:

You see, in science-fiction, the ordinary detective story is impossible; it can't be fair to the reader because of the very freedom of science-fiction that allows the author to invent new devices, even new cultural patterns, during the course of the story.[16]

Science fiction historian Sam Moskowitz enlarged on this theme:

Science fiction required only a single basic connection with reality, and the rest of the story could expand into outright fantasy provided the progression maintained a consistent logic. The detective story required that the reader be supplied with all the facts necessary to determine the perpetrator of the crime, and those not provided were implicit in the familiar world. The problem of a writer providing adequate background in the world of the future, a globe light-years off, or a technology that was capable of time travel, and still giving the reader a fair shake at guessing the ending, was monumental.[17]

That this problem is not insuperable has been demonstrated repeatedly in the work of Isaac Asimov, Larry Niven, and others. And if we abandon the very narrow interpretations of both "science fiction" and "detective stories" implicit in the preceding comments, we cannot help but notice that writers have been mixing sf and detective elements in fiction, with varying degrees of success, for almost as long as the two genres have been distinguishable as individual entities.

The most obvious early mixtures of sf and detection occurred in stories of "scientific detectives"—investigators who used scientific devices, either actual or fictional, in the solution of crimes. Among the first of these detectives was Luther Trant, created by Edwin Balmer and William MacHarg in the pages of *Hampton's Magazine* in 1909; a collection of nine Luther Trant stories was published in book form in the following year. Much more popular were Arthur B. Reeve's Craig Kennedy stories, which followed (and in some cases copied) the Trant series. Kennedy was a mainstay of *Cosmopolitan* magazine in the years just prior to World War I; the stories were syndicated in newspapers throughout the country and were reprinted in book editions which maintained their popularity until well into the 1930s. Craig Kennedy also appeared in silent movie serials such as *The Exploits of Elaine* (1914) and *The Romance of Elaine* (1915), whose scripts were turned into Sax Rohmerish novels featuring Oriental villains named Long Sin and Wu Fang. Imitators sprang up on all sides, and in 1930 there appeared a pulp magazine called *Scientific Detective Monthly,* devoted exclusively to stories of this type. Ten years earlier the magazine might have been a run-away success, but by 1930 the crest of the wave had passed. After five issues the magazine was retitled *Amazing Detective Tales,* and after five more issues it ceased publication.[18]

The scientific detective relied heavily on gadgets, such as exotic varieties of the lie detector, but the stories did not really blend genuine science-fictional elements into the mystery plot. A more substantial but less immediately noticeable amalgamation, however, was quietly taking place elsewhere. One of the most interesting types of science fiction is that which involves a puzzle or problem—Why did this alien civilization die? What is the purpose of this inexplicable artifact? What caused the disappearance of previous exploration parties on this supposedly uninhabited planet?—whose solution is gradually built up during the course of the story. The techniques of plotting and development necessary for this type of story are the same as those which underlie much of detective fiction (or indeed "structured" fiction of any kind), and many sf puzzle stories may legitimately be considered as mystery or detective stories. A good example is "Omnilingual" by H. Beam Piper,[19] which poses the problem of the decipherment of written records left by a civilized race on Mars which died out 50,000 years ago. The solution by the central character, Dr. Martha Dane, is armchair detection of the purest kind.

Many fine detective novels involve disguise, and characters who are masquerading as someone else. In a science fiction setting, this familiar plot device can take on a frightening dimension. The classic example is the novella "Who Goes There?" by John W. Campbell, Jr.[20] Scientists at an Antarctic base discover an extraterrestrial creature that has been frozen in the South Polar ice for twenty million years. They thaw it out—and discover too late that it is not only formidably intelligent and totally inimical, but also a shape-changer and mimic, able to assume the form, mannerisms, and speech of specific human beings. Once it is among them in disguise, how do they go about identifying and destroying it before it can escape to the outer world?

An extraterrestrial in disguise among humans is also the main character in Hal Clement's *Needle* (1950). Here the detective element is overt. A criminal member of an extraterrestrial race flees through space, pursued by a "policeman" known as the Hunter. Both fugitive and pursuer are symbiotes, accustomed to living within the body of a host creature, able to infiltrate the brain and nervous system of the host and, when necessary, control its actions. When their spaceships crash on Earth, the hosts are killed, and both symbiotes must seek new bodies. The Hunter, once established in his new host (a willing and adventurous fifteen-year-old), is faced with the problem of identifying his quarry, similarly hidden within a human shell—a veritable needle in the haystack of humanity.

The basic idea of "Who Goes There?" and *Needle*—Which one of Us is a Them?—has also been used in Frank M. Robinson's *The Power*, which we have already discussed, and in numerous other stories. In skilled hands, it is an infallible recipe for suspense and thrills.

Other types of detective and mystery fiction have appeared in science-fictional guise. The pyrotechnic novel *The Demolished Man* (1953) by Alfred Bester is an example of an "inverted" detective story, pioneered in "straight" mystery fiction by R. Austin Freeman. We know that Ben Reich, head of the most powerful business firm in the Solar System of the 24th century, has committed cold-blooded murder to save himself from ruin. The fascination of the story lies in Reich's battle to escape justice, in a society where crime detection is the province of the mind-reading Espers.

Murder in Millennium VI (1951) by Curme Gray is a science fiction mystery deserving of more attention from both sf and mystery enthusiasts. It is the only known fiction by this author, who is as much a mystery as anything in his book. The story is set roughly six thousand years in the future, in a matriarchal society so scientifically advanced that the very concept of "death" has disappeared from common usage. But then, one day, someone re-invents murder. . . . The remarkable thing about the book is that it is a first-person narrative told entirely in futuristic terms. Just as the writer of a story set in contemporary America takes for granted such everyday items as telephones, haircuts, and baseball, so Curme Gray writes as if his audience were familiar with "telement," "scooto," "communion," and other features of Millennium VI. The book is not entirely successful, either as science fiction or as a detective story, but it is a failure which stretches the mind at the same time that it entertains.[21]

Isaac Asimov, science fiction writer and author of a veritable library of books on subjects ranging from science to Shakespeare to off-color limericks, has had a long-standing interest in mystery fiction. He has published two contemporary mystery novels, as well as numerous short stories in the genre. He even took the idea of using a nationality as a pseudonym (Paul French) from Cornell Woolrich's alter ego, William Irish. In 1952, in response to a challenge from Horace Gold, editor of *Galaxy Science Fiction,* he embarked on a serious attempt to blend mystery fiction with science fiction. The result was a pair of novels, *The Caves of Steel* (1954) and *The Naked Sun* (1957), featuring detectives Elijah Baley, human, and R. Daneel Olivaw, robot. The pair would have been a trilogy if it had not been for Sputnik; while the third novel was still in its early stages, Asimov decided to divert his talents to science popularization rather than fiction, and it is in this area that the bulk of his subsequent writing has been done.

The Caves of Steel is a murder mystery set on Earth about three thousand years in the future, when the surface of the planet has been abandoned and humanity lives in vast subterranean complexes. People have been conditioned to feel comfortable in their "caves of steel" and to be psychologically incapable of venturing out on the free surface. It is this science fictional background that provides the framework for a double murder (of a human and a robot), which must be solved by Baley and Olivaw. In motive, method, and detection, the science fictional and mystery elements are inextricably bound together. The science fiction writer's task of exploring a strange society and the mystery writer's task of planting unobtrusive clues are carried out in parallel. Asimov also uses the mystery writer's technique of multiple solutions, so familiar from the work of Ellery Queen and John Dickson Carr.

The society depicted in *The Naked Sun* is opposite in every way to that in the preceding novel. Instead of a populous humanity served by a small number of robots, the planet Solaria has a sparse human population vastly outnumbered by robots. And instead of huddling together in subterranean cities, the inhabitants of Solaria shun personal contact—each individual lives on an estate hundreds of square miles in extent, communicating with others by three-dimensional TV and almost never meeting in person. Rikaine Delmarre is murdered on his isolated estate, skull crushed by the traditional blunt instrument which is absent from the scene of the crime. This is clearly an sf version of the English manor-house murder story, but once again it is the science fictional setting which makes this particular murder both psychologically and physically possible.[22]

In addition to the two robot novels, Asimov has written several science fiction mysteries in shorter lengths, most of which are collected in *Asimov's Mysteries* (1968). Of particular interest are the stories of Dr. Wendell Urth, a space-age equivalent of Baroness Orczy's Old Man in the Corner. Urth is a celebrated extraterrologist (expert in extraterrestrial matters) who not only has never been off the Earth but is so averse to travel that he refuses to ride in any mechanical conveyance. People bring their problems to him, he listens to the facts, asks a few questions, and provides the solutions in the best armchair detective tradition. "The Singing Bell" concerns a murder on the Moon, the main problem being how to break the chief suspect's lack of an alibi. (Yes, you read that correctly.) "The Talking Stone" deals with the whereabouts of a fortune in uranium, and "The Dying Night" with the theft of a scientific paper describing a revolutionary discovery.

Many other writers have worked in this unpredictable area where science fiction and mystery fiction overlap. Only a random sampling can be mentioned here. Frank Belknap Long's *John Carstairs, Space Detective* (1949) offers the unusual figure of a botanical detective: all of the cases which Carstairs investigates involve the odd properties of various extraterrestrial flora. In *Once Upon a Star* (1953) by Kendell Foster

Crossen we follow Manning Draco, an insurance investigator in the thirty-fifth century, as he pursues intergalactic con-being (well, what *do* you call a con-man who is not human?) Dzanku Dzanku through several broadly humorous escapades. Eric Frank Russell's *Wasp* (1957) is a straightforward tale of espionage in an interplanetary setting. *Sibyl Sue Blue* (1966) by Rosel George Brown is the story, by turns funny and tough, of a swinging, cigar-smoking female cop in the year 1990, pursuing drug pushers from another planet. *Too Many Magicians* (1967) by Randall Garrett offers an alternate world in which magic works, and in which the Anglo-French Empire now rules not only most of Europe but most of the Western Hemisphere as well. Lord Darcy, chief investigator for the Duke of Normandy, is handed a classic sealed room murder to solve, which he does in the finest tradition of Holmes and Nero Wolfe (who are gently parodied along the way). *A Werewolf Among Us* (1973) by Dean R. Koontz involves both Sherlockian pastiche and a variation on Asimov's Three Laws of Robotics in the solution of an *outré* murder. *Police Your Planet* (1975) by Lester del Rey and Erick van Lhin (a self-collaboration, since "van Lhin" is a pseudonym of del Rey's) is a "hard boiled" tough cop story set on Mars. Gene DeWeese and Robert Coulson's *Now You See It/Him/Them . . .* (1975) presents both murder and detection by means of psi powers, against the background of a convention of science fiction fans. Most recently we have *The Long ARM of Gil Hamilton* (1976) by Larry Niven, a collection of three novellas about UN investigator Gil Hamilton in a future world where the chief crime is kidnapping victims to obtain illegal spare parts for organ transplants. The book contains a commentary by the author in which he discusses the writing of science fiction detective stories.

The field of the sf mystery is a fertile one, which will undoubtedly produce as many interesting experiments in the future as it has in the past.

VI

A type of mystery fiction which often veers off into fantasy is that of the pastiche. As soon as the word is mentioned, we think inevitably of Sherlock Holmes, for there is probably no other fictional character who has inspired such a wealth of pastiche and parody. Some of the treatments are thoroughly pedestrian, some are imaginative without partaking of outright fantasy (an example in point is Stuart Palmer's irreverent explanation of Isadora Persano's "worm unknown to science"[23]), but many are genuinely fantastic. Indeed, by 1960 there were enough such pastiches to fill a book, *The Science Fictional Sherlock Holmes,* edited by Robert C. Peterson and published by the Denver scion society of the Baker Street Irregulars. The contents include Anthony Boucher's "The Anomaly of the Empty Man," discussed in an earlier section, and his delightful "The Greatest Tertian," which must be seen to be appreciated. There is also Poul Anderson's "The Martian Crown Jewels," whose theft is solved by the Martian detective Syaloch, of the Street of Those Who Prepare Nourishment in Ovens. And there are two off-trail adventures of August Derleth's

Holmes surrogate, Solar Pons: "The Adventure of the Snitch in Time" and "The Adventure of the Ball of Nostradamus," co-authored with sf writer Mack Reynolds.

The Adventure of the Peerless Peer (1974) by Philip José Farmer is a pastiche which takes Holmes and Watson to Africa during World War I, where they are involved with Tarzan and various characters out of the pulp magazines. Farmer has also written pastiches of Tarzan and Doc Savage, and in the "Department of Fictional Authors" in *The Magazine of Fantasy and Science Fiction* he has offered stories supposedly written by characters from other authors' fiction. "The Problem of the Sore Bridge—Among Others," by "Harry Manders" (September 1975), unites Holmes and Raffles, and offers explanations (of sorts) for Isadora Persano's worm, the disappearance of Mr. James Phillimore, and the fate of the cutter *Alicia*.

In *Sherlock Holmes's War of the Worlds* (1975) the father and son team of Manly W. Wellman and Wade Wellman offer four stories in which Sherlock Holmes and Professor Challenger are pitted against H. G. Wells's invading Martians.

Minor amusements, all of these, and yet they provide further evidence of the broad variety of themes, backgrounds, and purposes which can be supported by the framework of the mystery story.

NOTES

[1] "The Hound of the Baskervilles" by A. Conan Doyle, Chapter 14.

[2] "The Adventure of the Sussex Vampire" by A. Conan Doyle.

[3] "The Problem of Thor Bridge" by A. Conan Doyle.

⁴ Bantam Books #F2922, 1965, paperback.

⁵ "The Janus Resolution" by Frank D. McSherry, Jr., in *The Mystery Writer's Art*, edited by Francis M. Nevins, Jr., Bowling Green University Popular Press, 1971. Another essay by McSherry in the same volume, "The Shape of Crimes to Come," discusses the crime story in science fiction.

⁶ *The Exorcist* (1971) by William Peter Blatty; *Rosemary's Baby* (1967) by Ira Levin; *The Mephisto Waltz* (1969) by Fred Mustard Stewart. The first two titles are at least as well known in their film versions as in printed form; the film of *The Mephisto Waltz*, though equally skillful, made much less of an impact.

⁷ For further information on Sax Rohmer and his writings, consult: *Master of Villainy: A Biography of Sax Rohmer*, by Cay Van Ash and Elizabeth Sax Rohmer, edited with introduction, notes, and bibliography by Robert E. Briney, Bowling Green University Popular Press, 1972; "Sax Rohmer: An Informal Survey" by Robert E. Briney, in *The Mystery Writer's Art* (see Note 5).

⁸ *The Insidious Dr. Fu-Manchu*, Chapter 11. (Side note: in the first three Fu Manchu books the name was hyphenated; thereafter the hyphen was dropped.)

⁹ "Talk of the Town" column, *The New Yorker*, 29 November 1947.

¹⁰ *The Insidious Dr. Fu-Manchu*, Chapter XIII.

¹¹ "The Compleat Werewolf" and "The Pink Caterpillar" are contained in the collection *The Compleat Werewolf and Other Tales of Fantasy and Science Fiction*, Simon & Schuster, 1969; "Elsewhen" and "The Anomaly of the Empty Man" are contained in *Far and Away: eleven fantasy and science fiction stories*, Ballantine Books, 1955 (simultaneous hardcover and paperback editions).

¹² Cited on pp. 29–30 of *Cults of Unreason* by Dr. Christopher Evans, Farrar, Straus and Giroux, 1974.

¹³ *The Power* by Frank M. Robinson, Lippincott, 1956, Chapter Five.

¹⁴ An excellent biographical and critical study of Woolrich can be found in Francis M. Nevins's Introduction to *Nightwebs* by Cornell Woolrich, Harper & Row, 1971; revised edition, Equinox/Avon #19521, 1974, paperback.

¹⁵ Seabury Quinn's letters to Virgil Finlay are reproduced in facsimile in *Fantasy Collector's Annual–1975*, edited and published by Gerry de la Ree, Saddle River, N.J., 1974.

¹⁶ Introduction to *Who Goes There?* by John W. Campbell, Jr., Chicago: Shasta Publishers, 1948.

¹⁷ "The Sleuth in Science Fiction" by Sam Moskowitz, *Worlds of Tomorrow* (magazine), January 1966. In this and a subsequent article in the same magazine, "The Super-Sleuths of Science Fiction," March 1966, Moskowitz gives an excellent survey of detective themes in science fiction.

¹⁸ Much more information on early scientific detectives is contained in the articles by Sam Moskowitz cited above.

¹⁹ *Astounding Science Fiction*, February 1957; reprinted in *Where Do We Go from Here?*, edited by Isaac Asimov, Doubleday, 1971.

[20] *Astounding Science Fiction,* August 1938, under the pen-name "Don A. Stuart;" first book edition, 1948 (see Note 16); reprinted in *The Science Fiction Hall of Fame,* Volume Two A, edited by Ben Bova, Doubleday, 1973.

[21] A careful analysis of *Murder in Millennium VI* can be found in Chapter 20 (pp. 181–187) of *In Search of Wonder: Essays on Modern Science Fiction,* by Damon Knight, Second Edition, Chicago: Advent Publishers, 1967.

[22] A detailed discussion of *The Caves of Steel* and *The Naked Sun,* both as science fiction and as detective novels, can be found in *The Science Fiction of Isaac Asimov* by Joseph F. Patrouch, Jr., Doubleday, 1974, pp. 159–179.

[23] "The Adventure of the Remarkable Worm" by Stuart Palmer, first published in *The Misadventures of Sherlock Holmes,* edited by Ellery Queen, Little, Brown & Co., 1944; reprinted in *The Adventures of the Marked Man and one other,* by Stuart Palmer, The Aspen Press, 1973.

THIRTEEN

ALLEN J. HUBIN

*Allen J. Hubin is perhaps best
known in the mystery field as the
founder (in 1967) and editor-
in-chief of* THE ARMCHAIR
DETECTIVE, *a quarterly read by
mystery buffs throughout the
world. But his other distinctions
are numerous, including:
crime-fiction reviewer,* THE NEW
YORK TIMES (1968–71); *editor,*
BEST DETECTIVE STORIES OF THE
YEAR (1970–*to date*); *contributor,*
ENCYCLOPAEDIA BRITANNICA (*on
post-World War II mysteries*);
and contributing editor,
ENCYCLOPEDIA OF MYSTERY &
DETECTION. *Mr. Hubin, long
active in the Mystery Writers of
America, has served on numerous
Edgar Award committees.
An avid mystery fan since his
youth, Mr. Hubin has amassed
in his home what may be the
largest extant collection of mystery
stories in private hands, totalling
some 25,000 volumes.*

PATTERNS IN MYSTERY FICTION:
THE DURABLE SERIES CHARACTER

The established publishers and writers of mystery/detective fiction use a variety of recognition signals to the reader that another old friend in the genre is at hand. We shall discuss several significant devices of this sort, the most important of which is the series character.

1. PUBLISHERS. On occasion a publishing imprint will be created and set aside wholly for the sort of fiction indicated by its name: Mystery League, which published briefly during the early 1930s, and Mystery House, from the 1940s, come to mind, along with Doubleday's Crime Club in this country and Collins' corresponding imprint in England, both of which have been active for decades. For many years Doubleday also subdivided its mysteries with symbols to denote "chase and adventure" (gun); "something special" (!); "classic puzzler" (question mark); "damsel in distress" (dagger and flower); "suspense" (clock); and "favorite sleuth" (magnifying glass). Other publishers have printed guns, nooses, skulls, or the like on the spines

of their mysteries, or have established a subimprint for their books in this field. Here are some of them:

Subimprint	Publisher
Armchair Mystery	David McKay
Black Bat Mystery	Bobbs-Merrill
Bloodhound Mystery	Duell, Sloan & Pearce
Bloodhound Mystery	Boardman
Blue Streak Mystery	Dodge
Chantecler Mystery (Detective) Novel	Ives Washburn
Circle Mystery	M. S. Mill
Cloak and Dagger Mystery	Hammond Hammond
Clue Club Mystery	Hillman-Curl
Clue Mystery	Dutton
Cock Robin Mystery	Macmillan
Crime Circle Novels	Thornton Butterworth
Eagle Detective (Mystery)	Bles
Falcon's Head Mystery (Suspense)	World
Fingerprint Mystery	Ziff-Davis
Fingerprint Mystery	Alliance
Gargoyle Mystery	Coward-McCann
Guilt-Edged Mystery	Dutton
Inner Sanctum Mystery	Simon & Schuster
Main Line Mystery	Lippincott
Mask Mystery	Foulsham
Midnight Novel of Suspense	Houghton Mifflin
Midnight Thriller	Frederick Muller
Midnite Mystery	Books, Inc.
Murray Hill Mystery	Rinehart
Raven Book	Abelard Schuman
Red Badge Detective/Mystery	Dodd Mead
Red Circle Crime Novel	M. S. Mill
Red Mask Mystery	Putnam
Scarlet Thread Mystery	McBride

In addition, in recent years several publishers have regularly identified their offerings in this genre with such subtitles as "a novel of suspense" or "a novel of espionage."

2. AUTHORS. The name of a successful author becomes established in the public mind for the excellence of his storytelling—and for the type of story he tells. Thus the reader expects the same sort of fare as before when he picks up the latest Emma Lathen or Dick Francis. Writers who have become known in another field of literature will frequently choose a pseudonym if they turn their hands to mystery fiction, in order to keep the "signals" straight: J. I. M. Stewart writes his mainstream fiction under this, his real name, while issuing his detective fiction under his Michael Innes by-line. In addition, writers of crime fiction who turn to a different type within this broad genre will also sometimes choose a (new) pseudonym for the same reason; examples include the Gideon police procedurals written by John Creasey as J. J. Marric, the Mitch Tobin series by Donald Westlake as Tucker Coe, and the inverted murder stories written by Anthony Berkeley (Cox) as Francis Iles.

3. TITLES. Patterns can be found scattered throughout the titles used in mystery fiction. The table that follows lists their variety and frequency of appearance.

Title Pattern	Author	Example(s) (Number of titles in pattern)
Assignment—	Edward S. Aarons	Assignment—Angelina (40)
About the Murder of . . .	Anthony Abbot	About the Murder of a Startled Lady (6)
The . . . Contract	Philip Atlee	The Ill Wind Contract (19)
(Number Series)	Francis Beeding	The One Sane Man (14) The Two Undertakers
The Case of the . . .	Erle Stanley Gardner	The Case of the Howling Dog (90)
	Christopher Bush	The Case of the Flowery Corpse (56)

Title Pattern	Author	Example(s) (Number of titles in pattern)
Dark . . .	Peter Cheyney	Dark Bahama (6)
(Colors)	Frances Crane	The Flying Red Horse (25)
	John D. MacDonald	Dress Her in Indigo (16)
(Women's Names)	E. V. Cunningham	Alice (12)
The (Color) (Article of Clothing)	Pete Fry	The Orange Necktie (15)
The Black . . .	Constance and Gwenyth Little	The Black Curl (20)
	John Halstead	The Black Arab (6)
. . . Halfaday Creek	James B. Hendryx	Intrigue on Halfaday Creek Justice on Halfaday Creek (13)
(Consecutive Days of the Week)	Harry Kemelman	Friday the Rabbi Slept Late Saturday the Rabbi Went Hungry (5)
The Affair of the . . .	Clifford Knight	The Affair of the Circus Queen (18)
	Patrick O'Malley	The Affair of the Blue Pig (7)
Operation . . .	Dan J. Marlowe	Operation Fireball (10)
Kill Me in . . .	Earl Norman	Kill Me in Atami (7)
The Puzzle of the . . .	Stuart Palmer	The Puzzle of the Blue Banderilla (5)
. . . and the Detective	Allan Pinkerton	The Expressman and the Detective (14)
The (Nation) (Article) Mystery	Ellery Queen	The American Gun Mystery (9)
Puzzle for . . .	Patrick Quentin	Puzzle for Friends (6)
The Tragedy of (Letter)	Barnaby Ross	The Tragedy of X (3)
(References to Drawing)	Willetta Ann Barber and R. F. Schabelitz	The Deed Is Drawn Drawn Conclusion (7)
(Meter)	Hampton Stone	The Man Who Looked Death in the Eye The Babe with the Twistable Arm (19)
(Letter) as in . . .	Lawrence Treat	B as in Banshee D as in Dead (10)
The (Six-Letter Word) Murder Case	S. S. Van Dine	The Benson Murder Case (11)

Such title patterns as these usually accompany a series of books involving a continuing character and serve to increase the apparent unity of the series. The repetitive incorporation of such characters' names in titles serves the same purpose even more unambiguously and represents yet another title pattern, as does the titular use of such suggestive words as "murder," "death," "corpse," "body," "mystery," and "secret."

4. PLOT PATTERNS. Patterns—or, as they have sometimes (unkindly) been called, formulas—have flourished in, or even characterized, some of the subgenres within mystery fiction. For example, the heroine-walking-blithely-into-danger syndrome is well known in Gothic stories, a subgenre which Miss Phyllis A. Whitney discusses in detail elsewhere in this book. The common plot features of the formal, or golden age, detective story are also fondly remembered by fanciers of that hibernating form: the initial murder, preferably in a "closed" setting (such as a country house party); the lengthy questioning of suspects; the final gathering to hear the detective's exposition and identification of the guilty—even the "challenge to the reader" which was *de rigueur* in early Ellery Queen novels and also appeared in other mysteries between the World Wars.

5. SERIES CHARACTERS. Surely the strongest recognition device of all is the series character. Once he has been favorably established, a continuing protagonist can often triumphantly survive changes in authorship and media, retaining his legion of fanciers and attracting new ones in the process. As Sir Arthur Conan Doyle

found with Sherlock Holmes, a character can loom so large in the public mind that he assumes an independent existence, a greater reality even than his creator. Readers may demand more of the character's adventures than the creator is willing or able to produce. Furthermore, the series character offers the author possibilities for much greater depth of exploration of character and milieu than permitted in a single mystery novel—possibilities richly realized by such authors as Maj Sjöwall and Per Wahlöö, who collaborated on a series of Martin Beck novels.

If series characters are as important to mystery fiction and its readers as this, a chronology of the more durable of them may prove instructive in revealing trends and changes in public fancies. Such a chronology is provided below—and the pleasures of drawing conclusions from the data are left to the reader.

It is desirable to define the guidelines under which the chronology has been developed.

a. A "durable" series character is arbitrarily defined as one appearing in five or more books.* Magazines and dime novels are not here considered as books.

b. The chief series character is identified by name in each instance. It should be noted that this principal protagonist may well be surrounded by a large cadre

---

* It will be obvious that number of appearances is not the only criterion to judge the importance or popularity of a series character, inasmuch as the five-appearance requirement is not met by such characters of unquestioned significance as Poe's C. Auguste Dupin, Barnaby Ross's (Ellery Queen's) Drury Lane, and Dashiell Hammett's Sam Spade. In addition, current series creations which have already made their mark on mystery fiction in less than five appearances are thus also excluded; one outstanding example is John Ball's celebrated police detective, Virgil Tibbs, whose fifth book appearance did not come until after the 1975 cutoff year for this chronology.

of colleagues, antagonists, or Watsons; such recurring subordinate characters have not been identified in the chronology, even though in some instances their subordination might be open to dispute. Exceptions to this are those instances in which a subordinate series character subsequently becomes a main character; all appearances are then counted, so that a single book may be included in two different series.

c. Each character is placed in one of six categories: 1) amateur detective (who takes no pay for his involvement in crime solving and does not seek clients, but instead with awesome frequency happens upon bodies and other evidences of malefaction); 2) private investigator (who seeks clients, accepts pay for his services, and is not a member of an official law enforcement agency; thus both the likes of Sherlock Holmes and Mike Hammer are included here, as are investigators working for private firms—such as insurance companies—and lawyer-sleuths); 3) police investigator (including those from city, state, and national law enforcement agencies); 4) adventurer or knight-errant, one who—like Leslie Charteris' Simon Templar— battles the criminous ungodly chiefly out of love of adventure while not finding the monetary rewards necessarily repellent; in recent paperback manifestations the adventurer is likely to be driven by a consuming desire for revenge; 5) spy; and 6) criminal. Admittedly some of the categorizations in the chronology are fairly arbitrary. A good bit of pushing and shoving was necessary to fit certain characters into one of the six categories. But the alternative was a list of categories too large to be useful. A further complication is that a character will sometimes shift categories over the course of a series: a policeman will retire (or be dropped) from the force and become an amateur or a private eye, or a wartime spy will become a private investigator when peace arrives. In such instances the general objective here has been to categorize the character according to his initial occupation.

d. Entries are arranged in order of the year of first book appearance. Those year data that are in significant doubt—owing to the unavailability of the pertinent books for inspection—are enclosed in parentheses; the correct year in such cases may be earlier but not later. Those year data that would tend to mislead somewhat because the character involved had a much earlier existence in magazines or dime novels are marked with an asterisk. No significance attaches to the order in which characters are listed as appearing in a given year.

e. The number of book appearances for each character is given. Those in significant doubt are again enclosed in parentheses, and such numbers are minimums rather than maximums, in most instances. Original short-story collections (not multi-author anthologies) in which the series character appears in at least one story are included, but omnibus collections of works previously published separately or reshuffled short-story collections are not. Those numbers representing series not yet clearly concluded, and hence subject to upward adjustment in future years are marked with a +. For currently active series so marked, the data provided are intended to represent the number of appearances through the end of 1975.

f. Two additional variables are identified which may be useful in spotting trends and developments over the years of the chronology: the national source (or country for which the books were primarily written) of the series is identified, as is the original publishing format, either hardcover (HC) or paperback (PB). For national source the following code is used: A = American; B = British (including Australian); F = French; and S = Swedish.

An undertaking as large as this is always susceptible to errors of commission or omission. Corrections, and the removal of confessed uncertainties, with supporting data in either instance, will always be gratefully received for incorporation in subsequent editions of this book.

Year	Character	Type	Country/ Book Type	Number of Books	Author
1878	Ebenezer Gryce	police	A/HC	13	Anna Katharine Green
1878	James M'Govan	police	B/HC	7	James M'Govan
1887	Inspector Byrnes	police	A/HC	5	Julian Hawthorne
1887	Sherlock Holmes	private	B/HC	10	A. Conan Doyle (1954 collection by Adrian Conan Doyle and John Dickson Carr is included in the count)
1889	Nick Carter	private	A/PB	581	Nicholas Carter (house name)
1891	Old Sleuth	private	A/PB	(6)	Old Sleuth (house name)
1895	Dr. Nikola	criminal	B/HC	5	Guy Boothby
1898	Paul Beck	private	B/HC	5	M. McDonnell Bodkin
1899	Harrison Keith	private	A/PB	51	Nicholas Carter (house name)
1899	A. J. Raffles	criminal	B/HC	13+	E. W. Hornung (and Barry Perowne after 1933)
1904	Jim Godfrey	amateur	A/HC	5	Burton Stevenson
1906	Felix Boyd	private	A/PB	5	Scott Campbell

Year	Character	Type	Country/Book Type	Number of Books	Author
1907	Dr. John Thorndyke	private	B/HC	28	R. Austin Freeman
1907	Arsene Lupin	criminal	F/HC	17	Maurice Leblanc
1907	Joseph Rouletabille	amateur	F/HC	5	Gaston Leroux
1908	J. Rufus Wallingford	criminal	A/HC	5	George Randolph Chester
1909	Inspector Furneaux	police	B/HC	13	Gordon Holmes/ Louis Tracy
1909	Fleming Stone	private	A/HC	61	Carolyn Wells
1910	Hamilton Cleek	police	B/HC	11	Thomas W. Hanshew
1910	Inspector Hanaud	police	B/HC	6	A. E. W. Mason
1910	Jeff Clayton	private	A/PB	(13)	Willard Ward (house name)
1911	Father Brown	amateur	B/HC	5	G. K. Chesterton
1911	Commissioner Sanders	police	B/HC	13	Edgar Wallace (including three by Francis Gerard beginning in 1938)
1912	Smiler Bunn	criminal	B/HC	(7)	Bertram Atkey
1912	Edward Leithen	private	B/HC	7	John Buchan
1912	Judge Priest	amateur	A/HC	7	Irvin S. Cobb
1912	Craig Kennedy	private	A/HC	26	Arthur B. Reeve
1913	Dr. Fu Manchu	criminal	B/HC	14	Sax Rohmer
1914	Max Carrados	private	B/HC	5	Ernest Bramah
1914	Michael Lanyard (The Lone Wolf)	criminal	B/HC	8	Louis Joseph Vance
1915	Fantomas	criminal	F/HC	13	Marcel Allain (in part with Pierre Souvestre)
1915*	Sexton Blake	private	B/PB	100'S	various hands
1915	P. J. Davenant	amateur	B/HC	6	Lord Frederic Hamilton
1915	Richard Hannay	amateur	B/HC	5	John Buchan
1915	Dr. Syn	criminal	B/HC	7	Russell Thorndyke
(1916)	Detective (Inspector) Mitchell	police	A/HC	(10)	Natalie Sumner Lincoln
1917	Timothy McCarty	amateur	A/HC	5	Isabel Ostrander
1917	Jimmie Dale	adventurer	A/HC	5	Frank Packard
1918	Anthony Trent	criminal	B/HC	25	Wyndham Martyn
1919	Peter Clancy	amateur[1]	A/HC	59	Lee Thayer
1919	Pennington Wise	private	A/HC	7	Carolyn Wells
1920	Reggie Fortune	police	B/HC	21	H. C. Bailey
1920	Hercule Poirot	private	B/HC	41	Agatha Christie
1920	Bulldog Drummond	adventurer	B/HC	17	H. C. McNeile (including 7 by Gerard Fairlie beginning in 1938)
1921	John Bartley	private	A/HC	8	Charles Dutton
1921	Francis McNab	private	B/HC	6	John Ferguson

Year	Character	Type	Country/ Book Type	Number of Books	Author
1921	Cuthbert Vanardy (Grey Phantom)	adventurer	A/HC	5	Herman Landon
1921	Ephraim Tutt	private	A/HC	13	Arthur Train
1922	Tommy and Tuppence Beresford	amateur	B/HC	5	Agatha Christie
1922	Cheri-Bibi	adventurer	F/HC	5	Gaston Leroux
1923	Superintendent Henry Wilson	police	B/HC	19	G. D. H. Cole (with M. Cole after the first book)
(1923)	Jimgrim (James Schuyler Grim)	spy	B/HC	(11)	Talbot Mundy
1923	Inspector Luckraft	police	B/HC	6	Arthur J. Rees
1923	Lord Peter Wimsey	amateur	B/HC	14	Dorothy L. Sayers
1923	Aurelius Smith	spy	A/HC	7	R. T. M. Scott
1923	Dr. Adolph Grundt (Clubfoot)	spy	B/HC	8	Valentine Williams
1924	Jimmie Haswell	private	B/HC	9	Herbert Adams
1924	Colonel Wyckham Gore	amateur	B/HC	7	Lynn Brock
1924	Inspector Joseph French	police	B/HC	33	Freeman Wills Crofts
1924	Inspector Pointer	police	B/HC	23	A. Fielding
1924	Inspector (Superintendent) Sims	police	B/HC	13	Francis Grierson
1924	Anthony Ravenhill	amateur	B/HC	(7)	R. F. Foster
1924	Inspector Rason	police	B/HC	(11)	David Durham (also under Sefton Kyle by-line and under author's real name, Roy Vickers)
1924	Colonel Anthony Gethryn	amateur	B/HC	12	Philip MacDonald
1924	J. G. Reeder	police	B/HC	5	Edgar Wallace
1925	Superintendent Laurence Gilmartin	police	B/HC	(12)	Charles Barry
1925	Roger Sheringham	amateur	B/HC	10	Anthony Berkeley
1925	Charlie Chan	police	A/HC	6	Earl Derr Biggers
1925	Madame Rosika Storey	amateur	A/HC	7	Hulbert Footner
1925	Richard Verrell (Blackshirt)	criminal	B/HC	31	Bruce Graeme (including 20 beginning in 1952 by the originator's son Roderic Graeme)
1925	Sergeant Jasper Shrig	police	B/HC	(7)	Jeffrey Farnol
1925	Peter Creighton	private	B/HC	5	Armstrong Livingston
1925	Dr. Priestley	amateur	B/HC	72	John Rhode
1925	Trevor Dene	police	B/HC	5	Valentine Williams
1925	Dr. Eustace Hailey	amateur	B/HC	28	Anthony Wynne

Year	Character	Type	Country/ Book Type	Number of Books	Author
1926	Ludovic Travers	amateur	B/HC	63	Christopher Bush
1926	Ben	amateur	B/HC	8	J. J. Farjeon
1926	Superintendent Battle	police	B/HC	5	Agatha Christie
1926	Mortimer Sark	amateur	B/HC	5	John Hawk
1926	Nat Ridley	private	A/PB	12	Nat Ridley, Jr.
1926	Philo Vance	amateur	A/HC	12	S. S. Van Dine
1927	Jimmie Rezaire	private	B/HC	5	Anthony Armstrong
1927	Sir Clinton Driffield	police	B/HC	17	J. J. Connington
1927	Race Williams	private	A/HC	7	Carroll John Daly
1927	Anthony Bathurst	amateur	B/HC	(54)	Brian Flynn
1927	Scott Egerton	amateur	B/HC	10	Anthony Gilbert
1927	Paul Vivanti	criminal	B/HC	6	Sydney Horler
1927	Miles Bredon	amateur	B/HC	5	Ronald Knox
1927	Chandos	adventurer	B/HC	(8)	Dorford Yates
1928	Colonel Alistair Granby	spy	B/HC	17	Francis Beeding
1928	Sergeant (Inspector) Patrick Aloysius McCarthy	police	B/HC	(43)	John G. Brandon
1928	Simon Templar (The Saint)	adventurer	B/HC	45+	Leslie Charteris
1928	Gilbert Larose	police	B/HC	25	Arthur Gask
1928	Inspector Cuthbert Higgins	police	B/HC	33	Cecil Freeman Gregg
1928	Professor Luther Bastion	amateur	B/HC	(16)	Gavin Holt
1928	Martin Dale (The Picaroon)	criminal	B/HC	7	Herman Landon
1928	Inspector Shane	police	B/HC	5	Seldon Truss
1928	Lynn MacDonald	private	A/HC	6	Kay Cleaver Strahan
1928	Inspector Napoleon Bonaparte	police	B/HC	29	Arthur W. Upfield
1928	Maud Silver	private	B/HC	32	Patricia Wentworth
1928	Sir Leonard Wallace	spy	B/HC	(8)	A. D. Wilson
1929	Albert Campion	amateur	B/HC	25	Margery Allingham (including two by her husband, Youngman Carter, beginning in 1969)
1929	Jim Sands	amateur	A/HC	5	Robert J. Casey
1929	Inspector Williams	police	B/HC	(5)	Hugh Clevely
1929	Inspector Hugh Collier	police	B/HC	(8)	Moray Dalton
1929	Harley Manners	amateur	A/HC	6	Charles Dutton
1929	Sarah Keate	amateur	A/HC	7	Mignon Eberhart
1929	Inspector McLean	police	B/HC	55	George Goodchild
1929	Gunston Cotton	spy	B/HC	14	Rupert Grayson
1929	Inspector (Superintendent) Anthony Slade	police	B/HC	(28)	Leonard Gribble

Year	Character	Type	Country/ Book Type	Number of Books	Author
1929	Continental Op	private	A/HC²	10	Dashiell Hammett
1929	Inspector Silver	police	B/HC	(13)	Henry Holt
1929	Lieutenant Valcour	police	A/HC	11	Rufus King
1929	Jimmy Traynor	private	B/HC	5	Armstrong Livingston
1929	Peter Piper	amateur	A/HC	5	Nancy Barr Mavity
1929	Mrs. (Dame) Beatrice Bradley	amateur	B/HC	49+	Gladys Mitchell
1929	Tommy Rankin	police	A/HC	14	Milton Propper
1929	Inspector Carter and Sergeant Bell	police	B/HC	5	E. R. Punshon
1929	Ellery Queen	amateur	A/HC	43	Ellery Queen
1929	Colonel Duncan Grant	spy	B/HC	6	Graham Seton
1929	Inspector Alan Grant	police	B/HC	5	Gordon Daviot (thereafter under the author's real name Josephine Tey)
1929	Inspector Frost	police	B/HC	7	H. Maynard Smith
1929	Inspector John Poole	police	B/HC	8	Henry Wade
1929	Montrose Arbuthnot	private	B/HC	(5)	N. A. Temple-Ellis
1930	Thatcher Colt	police	A/HC	8	Anthony Abbot
1930	Philip Tracy	amateur	A/HC	7	H. Ashbrook
1930	James F. "Bonnie" Dundee	police	A/HC	5	Anne Austin
1930	Joshua Clunk	private	B/HC	11	H. C. Bailey
(1930)	Commissioner Denzil Grigson	police	B/HC	(5)	Adam Broome
1930	Desmond Merrion	amateur	B/HC	(61)	Miles Burton
1930	Henri Bencolin	police	A/HC	5	John Dickson Carr
1930	Jane Marple	amateur	B/HC	14+	Agatha Christie
1930	Hugh Carding	private	B/HC	(6)	Gilbert Collins
1930	Dennis Tyler	police	A/HC	7	Diplomat
1930	Amos Lee Mappin	amateur	A/HC	10	Hulbert Footner
1930	Evan Pinkerton	amateur	A/HC	11	David Frome
1930	Inspector John Swinton	police	B/HC	5	Ian Greig
1930	Inspector Reynolds	police	B/HC	(9)	Elaine Hamilton
(1930)	Jerry Scant	amateur	B/HC	5	L. A. Knight
1930	Captain (Major, Colonel) Hugh North	spy	A/HC	25	Van Wyck Mason
1930	Inspector Christopher McKee	police	A/HC	31	Helen Reilly
1930	Inspector Kane	police	A/HC	5	Roger Scarlett
1930	Professor Henry Arthur Fielding	amateur	B/HC	(9)	David Sharp
1931	Gordon Muldrew	police	B/HC	(6)	Luke Allan
1931	Peter Shane	amateur	A/HC	8	Francis Bonnamy
1931	Major Peter Castle	spy	B/HC	(12)	Gilderoy Davison

Year	Character	Type	Country/ Book Type	Number of Books	Author
1931	Colonel Peter Gantian (Leathermouth)	spy	B/HC	11	Carlton Dawe
1931	Ronald Camberwell	private	B/HC	10	J. S. Fletcher
1931	Mr. Jellipot	private	B/HC	(9)	Sydney Fowler
1931	Asaph Clume	private	A/HC	5	Raymond Leslie Goldman
1931	Inspector (Superintendent) Stevens and Inspector Allain	police	B/HC	13	Bruce Graeme
1931	The Shadow	adventurer	A/PB	30+	Maxwell Grant
1931	Inspector (Superintendent) MacDonald	police	B/HC	47	E. C. R. Lorac
1931	Hildegarde Withers	amateur	A/HC	17	Stuart Palmer
1931	Clay Harrison	private	B/HC	(5)	Clifton Robbins
1931	Asey Mayo	amateur	A/HC	24	Phoebe Atwood Taylor
1931	Inspector Wilton Jacks	police	A/HC	6	J. H. Wallis
1931	Inspector Jules Maigret	police	F/HC	75	Georges Simenon
1932	Department Z (Gordon Craigie)	spy	B/HC	28	John Creasey
1932	Lessinger	criminal	B/HC	7	Richard Essex
1932	Tiger Standish	spy	B/HC	11	Sydney Horler
1932	Mick Cardby	private	B/HC	(25)	David Hume
1932	Inspector Barnard	police	B/HC	(9)	T. C. H. Jacobs
1932	Inspector Archie Burford	police	B/HC	6	Victor MacClure
1932	Christopher Hand	private	A/HC	5	Stanley Hart Page
(1932)	Inspector Andy Frampton	police	B/HC	(38)	T. Arthur Plummer
1932	Amos Petrie	police	B/HC	7	J. V. Turner
1932	Philip Tolefree	private	B/HC	22	R. A. J. Walling
1933	Arthur Stukely Pennington	amateur	B/HC	(23)	John G. Brandon
1933	Dr. Gideon Fell	amateur	A/HC	26	John Dickson Carr
1933	Hugh Rennert	police	A/HC	7	Todd Downing
1933	Perry Mason	private	A/HC	85	Erle Stanley Gardner
1933	Rex Coulson	adventurer	B/HC	6	Jack Mann
1933	Christopher Bond	private	B/HC	9	Wyndham Martyn
1933	Constable (Inspector, Commander) Bobby Owen	police	B/HC	35	E. R. Punshon
1933	Phineas Spinnet	private	B/HC	(7)	Andrew Soutar
1933	P. C. (Inspector, Superintendent) Richardson	police	B/HC	8	Basil Thomson
1933	Trever Lowe	amateur	B/HC	(14)	Gerald Verner
(1933)	Colonel Ormiston	spy	B/HC	(8)	J. M. Walsh

Year	Character	Type	Country/ Book Type	Number of Books	Author
1933	Duke de Richleau	spy	B/HC	(11)	Dennis Wheatley
1934	Major Jack Atherley	amateur	B/HC	(8)	Charles Ashton
1934	Sergeant (Inspector, Superintendent) Geoffrey Boscobell	police	B/HC	13	Cecil M. Wills
1934	Richard Herrivell	amateur	B/HC	9	John Bentley
(1934)	Daphne Wrayne	private	B/HC	(47)	Mark Cross
1934	Judge Ephraim Peabody Peck	amateur	A/HC	9	August Derleth
1934	Sir Henry Merrivale	amateur	A/HC	24	Carter Dickson
1934	Grace Latham and/or John Primrose	amateur	A/HC	16	Leslie Ford
1934	Inspector Michael Lord	police	A/HC	6	C. Daly King
1934	Bill Crane	private	A/HC	5	Jonathan Latimer
1934	Tim Terrell	spy	B/HC	(9)	Stephen Maddock
1934	Inspector Roderick Alleyn	police	B/HC	28+	Ngaio Marsh
1934	Mr. Swan	amateur	B/HC	(5)	R. Philmore
1934	Nero Wolfe	private	A/HC	46	Rex Stout
1934	Superintendent Robert Budd	police	B/HC	(24)	Gerald Verner
1934	Inspector Head	police	B/HC	(12)	E. Charles Vivian
1934	Inspector Treadgold	police	B/HC	7	Anthony Weymouth
1934	Gregory Sallust	spy	B/HC	11	Dennis Wheatley
1935	Laurie Fenton	spy	B/HC	15	Michael Annesley
1935	Lieutenant Peter Quint	police	A/HC	5	Hugh Austin
1935	Inspector Schmidt	police	A/HC	38+	George Bagby
1935	Nigel Strangeways	private	B/HC	16	Nicholas Blake
(1935)	Dixon Hawke	private	B/PB	20	anonymous
1935	Inspector Meredith	police	B/HC	(9)	John Bude
1935	Kent Murdock	amateur	A/HC	21	George Harmon Coxe
1935	Percy Huff	amateur	B/HC	(6)	Charman Edwards
1935	Inspector Victor Bondurant	police	A/HC	8	James G. Edwards
1935	James Greer	amateur	B/HC	5	Newton Gayle
(1935)	Paul Templeton	private	B/HC	(6)	Richard Goyne
(1935)	Peter Mohune	spy	B/HC	(10)	Pelham Groom
1935	Lieutenant Bill French	police	A/HC	13	Christopher Hale
1935	Elisha Macomber	amateur	A/HC	17	Kathleen Moore Knight
1935	Mr. Moto	spy	A/HC	6	John P. Marquand
1935	Mrs. Palmyra Pym	police	B/HC	22	Nigel Morland
1935	Freddie Brown	amateur	B/HC	(8)	Michael Poole
1935	Sheriff Rocky Allan	police	A/HC	6	Virginia Rath
1935	Jane Amanda Edwards	amateur	A/HC	11	Charlotte Murray Russell

Year	Character	Type	Country/ Book Type	Number of Books	Author
1935	Henry Hyer	private	A/HC	9	Kurt Steel
1936	Roger Bennion	amateur	B/HC	28	Herbert Adams
1936	Sergeant William Beef	police	B/HC	8	Leo Bruce
1936	Lemmy Caution	police	B/HC	12	Peter Cheyney
1936	Theocritus Lucius Westborough	amateur	A/HC	10	Clyde B. Clason
1936	Inspector Cheviot Burmann	police	B/HC	(27)	Belton Cobb
1936	Dick Pemberty	spy	B/HC	(6)	Philip Conde
1936	Jupiter Jones	amateur	A/HC	5	Timothy Fuller
1936	Sir John Meredith	police	B/HC	16	Francis Gerard
1936	Arthur Crook	private	B/HC	50	Anthony Gilbert
1936	Robin Bishop	amateur	A/HC	5	Geoffrey Homes
1936	Sir John Appleby	police	B/HC	28+	Michael Innes
1936	Clive Conrad (Dormouse)	private	B/HC	(21)	Frank King
(1936)	Inspector Wake	police	B/HC	(5)	Charles Kingston
1936	Gregory George Gordon Green (Gees)	private	B/HC	7	Jack Mann
1936	Inspector Edward Beale	police	B/HC	8	Rupert Penny
1936	Peter Duluth	amateur	A/HC	9	Patrick Quentin
1936	Tony Woolrich	amateur	A/HC	5	Milton M. Raison
(1936)	Inspector Shelley	police	B/HC	(8)	John Rowland
1936	Barney Gantt	amateur	A/HC	7+	John Stephen Strange
1936	Inspector Gidleigh	police	B/HC	23	Seldon Truss
1936	Dr. Septimus Dodds	private	B/HC	(10)	Sutherland Scott
1937	Simon Brade	amateur	A/HC	7	Harriette Campbell
1937	Sergeant Johnny Lamb	police	B/HC	5	John Donavan
1937	Peter Justice	adventurer	B/HC	5	Francis Duncan
1937	Doug Selby	police	A/HC	9	Erle Stanley Gardner
1937	Inspector John Mallett	police	B/HC	6	Cyril Hare
1937	Sergeant (Inspector) Hemingway	police	B/HC	8	Georgette Heyer
1937	Gerald Frost (Nighthawk)	adventurer	B/HC	7	Sydney Horler
1937	Captain Ben Lucias	police	A/HC	6	Royce Howes
1937	Captain Duncan Maclain	private	A/HC	13	Baynard Kendrick
1937	Huntoon Rogers	amateur	A/HC	18	Clifford Knight
1937	John Mannering (The Baron)	criminal	B/HC	47	Anthony Morton
1937	Jason Cordry	amateur	A/HC	5	James O'Hanlon
1937	Dr. Hugh Westlake	amateur	A/HC	9	Jonathan Stagge
1937	Leonidas Witherall	amateur	A/HC	8	Alice Tilton
1937	Rampion Savage	amateur	B/HC	(9)	James Turner

Year	Character	Type	Country/ Book Type	Number of Books	Author
1937	Oliver "O.K." Keene	spy	B/HC	(8)	J. M. Walsh
1937	Inspector Harry Charlton	police	B/HC	10	Clifford Witting
1937	Inspector Steven Mitchell	police	B/HC	12	Josephine Bell
1937	Dr. David Wintringham	amateur	B/HC	13	Josephine Bell
1938	Slim Callaghan	private	B/HC	10	Peter Cheyney
1938	Maxwell Archer	adventurer	B/HC	(7)	Hugh Clevely
1938	Richard Rollison (The Toff)	adventurer	B/HC	55	John Creasey
1938	Cyrus Hatch	amateur	A/HC	8	Frederick C. Davis
1938	Tony Hunter	private	A/HC	10	Robert George Dean
1938	Anne and Jeffrey McNeill	amateur	A/HC	16	Theodora DuBois
1938	Paul Temple	amateur	B/HC	9	Francis Durbridge
1938	Inspector Septimus Finch	police	B/HC	20+	Margaret Erskine
1938	Superintendent (Inspector) Mallet	police	B/HC	(18)	Mary Fitt
1938	Norman Conquest	adventurer	B/HC	51	Berkeley Gray
1938	Inspector George Muir	police	B/HC	9	Francis Grierson
1938	Humphrey Campbell	private	A/HC	5	Geoffrey Homes
1938	Basil Willing	amateur	A/HC	12+	Helen McCloy
1938	Lieutenant Stephen Mayhew	police	A/HC	7	D. B. Olsen
1938	Mary Carner	private	A/HC	5	Zelda Popkin
1938	Michael Dundas	amateur	A/HC	7	Virginia Rath
1938	Mr. Pendlebury	amateur	B/HC	(8)	Anthony Webb
1939	Patrick Dawlish	spy	B/HC	50	Gordon Ashe
1939	Fergus O'Breen	private	A/HC	5	Anthony Boucher
1939	Jim Steele	amateur	A/HC	(7)	Dana Chambers
1939	Philip Marlowe	private	A/HC	7	Raymond Chandler
1939	Sheriff Jess Roden	police	A/HC	21	A. B. Cunningham
1939	Peter and Janet Barron	amateur	A/HC	5	Ruth Darby
1939	Bruce Murdoch	spy	B/HC	6	Norman Deane
1939	Donald Lam	private	A/HC	29	A. A. Fair
1939	Inspector Bill (Ironsides) Cromwell	police	B/HC	43	Victor Gunn
1939	Mike Shayne	private	A/HC[3]	67+	Brett Halliday
1939	Edward Trelawny	police	A/HC	(5)	Amelia Reynolds Long
1939	Matt Winters	amateur	A/HC	6	Inez Oellrichs
1939	Rachel and Jennifer Murdock	amateur	A/HC	13	D. B. Olsen
1939	Homer Evans	amateur	A/HC	9	Elliot Paul
1939	John J. Malone	private	A/HC	14	Craig Rice
1939	Alister Woodhead	spy	B/HC	13	E. H. Clements

Year	Character	Type	Country/ Book Type	Number of Books	Author
1940	Rex McBride	private	A/HC	6	Cleve F. Adams
1940	Christopher Storm	amateur	A/HC	7	Willetta Ann Barber and R. F. Schabelitz
1940	Dick Marlowe	private	B/HC	(8)	John Bentley
1940	Harvey Tuke	police	B/HC	7	Douglas Browne
1940	Tommy Hambledon	spy	B/HC	26	Manning Coles
1940	Saturnin Dax	police	B/HC	(34)	Marten Cumberland
1940	Henry Gamadge	amateur	A/HC	16	Elizabeth Daly
1940	Toby Dyke	amateur	B/HC	5	E. X. Ferrars
1940	Johnny Fletcher and Sam Cragg	amateur	A/HC	14	Frank Gruber
1940	Desmond Shannon	private	A/HC	17	M. V. Heberden
(1940)	Inspector William Austen	police	B/HC	(29)	Anne Hocking
1940	Pam and Jerry North	amateur	A/HC	26	Frances and Richard Lockridge
1940	Peter Greyleigh	adventurer	B/HC	13	Colin Robertson
1940	Haila and Jeff Troy	amateur	A/HC	9	Kelley Roos
1940	Captain (Lieutenant) Bill Grady	police	A/HC	(7)	Ione Sandberg Shriber
1940	Elsie May Hunt and Tim Mulligan	amateur	A/HC	18	Aaron Marc Stein
1941	Inspector Thomas Littlejohn	police	B/HC	54+	George Bellairs
1941	John Bent	private	A/HC	7	H. C. Branson
1941	Quinny Hite	private	A/HC	5	Richard Burke
1941	Pat and Jean Abbott	amateur	B/HC	(26)	Frances Crane
1941	Theodore I. Terhune	amateur	B/HC	7	Bruce Graeme
1941	Lieutenant (Captain, Inspector) Merton Heimrich	police	A/HC	23	Frances and Richard Lockridge
1941	Liz Parrott	amateur	A/HC	(7)	Manning Long
1942	Inspector Cockrill	police	B/HC	7	Christianna Brand
1942	Jack (Flashgun or Flash) Casey	amateur	A/HC	6	George Harmon Coxe
1942	Inspector (Superintendent) Roger West	police	B/HC	43	John Creasey
1942	Dr. Stanislaus Alexander Palfrey	spy	B/HC	34	John Creasey
1942	Inspector Gridley Nelson	police	A/HC	13	Ruth Fenisong
1942	Francis Pettigrew	private	B/HC	5	Cyril Hare
1942	Paul Kilgerrin	private	A/HC	11	Charles B. Leonard
1942	Lieutenant Richard Tuck	police	A/HC	5	Lange Lewis
1942	Marshal Ben Pedley	police	A/HC	9	Steward Sterling

Year	Character	Type	Country/ Book Type	Number of Books	Author
(1943)	Inspector Alan Fraser	police	B/HC	(23)	Hugh Desmond
1943	Dr. Morelle	amateur	B/HC	14	Ernest Dudley
1943	Inspector Carl Knickman	police	A/HC	(6)	Alfred Eichler
1943	Martin Ames	amateur	A/HC	(5)	Alfred Eichler
1943	Superintendent John Bellamy	police	B/HC	(6)	T. C. H. Jacobs
1943	Arab and Andy Blake	amateur	A/HC	5	Richard Powell
1944	Lydford Long	amateur	B/HC	(9)	Henry Carstairs
1944	Gervase Fen	amateur	B/HC	9	Edmund Crispin
1944	Kit Acton	amateur	A/HC	5	Marion Bramhall
1944	Buddy Mustard	private	B/HC	(7)	Roland Daniel
1944	Abbie Harris	amateur	A/HC	6	Amber Dean
1944	Dr. Harry Manson	police	B/HC	(26)	E. and M. Radford
1944	Garry Dean	amateur	A/HC	6	Paul Whelton
1945	Professor John Stubbs	amateur	B/HC	(9)	R. T. Campbell
1945	Solar Pons	private	A/HC	12	August Derleth
1945	Sergeant (Inspector) Peter Bradfield	police	B/HC	5	Clifford Witting
1945	Ben Helm	private	A/HC	5	Bruno Fischer
1945	Jenny Gilette (Lewis) and Hunter Lewis	amateur	A/HC	6	Robin Grey (later as paperback origi- nals under author's real name, Elizabeth Gresham)
1945	Patrick Laing	amateur	A/HC	6	Patrick Laing
1945	Professor A. Penny- feather	amateur	A/HC	6	D. B. Olsen
1945	Steve Silk	private	B/HC	(9)	J. B. O'Sullivan
1945	Mitch Taylor	police	A/HC	8	Lawrence Treat
1946	Inspector Julian Rivers	police	B/HC	11	Carol Carnac
1946	Jeff DiMarco	amateur	A/HC	6	Doris Miles Disney
1946	Inspector William Bastion	police	B/HC	5	Richard Harrison
1946	Major Brains Cunning- ham	spy	B/HC	(14)	E. P. Thorne
1946	Superintendent Folly	police	B/HC	6	Jeremy York
1947	Ed and Am Hunter	amateur	A/HC	7	Fredric Brown
1947	Superintendent Arthur Manning	police	B/HC	(6)	Belton Cobb
1947	Inspector Hazelrigg	police	B/HC	7	Michael Gilbert
1947	Mac	private	A/HC	17	Thomas B. Dewey
1947	John and Suzy Marshall	private	A/HC	10	James M. Fox
1947	Johnny Liddell	private	A/HC[4]	31	Frank Kane
1947	Peter Chambers	private	A/HC[5]	29	Henry Kane
1947	Silas Booth	private	A/HC	7	J. Lane Linklater

Year	Character	Type	Country/ Book Type	Number of Books	Author
1947	Inspector Lancelot Carolus Smith	police	B/HC	5	Norman Berrow
1947	Scott Jordan	private	A/HC	11	Harold Q. Masur
1947	Max Thursday	private	A/HC	6	Wade Miller
1947	Captain Steve Johnson	police	A/HC	5	Hugh Lawrence Nelson
1947	Julia Tyler	amateur	A/HC	7	Louisa Revell
1947	Mike Hammer	private	A/HC	10+	Mickey Spillane
(1947)	Inspector Arthur "Duck" Mallard	police	B/HC	(5)	Andrew Spiller
1947	Gil Vine	private	A/HC	8	Stewart Sterling
1948	Jane and Dagobert Brown	amateur	B/HC	12	Delano Ames
1948	Doc Connor	amateur	A/HC	5	Jack Dolph
1948	Steve Drake	private	A/HC	5	Richard Ellington
1948	Superintendent Andrew Ash	police	B/HC	8	Francis Grierson
1948	Eve Gill	amateur	B/HC	7	Selwyn Jepson
1948	Inspector Andy McMurdo	police	B/HC	(9)	Nigel Morland
(1948)	Inspector Grogan	police	B/HC	(12)	Margot Neville
1948	Reverend Martin Buell	amateur	A/HC	(6)	Margaret Scherf
1948	Jeremiah X. Gibson	police	A/HC	18	Hampton Stone
1949	Mark Corrigan	spy	B/HC	30	Mark Corrigan
(1949)	Superintendent Sandyman	police	B/HC	(5)	Neill Graham
1949	Dr. Douglas Baynes	amateur	B/HC	6	Vicars Bell
1949	Temple Fortune	private	B/HC	(18)	T. C. H. Jacobs
1949	Jim Dunn	private	A/HC	8	Hugh Lawrence Nelson
1949	Miriam Birdseye	amateur	B/HC	(5)	Nancy Spain
1949	Carney Wilde	private	A/HC	7	Bart Spicer
1949	Judge Dee	police	B/HC	17	Robert van Gulik
1949	Lew Archer	private	A/HC	18+	John Macdonald[6]
(1950)	Danny Spade	private	B/PB	(30)	Dail Ambler
1950	Sumuru	criminal	A/PB	5	Sax Rohmer
1950	Inspector Ronald Price	police	B/HC	5	Joanna Cannan
(1950)	Inspector (Superintendent) Flagg	police	B/HC	(30)+	John Cassells
1950	Schuyler Cole and Luke Speare	private	A/HC	6	Frederick C. Davis
1950	Shell Scott	private	A/PB	36+	Richard S. Prather
1950	John Cornelius Franklin Scotter	private	B/HC	7	Thurman Warriner
(1950)	Superintendent Roger Ellerdine	police	B/HC	(5)	Cecil M. Wills
1951	Timothy Dane	private	A/HC	9	William Ard
1951	Laura Scudamore (The Sinister Widow)	criminal	B/HC	7	Raymond Armstrong

Year	Character	Type	Country/ Book Type	Number of Books	Author
1951	Captain Wade Paris	police	A/HC	10	Ben Benson
1951	Sir Abercrombie Lewker	amateur	B/HC	(15)	Glyn Carr
1951	Rex Banner	amateur	B/HC	(7)	Robert Chapman
1951	Hiram Potter	amateur	A/HC	10	Rae Foley
1951	Montague Cork	amateur	B/HC	5	Macdonald Hastings
1951	Johnny Maguire	private	A/PB	7	Richard Himmel
1951	Glenn Bowman	private	B/HC	(26)+	Hartley Howard
1951	Steve Conacher	private	A/HC	8	Adam Knight
1951	Chico Brett	private	B/HC	16	Kevin O'Hara
1951	Hugo Bishop	amateur	B/HC	6	Simon Rattray
1951	Vicky McBain	private	B/HC	8	Colin Robertson
1951	Carl Good	private	A/PB	(5)	Robert O. Saber
1952	John Piper	private	B/HC	(33)+	Harry Carmichael
1952	Hooky Heffern(m)an	private	B/HC	7+	Laurence Meynell
1952	Milo March	private	A/HC	21+	M. E. Chaber
1952	Inspector Smith	police	B/HC	(5)	Simon Troy
1952	Father Shanley	amateur	A/HC	9	Jack Webb
1952	Steve Craig	private	B/HC	(6)	Bevis Winter
1953	Ed Noon	private	A/HC[7]	29+	Michael Avallone
1953	Ralph Lindsey	police	A/HC	7	Ben Benson
1953	Barney Hyde	private	B/HC	8	Nigel Brent
1953	Johnny Fedora	spy	B/HC	(10)	Desmond Cory
1953	Johnny Macall	private	B/HC	6	Gerard Fairlie
1953	Inspector (Superintendent) Patrick Duffy	police	B/HC	8	Nigel Fitzgerald
1953	James Bond	spy	B/HC	15	Ian Fleming (including a 1968 novel by Robert Markham)
1953	Brad Dolan	adventurer	A/PB	6	William Fuller
1953	Gregory Quist	private	A/HC	8	William Colt MacDonald
1953	Jim Bennett	private	A/HC	10	Robert Martin
1953	Mark Brandon	private	B/HC	(12)	Vernon Warren
1954	Bart Hardin	amateur	A/HC	8	David Alexander
1954	John and Sally Strang	amateur	B/HC	(5)	Henry Brinton
1954	Ludovic Saxon (The Picaroon)	adventurer	B/HC	(20)+	John Cassells
1954	Don Cadee	private	A/HC	9	Spencer Dean
1954	Horatio Green	amateur	B/HC	5	Beverley Nichols
1954	Inspector Harry Martineau	police	B/HC	(14)	Maurice Procter
1954	Inspector (Superintendent) Simon Manton	police	B/HC	(14)	Michael Underwood
1955	Sam Durell	spy	A/PB	40+	Edward S. Aarons
1955	Carolus Deene	amateur	B/HC	23+	Leo Bruce

Year	Character	Type	Country/ Book Type	Number of Books	Author
1955	John Chadwick	private	B/HC	(6)	Guy Cobden
1955	Pete Selby	police	A/PB	9	Jonathan Craig
1955	Brock Callahan	private	A/HC	7	William Campbell Gault
1955	Solo Malcolm	private	B/HC	(31)+	Neill Graham
1955	Inspector (Superintendent) George Herbert Gently	police	B/HC	23+	Alan Hunter
1955	Chester Drum	private	A/PB	18	Stephen Marlowe
1955	Commander George Gideon	police	B/HC	21	J. J. Marric
1955	Mavis Seidlitz	private	B/PB	(12)+	Carter Brown
1955	Sugar Kane	private	B/HC	27+	Lovat Marshall
1955	Miss Hogg	private	B/HC	9	Austin Lee
(1955)	San Antonio	police	F/HC	(8)	San Antonio
1956	Morocco Jones	private	A/PB	5	Jack Baynes
1956	Julia Probyn	spy	B/HC	8+	Ann Bridge
1956	Dorian Silk	spy	B/HC	12+	Simon Harvester
1956	Steve Carella (87th Precinct)	police	A/PB[8]	29+	Ed McBain
(1956)	Inspector (Superintendent) William Baker	police	B/HC	(5)	Osmington Mills
1956	Quentin Eady	amateur	B/HC	(6)	E. P. Thorne
1956	Daye Smith	amateur	B/HC	(12)	Frank Usher
(1956)	Al Wheeler	police	B/PB	(44)+	Carter Brown
1957	Inspector John Coffin	police	B/HC	13+	Gwendoline Butler
1957	Steve Bentley	amateur	A/PB	9	Robert Dietrich
1957	Honey West	private	A/PB	11	G. G. Fickling
1957	Pete Fry	private	B/HC	15	Pete Fry
1957	Inspector (Superintendent) Bradbury	police	B/HC	5	Norman Longmate
1957	Mark Raeburn	private	B/HC	6	Malcolm Gair
1957	Grave-Digger Jones and Coffin Ed Johnson	police	A/PB[9]	8	Chester Himes
1957	Colin Thane and Bill Moss	police	B/HC	14+	Bill Knox
1957	Inspector Michael Hornsley	police	B/HC	5	Elizabeth Salter
1957	Inspector Lovick	police	B/HC	(11)	G. M. B. Wilson
1958	Marc Brody	amateur	B/PB	(22)	Marc Brody
1958	Hubert Bonnisseur de la Bath	spy	F/HC	(17)	Jean Bruce
1958	Bill Banning	private	B/HC	6	Nat Easton
1958	Joe Puma	private	A/PB	6	William Campbell Gault
1958	Inspector Gregory Pellew	police	B/HC	11+	Val Gielgud
1958	Colonel Charles Russell	spy	B/HC	16+	William Haggard

Year	Character	Type	Country/Book Type	Number of Books	Author
1958	Max Heald	spy	B/HC	6	Harry Hossent
1958	Ben Gates	private	A/PB	5	Robert Kyle
1958	Jeff Green	private	A/HC	5	Carlton Keith
1958	Tony Costaine and Bert McCall	private	A/PB	7	Neil MacNeil
1958	Jake Barrow	private	A/PB	5	Nick Quarry
1958	Matt Erridge	amateur	A/HC	10+	Aaron Marc Stein
1958	Inspector Purbright	police	B/HC	8+	Colin Watson
1958	Richard Graham	amateur	B/HC	(6)	John Welcome
1958	M. Pinaud	police	B/HC	17+	Pierre Audemars
(1958)	Danny Boyd	private	B/PB	(28)+	Carter Brown
1959	Lou Largo	private	A/PB	6	William Ard
(1959)	Pete Schofield	private	A/PB	(8)	Thomas B. Dewey
1959	McHugh	spy	A/PB	5	Jay Flynn
1959	Mark Kilby	private	A/PB	6	Robert Caine Frazer
1959	Father Joseph Bredder	amateur	A/HC	10+	Leonard Holton
1959	Johnny Killain	private	A/PB	5	Dan J. Marlowe
1959	Inspector Broom	police	B/HC	(7)	Freda Hurt
1959	Inspector (Superintendent) Henry Tibbett	police	B/HC	12+	Patricia Moyes
1959	Clutha	private	B/HC	5+	Hugh Munro
1959	Burns Bannion	private	A/PB	7	Earl Norman
1959	Inspector Fadiman Wace	police	B/HC	(6)+	Roger Simons
1959	Monty Nash	spy	A/PB	5	Richard Telfair
1959	Chief Fred Fellows	police	A/HC	10	Hillary Waugh
1959	Rocky Steele	private	A/PB	6	John B. West
1960	Michael Grant	private	B/HC	(5)	Roland Daniel
1960	Giff Speer	police	A/PB	(6)+	Don Tracy
1960	Matt Helm	spy	A/PB	17+	Donald Hamilton
1960	Commander Esmonde Shaw	spy	B/HC	(12)+	Philip McCutchan
1960	Sergeant Caleb Cluff	police	B/HC	11+	Gil North
1960	Lieutenant Luis Mendoza	police	A/HC	26+	Dell Shannon
1961	Inspector George Felse (and family)	police	B/HC	11+	Ellis Peters
1961	Paul Harris	amateur	B/HC	11+	Gavin Black
(1961)	Rick Holman	private	B/PB	(31)+	Carter Brown
1961	Mark Preston	private	B/HC	16+	Peter Chambers
1961	Jesse Falkenstein	private	A/HC	5	Lesley Egan
1961	Vic Varallo	police	A/HC	7	Lesley Egan
1961	Dale Shand	private	B/HC	(7)+	Douglas Enefer
1961	John Putnam Thatcher	amateur	A/HC	16+	Emma Lathen
1961	Adam Flute	private	B/HC	6	Droo Launay
1961	George Smiley	spy	B/HC	5+	John LeCarre

Year	Character	Type	Country/ Book Type	Number of Books	Author
1961	Harrigan and Hoeffler	spy	A/HC	7	Patrick O'Malley
1961	Superintendent Bradley	police	B/HC	6	Colin Robertson
1961	Stephen Dain	police	A/PB	5	Robert Sheckley
1961	David Danning	private	A/PB	8	Don von Elsner
1962	Mr. Holmes	spy	B/HC	7	Conrad Voss Bark
1962	Nameless (known as Harry Palmer in the films)	spy	B/HC	6+	Len Deighton
1962	Paul Chavasse	spy	B/HC	6	Martin Fallon
1962	Adam Ludlow	amateur	B/HC	5	Simon Nash
1962	Captain Jose da Silva	police	A/HC	10+	Robert L. Fish
1962	Inspector (Commissaire) Van der Valk	police	B/HC	10	Nicholas Freeling
1962	Superintendent Adam Dalgliesh	police	B/HC	6+	P. D. James
1962	Earl Drake	criminal	A/PB	11+	Dan J. Marlowe
(1962)	Slade McGinty	private	B/HC	(5)	Jacques Pendower
1962	Pierre Chambrun	amateur	A/HC	11+	Hugh Pentecost
1962	Ian Firth	private	B/HC	(6)	Ludovic Peters
1962	Parker	criminal	A/PB[10]	16+	Richard Stark
1962	Inspector Joshua Smarles	police	B/HC	8	MacGregor Urquhard
1962	Antony Maitland	private	B/HC	23+	Sara Woods
1963	Joe Gall	spy	A/PB	19+	Philip Atlee
1963	Larry Baker	amateur	B/PB	(6)+	Carter Brown
1963	Detective Inspector George Judd	police	B/HC	5	Eric Bruton
1963	Superintendent Donald Reamer (The Dreamer)	police	B/HC	13+	W. Murdoch Duncan
1963	David Grant	spy	B/HC	10+	George Mair
1963	Bart Gould	spy	A/PB	8	Joseph Milton
1964	Mark Hood	spy	B/PB	13	James Dark
1964	Inspector Salvador Borges	police	B/HC	5	John and Emery Bonett
1964	Boysie Oakes	spy	B/HC	8+	John Gardner
1964	Inspector Ganesh Ghote	police	B/HC	9+	H. R. F. Keating
1964	Nick Carter	spy	A/PB	101+	Nick Carter (house name)
1964	Rabbi David Small	amateur	A/HC	5+	Harry Kemelman
1964	Webb Carrick	police	B/HC	8+	Bill Knox
1964	Dr. Jason Love	spy	B/HC	7+	James Leasor
1964	Sergeant Ivor Maddox	police	A/HC	7+	Elizabeth Linington

Year	Character	Type	Country/ Book Type	Number of Books	Author
1964	Nathan Shapiro	police	A/HC	6+	Frances and Richard Lockridge (later Richard Lockridge)
1964	Travis McGee	adventurer	A/PB[10]	16+	John D. MacDonald
1964	Talos Cord	spy	B/HC	6+	Robert MacLeod
1964	Peter Styles	amateur	A/HC	11+	Judson Philips
1964	Inspector Wilfred Dover	police	B/HC	7+	Joyce Porter
1964	Lieutenant Lee Barcello	police	A/HC	5	Stephen Ransome
1964	Inspector Reg Wexford	police	B/HC	9+	Ruth Rendell
*1964	Doc Savage	adventurer	A/PB	80+	Kenneth Robeson (house name)
1965	Joaquin Hawks	spy	A/PB	5	Bill S. Ballinger
1965	John Keith	spy	A/PB	5	Norman Daniels
1965	Quiller	spy	B/HC	6+	Adam Hall
1965	Inspector Harry James	police	B/HC	9	Kenneth Giles
1965	Dr. Emmanuel Cellini	amateur	B/HC	11	Kyle Hunt (Michael Halliday in England)
1965	Inspector Bill Houghton	police	B/HC	5	Maurice Culpan
1965	Maxwell Smart	spy	A/PB	9	William Johnston
1965	Bernard Simmons	police	A/HC	5	Frances and Richard Lockridge
1965	Modesty Blaise	spy	B/HC	7+	Peter O'Donnell
1965	John Jericho	amateur	A/HC	6+	Hugh Pentecost
1965	Peter Ward	spy	A/PB	10	David St. John
1965	Alan Grofield	criminal	A/PB[11]	7+	Richard Stark
1965	Kelly Robinson and Alexander Scott	spy	A/PB	7	John Tiger
*1965	Dick Van Loan (The Phantom Detective)	adventurer	A/PB	(22)	Robert Wallace
(1965)	Richard Quintain	spy	B/PB	(5)	W. Howard Baker
1965	Napoleon Solo (The Man from U.N.C.L.E.)	spy	A/PB	(25)	various hands
1966	Evan Tanner	spy	A/PB	7+	Lawrence Block
1966	Inspector Christopher Dennis Sloan	police	B/HC	6+	Catherine Aird
1966	Pete McGrath	private	A/PB	10	Michael Brett
1966	Mitch Tobin	amateur	A/HC	5	Tucker Coe
*1966	Secret Agent X	spy	A/PB	7	Brant House (house name)
1966	Phil Kramer	private	A/HC	5+	Paul Kruger
1966	Timothy Herring	amateur	B/HC	6	Malcolm Torrie
1966	Tim Corrigan	police	A/PB	6	"Ellery Queen"

Year	Character	Type	Country/ Book Type	Number of Books	Author
1966	Mike Brooks	spy	B/HC	5	H. T. Rothwell
*1966	James Christopher (Operator 5)	spy	A/PB	10	Curtis Steele (house name)
1966	Knute Severson	police	A/HC	14+	Tobias Wells
1966	Jonas Wilde	spy	B/HC	8+	Andrew York
1967	Dr. Davie	amateur	B/HC	5	V. C. Clinton-Baddeley
1967	Dan Fortune	private	A/HC	7+	Michael Collins
1967	Mike Faraday	private	B/HC	20+	Basil Copper
1967	Dave Cannon and Bob Eddison	amateur	A/HC	5+	Michael Delving
1967	Sergeant Bob Reed	police	B/HC	5	Charles Drummond
1967	Superintendent Tom Pollard	police	B/HC	7+	Elizabeth Lemarchand
1967	Paul Muller	private	B/HC	14+	Paul Muller
1967	Martin Beck	police	S/HC	8+	Maj Sjöwall and Per Wahlöö
1968	Superintendent Charles Wycliffe	police	B/HC	6+	W. J. Burley
1968	Mod Squad	police	A/PB	5	Richard Deming
1968	Superintendent James Pibble	police	B/HC	5	Peter Dickinson
1968	Mark Savage	spy	B/HC	(5)+	Matthew Eden
1968	Inspector William Aveyard	police	B/HC	7+	James Fraser
1968	Phil Sherman	spy	A/PB	16+	Don Smith
1968	Angel	?	B/HC	12+	Graham Montrose
1968	Miss Emily Seeton	amateur	B/HC	5+	Heron Carvic
1968	Kane Jackson	private	A/HC	5+	William Arden
1969	Cabot Caine	adventurer	A/PB	5+	Alan Caillou
1969	Inspector George Masters	police	B/HC	6+	Douglas Clark
1969	Jennifer Norrington, Allexandro di Ganzarello, and Coleridge Tucker III	adventurer	B/HC	5+	Ivor Drummond
1969	Bill Cartwright	spy	A/PB	8	Patrick Morgan
1969	Mark Bolan (The Executioner)	adventurer	A/PB	23+	Don Pendleton
1969	Lieutenant Frank Hastings	police	A/HC	6+	Colin Wilcox
1969	Peter Craig	spy	B/HC	6+	Kenneth Benton
1970	The Butcher	police	A/PB	16+	Stuart Jason
1970	Tessa Chrichton (Price)	amateur	B/HC	8+	Ann Morice
1970	Richard Abraham Spade	adventurer	A/PB	5	B. B. Johnson

Year	Character	Type	Country/ Book Type	Number of Books	Author
1970	Superintendent Andrew Dalziel	police	B/HC	5+	Reginald Hill
1970	Sergeant Cribb	police	B/HC	6+	Peter Lovesey
1970	Spider Scott	criminal	B/HC	5+	Kenneth Royce
1970	Max Roper	private	A/HC	5+	Kin Platt
1970	Tiger Shark	spy	A/PB	11	Ken Stanton
1970	Dr. David Audley	spy	B/HC	6+	Anthony Price
1970	John Shaft	private	A/HC	7+	Ernest Tidyman
1971	Remo Williams (The Destroyer)	police	A/PB	20+	Richard Sapir and Warren Murphy
(1971)	Randall Roberts	private	B/PB	(5)+	Carter Brown
1971	Jim Larkin	amateur	B/HC	5+	Martin Russell
*1972	Dick Benson (The Avenger)	adventurer	A/PB	36	Kenneth Robeson (house name)
1972	Richard Carnellion (The Death Merchant)	spy	A/PB	13+	Joseph Rosenberger
1973	Jefferson Boone (The Handyman)	adventurer	A/PB	6+	Jon Messmann
1973	Ben Martin (The Revenger)	adventurer	A/PB	6+	Jon Messmann
1973	Dakota	private	A/PB	5+	Gilbert Ralston
1973	Malko Linge	spy	F/PB	10+	Gerald de Villiers
1973	Mark Hardin (The Penetrator)	adventurer	A/PB	11+	Lionel Derrick
1973	Ed Razoni and William Jackson	police	A/PB	5+	W. B. Murphy
1973	John Bolt (Narc)	police	A/PB	9+	Robert Hawkes
1973	Burt Wulff (The Lone Wolf)	adventurer	A/PB	13+	Mike Barry
1973	Philip Magellan (The Marksman)	adventurer	A/PB	19+	Frank Scarpetta
1973	John Eagle (The Expediter)	spy	A/PB	9+	Paul Edwards
1973	Deputy Marshal Sam McCloud	police	A/PB	6+	Collin Wilcox, later David Wilson
1974	Johnny Rock (The Sharpshooter)	adventurer	A/PB	16+	Bruno Rossi
1974	Lieutenant Kojak	police	A/PB	9+	Victor B. Miller
1974	Sergeant Joe Ryker	police	A/PB	5+	Nelson DeMille
1974	Francis Xavier Killy	spy	A/PB	6+	Simon Quinn
1974	Jim Hardman	private	A/PB	7+	Ralph Dennis
1974	Agent for Cominsec	spy	A/PB	5+	Ralph Hayes
1975	Huntington Cage	private	A/PB	6+	Alan Riefe

NOTES

[1] Note that after one book as a (boy) amateur detective, Clancy became for a brief period a policeman, and then was a private detective through more than fifty books.

[2] After the first two titles, the series appeared in digest-size paperback originals.

[3] The series went into paperback originals after the forty-fifth volume.

[4] The last twenty books in the series were paperback originals.

[5] The last twenty-three books in the series were paperback originals.

[6] After one title under this by-line and four as John Ross Macdonald, all volumes have appeared under the name Ross Macdonald.

[7] After the first three, all have been paperback originals in the United States though largely hardcover in England.

[8] After the seventh book the series went into hardcovers.

[9] After the fifth book the series went into hardcover.

[10] Switched to hardcover with the fifteenth volume.

[11] Only the first two were paperback original appearances.

FOURTEEN   OTTO PENZLER

*(A biographical sketch of
Mr. Penzler, who contributed two
chapters to this book,
appears on page 82.)*

THE GREAT CROOKS

It may be accepted as an irrefutable, if obvious, maxim that the detective story requires a detective, and the detective must have something to detect. Presuming a crime of some type requires someone to commit that crime. Therefore the crook is more important to the mystery story than the detective. The crook can exist independently; the detective requires the prior existence—and action—of the crook. Although frequently offstage, there must be a crook in each detective story before there can be a story, otherwise there would be nothing for the detective to do.

Historically, crooks precede detectives. There were criminals before detectives, who have a history of substantially less than two hundred years in fact, and less than that in fiction. Some of the great characters in early literature and legend are crooks, including Robin Hood, Gil Blas, Dick Turpin, Moll Flanders—all famous before the first detective picked up a magnifying glass. And the great names in more recent literature that ignite a spark of instant recognition are liberally sprinkled with great crooks and rogues: Dr. Fu Manchu, The Saint, Raffles, Count Dracula, Professor Moriarty, The Lone Wolf, Arsene Lupin, Boston Blackie.

Why then are they ignored as much as they have been? The first anthology devoted exclusively to crime stories was edited by Ellery Queen (of course) in 1945[1]—more than a hundred years after the creation of the detective story and about sixty years after the first detective-story anthology.[2] In that criminal anthology, Queen gave his definition of what constitutes a crook story: "It must contain a crook who crooks; the crook should be the protagonist; and almost invariably the crook should triumph over the forces of the law, amateur or official. In a phrase, a crook story is 'detection in reverse.'" No one has come up with a better definition in three decades, although the last of the three stipulations may be unnecessary. Does Fu Manchu ever really triumph? He escapes capture, he frustrates every legal and some extralegal efforts to rid the world of his presence, yet it would be unrealistic to suggest that he has ever succeeded. His goal, of course, is world domination, and no sinister Oriental— including Mao—has yet succeeded. Yet one would have to agree that Fu Manchu is a crook. It might be argued that Sir Denis Nayland Smith is the protagonist in Sax Rohmer's melodramatic adventure tales, but what a helpless, overmatched pawn he is. Although we see much of the action from his point of view, Fu Manchu's presence, physical or spiritual, overwhelms the stage.

There are two kinds of crooks in mystery fiction— the bad guys and the good guys. Fu Manchu and Professor Moriarty are bad guys; Raffles and The Saint are good guys. The bad guys are villains, and the books and stories in which they appear are rarely told from their point of view. It is a truth that an audience, whether reading a book, watching a movie, or listening to a person explain why he just got divorced, tends to side with the point of view it is attending. In "big caper" films and books, we tend to identify with the crooks. I've yet to meet the person whose sympathies lay against the gang of thieves who tried to loot Topkapi Palace. At the same time, everyone roots for the police when they begin to assemble bits of information in the police procedural or other, less precise forms of detective fiction. Perhaps the best suspense novels are those that shift between the criminal and the police as a plan is conceived and developed on the one hand, and steps are taken to discover and prevent it on the other, as with *The Day of the Jackal*[3] and such Cornell Woolrich novels as *The Bride Wore Black*.[4]

So we can often sit back and root against villains because the stories are told from the angle of Nayland Smith or Sherlock Holmes. When Raffles decides to steal a necklace, or when Simon Templar (The Saint) prepares to break into a safe, we lend our sympathetic attention because we know why the crime is being committed. If the story is told properly, we will identify with the crook because he needs the money for a good cause, and he's probably stealing it from a no-goodnick to begin with.

One characteristic of most villains is a hyperactive sense of greatness, or grandeur. Fu Manchu wants to conquer the world. Moriarty controls most of the crime in London, as Holmes demonstrates in the stories written by John H. Watson, M.D., and has far greater plans (as John Gardner shows in his splendid books about the evil professor),[5] which include controlling all the crime in Europe and, ultimately, the world. Carl Peterson, Bulldog Drummond's adversary in four novels, also has plans to rule the world, and more than one of James Bond's opponents employs veritable armies with the same end in sight. Cesare Bandello, known as "Little Caesar," thought he was smart enough and tough enough to rule the entire Chicago underworld.

Dr. Fu Manchu is the most enduring of a long succession of sinister Oriental villains. Sax Rohmer had been writing with indifferent success when he reportedly heard about an actual historical character pseudonymously named "Mr. King," a criminal of legendary power in London's Limehouse district. Researching a newspaper article, Rohmer waited in hidden doorways for the opportunity to see "Mr. King" and he claims to have seen him—from a distance and on a foggy night. When he saw the face of the man who ruled the tongs which controlled the crime, drugs, and gambling in Limehouse, the face embodied all the evil known to man. The fact that the Boxer Rebellion a few years before had frightened the Western world, particularly England, of a "Yellow Peril" may also have influenced Rohmer to write about the Devil Doctor, a Chinese fiend intent on world domination.

The first book about Fu Manchu was *The Mystery of Dr. Fu-Manchu*.[6,7] There are thirteen novels in which he appears, one in which his presence is known but remains unnamed *(The Golden Scorpion)*,[8] and four short stories. Throughout the saga, the satanic doctor remains the most ruthless and diabolical archvillain ever created, although in later episodes he abandons his plans for world conquest long enough to join forces with the West to thwart the spread of imperialistic communism.

Physically, he is tall and slim (although often played by somewhat corpulent actors, such as Warner Oland, in films) and clean-shaven—"Fu Manchu" mustaches were the invention of motion picture make-up men, not of Sax Rohmer, who wanted nothing to interfere with the insidious doctor's many disguises.

Fu Manchu had been anticipated by Dr. Nikola, the archcriminal in five novels by Guy Boothby, beginning with *A Bid for Fortune, or Dr. Nikola's Vendetta*.[9] Like Fu Manchu, Nikola has hypnotic eyes that can cause almost anyone in his presence to execute his wishes.

Sinister Orientals were one of the great clichés of the more lurid pulp magazines, with Dr. Yen Sin and Wu Fang even rating their own magazines.

The most sinister of the female of the species is Sumuru, also a creation of Sax Rohmer, but her adventures never achieved anywhere near the popularity of Rohmer's Fu Manchu stories. In *Sumuru*,[10] she is described as "more dangerous than the atom bomb," which, when compared with a catalogue of her crimes, may not be terribly hyperbolic. "This woman Sumuru," explains her pursuer, "employs some of the most ghastly weapons ever invented. She's an adept in the use of obscure poisons. Some of her victims have been blinded by a mere puff of powder; others struck dumb.

And there's a horrible thing called *rigor kubus,* a sort of fungus which invades the system and apparently turns the body to something like stone."

Only slightly less sinister is James Moriarty, the evil professor with whom Sherlock Holmes battles, first intellectually, then physically in a titanic struggle at the edge of the Reichenbach Falls. Initially, both men were reported killed,[11] but Holmes later returned and explained how he survived.[12] In 1973, John Gardner, famous for his series about Boysie Oakes, the James Bond-ish secret-service assassin who turns ill at the sight of blood, decoded the notebooks of Moriarty and the world learned that the professor, too, had survived the alleged plunge from Reichenbach. In *The Return of Moriarty,* we see, for the first time, what Moriarty is really like. One of three brothers (all named James), he is jealous of his smarter older brother and eventually kills him. A fratricide is rarely the most lovable (or even likable) of characters, but we do see that James, as the head of a large "family" of dips, dolly-mops, lurkers, and other criminals, has his tender moments. He is a Victorian Godfather, dispensing favors and attending weddings one day, killing and torturing his enemies and the unfaithful the next.

Known to Sherlock Holmes as "The Napoleon of Crime," and compared by the great detective to a giant spider at the center of the web of crime which embraces all of London, Moriarty poses as a gentle mathematics professor, author of a significant paper on the dynamics of an asteroid. Clean-shaven and ascetic-looking, he is "forever slowly oscillating from side to side in a curiously reptilian fashion."

Outwardly less cerebral than his villainous peers, Carl Peterson is distinguished for his hands: "large and white and utterly ruthless" according to Phyllis Benton, Bulldog Drummond's future girl friend and wife. Peterson is frustrated in four successive novels, beginning with the first Drummond novel by "Sapper" (H. C. McNeile), *Bull-Dog Drummond*.[13] His plans for world domination end with his death in the fourth,[14] but then his maddened widow attempts revenge by kidnaping Hugh's wife in *The Female of the Species*.[15]

The great villains were created by English authors, but none of them is English. Fu Manchu is Oriental, Moriarty is Irish, and Peterson is dismissed with scorn as a phony who took the "sound old English name" of Peterson as a cover-up. All of the detectives and adventurers who combat their villainy are English. Very English. Even lesser villains created by English authors are given foreign names or backgrounds. Hesketh Prichard's Don Q[16] (full name: Don Quebranta Huesos, or the bone-smasher) is a Spaniard who follows the Robin Hood syndrome of being vicious to the rich and kindly to the poor, as if the rich are inherently evil. L. T. Meade's Madame Sara has the distinction of being the first "mass murderer" in short mystery fiction. Each of the stories in *The Sorceress of the Strand*[17] deals with a murder planned by the angelic-looking Sara. Although she is described as having a mass of rippling golden hair, she is quickly identified as "a mixture of Italian and Indian." The same author (aided by Robert

Eustace) also wrote a series of stories about Katherine, later known as Mme. Koluchy, the head and queen of a secret society, The Brotherhood of the Seven Kings.[18] Again, although the society operated in the middle of London, the girl is described as Italian on the second page.

Writers in other countries besides England created a few really nasty villains. In the United States, Melville Davisson Post, who later created Uncle Abner, gave us the unscrupulous lawyer *par excellence,* Randolph Mason.[19] He uses the shortcomings of the law to defeat justice and free his clients. The criminals in his cases do not make any effort to avoid being caught for their crimes; unlike most criminals, their aim was not to elude capture, but to avoid punishment. Mason once explained his viewpoint: "No man who has followed my advice has ever committed a crime. Crime is a technical word. It is the law's term for certain acts which it is pleased to define and punish with a penalty. What the law permits is right, else it would prohibit it. What the law prohibits is wrong, because it punishes it. The word moral is a purely metaphysical one." Although he has actually advised a client to commit murder, Mason later shifted position and worked for the ends of justice, rather than for the end of it.

In France, Fantomas was known as the Lord of Terror.[20] The series of novels recounting his exploits were first written by Marcel Allain and Pierre Souvestre, later by Allain himself. Although a criminal mastermind, Fantomas directed his skills not to world conquest, but to the more prosaic occupations of bank robberies and safecrackings. Relentlessly pursued by Juve, the detective, Fantomas is described as a modern Mephistopheles who spreads terror wherever he treads, but he's not in the same league as Fu Manchu or even Carl Peterson.

The patriotic zeal of English writers to ascribe villainies to foreigners does not extend to their likable rogues. The good crooks, the gentlemen cracksmen and amateur jewel thieves, are invariably countrymen.

They are all extremely handsome (or, in the case of female crooks, beautiful and innocent-looking), immaculately groomed and dressed, with a sense of good sportsmanship and honor that would keep clergymen hard-pressed.

The greatest of the amateur cracksmen is, of course, A. J. Raffles. Created by E. W. Hornung as a tongue-in-cheek inversion of his brother-in-law's famous detective (Arthur Conan Doyle's Sherlock Holmes), the cricket-playing jewel thief rivaled, for a time, the popularity of his more legal counterpart. The first volume devoted to Raffles is dedicated to Conan Doyle with the words: "To A. C. D. This sincerest form of flattery."[21]

Suave, sophisticated, handsome, and one of England's greatest cricket players, Raffles is always a welcome guest at weekend parties given by the wealthy. His code of honor prohibits him from stealing from his host, although other guests are not safe from his larcenous inclinations.

His partner in crime is Bunny Manders, once a schoolmate of the man he reveres. Bunny becomes an accomplice in the first story, *The Ides of March*, when Raffles prevents him from committing suicide over a gambling debt. That incident is one of many in which Raffles steals to help a friend in need, or for some purpose more worthwhile than lining his own pockets.

Before committing his very first criminal act, Raffles was penniless and desperate. After "tasting blood," as he put it, he found that he liked stealing. Explaining his motivations to Bunny, he said: "Why settle down to some humdrum, uncongenial billet when excitement, romance, danger and a decent living were all going begging together? Of course it's all very wrong, but we can't all be moralists, and the distribution of wealth is very wrong to begin with."

Later, particularly in the novel that concludes Hornung's adventures of the cracksman, Raffles joins the side of law and order.[22]

Some years later, Barry Perowne made an arrangement with the Hornung estate and used Raffles for a series of novelettes for *The Thriller* magazine, beginning in 1932. These somewhat unsuccessful adventure tales made the character contemporary, pulling him out of the environment to which he was so uniquely suited. World War II terminated the existence of *The Thriller* and Raffles, until Frederic Dannay convinced Perowne to revive him for the pages of *Ellery Queen's Mystery Magazine*. But this time he was put back in Victorian and Edwardian London—the time to which he belongs. Scores of stories followed, many the equal or superior of Hornung's own invention, but Raffles was a new person. Very loosely patterned after a real-life sportsman, C. B. Fry, Perowne's Raffles never robbed purely for personal gain. He stole to help others, or to provide justice when a weak legal community was unable or unwilling to punish evil.

Perhaps the most striking element of the new Raffles is that he did not turn detective. Virtually every rogue in mystery fiction eventually turns his attention to the detection of crime, and away from the commission of it.

Simon Templar, The Saint, has all the makings of a splendid crook. His physical attributes are on a grand scale—six feet two inches tall, broad-shouldered, and muscular. An expert in many sports, he has, in short, every skill an adventurer could need. Intellectually, he is also a giant, with a vast store of knowledge in diverse fields and fluency in several languages. He is an immaculate and impeccable dresser, fond of all the best things life has to offer, and he is able to afford them. Add to this the soul of a romantic adventurer. He is quoted once as saying: "I'm mad enough to believe in romance. And I'm sick and tired of this age—tired of the miserable little mildewed things that people racked their brains about, and wrote books about, and called life. I wanted something more elementary and honest—battle, murder, sudden death, with plenty of good beer and damsels in distress, and a complete callousness about blipping the ungodly over the beezer. It mayn't be life as we know it, but it ought to be." There you have the makings of the perfect rogue.

Although Templar often breaks the law in his adventures, he is really as much a detective as he is a thief, most of his exploits resulting in the foiling of criminals and the ultimate turning over of them to Scotland Yard.

Although his background is steeped in the nether side of the law, The Lone Wolf, Louis Joseph Vance's debonair cracksman, likewise turns to the solution of crime rather than its perpetration. Born Michael Lanyard and raised as Michael Troyon, an impoverished child in Paris, he once tried to steal from a professional thief, who caught him, liked him, and taught him the skills of his profession. In addition to the techniques of stealing and chicanery, he taught him the "three cardinal principles of successful cracksmanship: Know your ground thoroughly before venturing upon it; strike and retreat with the swift precision of a hawk; be friendless. And the last of these is the greatest." Thus was The Lone Wolf born, but he did not remain alone long, for he met a beautiful girl who proved to be his undoing as a crook; he became a crime solver instead.

Bruce Graeme's Blackshirt, or Richard Verrel, is a direct descendant of Raffles and follows in the footsteps of The Saint and The Lone Wolf. Also a daring cracksman and a cultivated gentleman comfortable in the plushest club, he is forced to forego his life of crime when a young woman discovers his identity. Like Lanyard, he was raised by people not his parents and ultimately marries the woman who transforms him from a crook to a detective. Unlike other thieves *cum* detectives, the decision is not his. He is blackmailed into shifting position by anonymous telephone calls from his future wife. The audacious burglar gets his name because of the costume he affects when working: He dresses entirely in black, including the mask that covers his face.

John Creasey created The Baron in the same image as the other great crooks. Early in his career, John Mannering led the usual double life: a respectable gentleman by day (an antiques dealer) and a flamboyant jewel thief by night. In all his later cases The Baron is on the side of the law. The Toff, Richard Rollison, is another Creasey detective who had a checkered past and who employed tactics that would raise the eyebrows of any but the most blasé.

The first purely fictional crook invention to appear in a short-story collection (preceding Raffles by fully two years) is Colonel Clay, who bilks the titular character of *An African Millionaire* in a series of thefts that rely largely on Clay's skillful disguises; he normally has an open, honest countenance that embodies innocence itself.[23]

Hamilton Cleek, the creation of Thomas W. Hanshew, resented being called a cracksman, claiming that sobriquet was analogous to calling Paganini a fiddler. The boldest criminal of his time, he asked journalists to refer to him as "The Man Who Calls Himself Hamilton Cleek." In exchange for that courtesy, he supplies them with information about his forthcoming robberies. Cleek is known as "The Man of the Forty Faces" because of a rubberized skin texture that enables him to contort his face into any number of disguises without the use of make-up. He, too, sides with Scotland Yard and the British government in later cases.

The central character in Arnold Bennett's *The Loot of Cities*[24] is Cecil Thorold, a full-fledged millionaire who steals, blackmails, and otherwise makes life difficult for other crooks. In his first recorded episode, he extracts 50,000 pounds from a crook, then makes a *grand geste* before the startled eyes of a pretty girl by flinging the notes onto a roaring fire.

Anthony Trent is a brilliant writer of crime stories

who is called "The Master Criminal" by the police who are unable to trace his real name. Wyndham Martin's brilliant crook, like Blackshirt, The Lone Wolf, and other cultivated thieves, is also reformed by the love of a good woman.

R. Austin Freeman's most noted literary invention is, of course, Dr. Thorndyke, but he also enjoyed working the other side of the road. Under the collaborative (with John J. Pitcairn) pseudonym Clifford Ashdown, he created Romney Pringle.[25] While Blackshirt and Trent are authors, Pringle poses as a literary agent, an occupation which some might describe as a form of thievery in its own right. As innocent-looking as most successful rogues, Pringle, like Thorold, is a specialist at mulcting other crooks. Other interesting crooks created by Freeman are Danby Croker,[26] who is the virtual blond twin of dark-haired Tom Nagget (they dye their hair to impersonate each other in various nefarious schemes), and the grisly Humphrey Challoner,[27] who avenges his wife's death at the hands of an unknown burglar by setting traps for other burglars, killing them, and forming a macabre museum of their shrunken heads and skeletons.

Bertram Atkey's Smiler Bunn is another crook with the redeeming quality of stealing only from those who are not really entitled to retain possession of their wealth, either because they, too, operate outside the limitations of the law, or because they are so hopelessly foolish they virtually beg to be lightened of their purses. Unlike most other crooks of English literature, who are suave and handsome, Bunn is middle-aged and rather fat, and is not above placing himself in ridiculous positions to gain his ends.

Some of the most brilliant and successful literary rogues are female. Fidelity Dove, Roy Vickers's beautiful, violet-eyed, angel-faced creation, appears in only one book, but she is a memorable character nonetheless.[28] Detective Inspector Rason, who is later successful as head of the Department of Dead Ends, is totally frustrated by Fidelity, calling her "the coolest crook in London, and then some." She always wears gray, partly because it looks good with her violet eyes, and partly because it reflects her strictly puritanical attitude.

Edgar Wallace's Four-Square Jane is another beautiful and very young girl who engineers successful crimes, with no selfish motives, throughout a series of short stories.[29] Hulbert Footner's Madame Rosika Storey first appeared in 1925.[30] Also a stunningly beautiful young woman, she is described as "a practical psychologist—specializing in the feminine." Although she often profits from her efforts, she is really a detective, solving crimes involving villainous master-minds and sinister criminals. Footner's fertile imagination provided the exotic Mme. Storey with a fantastically dressed black ape which sat upon her arm in public.

The year 1925 also saw the first publication of *The Notorious Sophie Lang* by Frederick Irving Anderson.[31] Although the book was published only in England — an incredible oversight when one considers the talent of the author—Sophie is an American crook whose exploits are chronicled by an American author. She is so adroit that she is often regarded as a legend, and her major adversary, Deputy Parr, enjoys telling of the excellent young policemen assigned to her case who fail so badly that they feel as if they had been sent after a nonexistent object, as schoolboys are sent to fetch left-handed monkey wrenches.

Anderson is also the creator of the greatest of all American crooks, The Infallible Godahl.[32] Godahl, as his sobriquet implies, is the consummate criminal, so nearly perfect, so flawless, that he has never even been suspected of a crime, much less accused or arrested for one. Deputy Parr has the misfortune to be matched against Godahl, with the same lack of success he brings to the Sophie Lang adventures. The possessor of a giant intellect, Godahl is the perfect thinking machine, able to take any problem and break it down to its simplest components and solve each of them. He leaves nothing to chance and does not believe in luck, superstition, or intuition. He believes, or rather he knows, that he is infallible and the intellectual superior of any potential adversary. His only fear is of the afflicted, because he believes that anyone who loses the use of one sense acquires greater strength in those that remain.

Godahl is the best of a fine assortment of American crooks who break the law and fill their pockets in any number of ingenious ways. Get-Rich-Quick Wallingford is a confidence man of the first rank. He has the appearance of an affluent businessman and encounters little trouble in finding potential investors in his schemes. Using nearly legal business methods, he manages to separate funds from those who believe they can ride his coattails to a fortune. George Randolph Chester's gentleman con artist first appeared in *Get-Rich-Quick Wallingford*.[33] The methods of Amos Clackworthy[34] bear an extraordinary resemblance to Wallingford's. O. Henry's Jeff Peters teams up with

Andy Tucker in *The Gentle Grafter*, a collection of short stories "built about a single theme: the separation of the fool and his money."[35]

Reformed safecrackers appeared in goodly numbers during the early part of this century. Jimmy Valentine, O. Henry's glorious young man, started the trend when he appeared in *A Retrieved Reformation*[36] and subsequently in the popular stage play, *Alias Jimmy Valentine*. A handsome and charming safecracker, he, too, reforms for the love of a pretty girl. In the now familiar tale, he must crack open a safe to save the life of a child while a detective waits for him to reveal his identity by reverting to his illicit profession.

Boston Blackie had declared war on society and had broken its rules by becoming a safecracker and a dangerous criminal before he reformed and spread the gospel of reform among his underworld friends and acquaintances. Strangely, in the only book about him, the adventures were set in San Francisco, and Boston has no connection with either the character or the action.[37]

Like Jimmy Valentine, his namesake, Frank Packard's Jimmie Dale learned about safes from his father's business, which was the manufacturing of them. A gentleman thief who rights injustices through extralegal methods, Dale is known as the Gray Seal because he leaves that identifying mark behind after every job.

Bill Parmelee, who appears in Percival Wilde's *Rogues in Clover*,[38] and Careful Jones, who appears in short stories by Thomas Costain (under the pseudonym Pat Hand) are both cardsharps. Parmelee specializes in solving crimes, while Jones specializes in "trimming the rich to help the poor" while doing pretty well for himself in the bargain.

Edward D. Hoch has created a popular modern-day crook in Nick Velvet, who has appeared in dozens of short stories, mostly published in *Ellery Queen's Mystery Magazine* and in two collections, *The Spy and the Thief*[39] and *The Thefts of Nick Velvet*.[40] Velvet steals only extraordinary items that have no value—for a minimum $20,000 fee. He has stolen a baseball team, water from a swimming pool, a sea serpent, and even made a theft from an empty room.

Another outstanding contemporary crook is Kek Huuygens, a smuggler whose adventures have appeared in four novels and one short-story collection, *Kek Huuygens, Smuggler*.[41] Robert L. Fish's international thief was born in Poland, took a Dutch name while in Holland during World War II, and now has an American passport.

Since Eugene Francois Vidocq changed his way of earning a living from being one of France's most active criminals to being the founder of the Sûreté, French crooks have followed the pattern and switched allegiances during mid-career.

The most famous of France's fictional crooks is Arsene Lupin, Maurice Leblanc's handsome rogue who dances merrily through more than a dozen volumes. A master of disguises, he assumes many identities and has an unbroken string of successes, even when pitted against Sherlock Holmes in several instances. Later in his career, he shifts to the side of law and order, mainly because of the influence of a beautiful girl with whom he falls in love (and doesn't *that* sound familiar?).

A subsidiary character who has achieved some degree of fame in his own right is Flambeau, the brilliant thief pursued and captured by Father Brown in G. K. Chesterton's first story about the Yorkshire clergyman.[42] Once outsmarted, Flambeau is surprised and grateful when Father Brown does not turn him over to the police, and he repents his evil ways and later assists the gentle priest in solving other crimes.

Some other subsidiary characters who have turned out to be memorable crooks are Auric Goldfinger, James Bond's adversary in *Goldfinger*,[43] and Casper Gutman, who pursues the fabulous black bird in Dashiell Hammett's *The Maltese Falcon*.[44]

Perhaps they don't really count as crooks in the usual sense, but it would be difficult (and a little unfair) to ignore some of the more flamboyant villains who appear in works which border the mystery story. It would be indecent to fail to give proper credit to the delicious villainies of Count Dracula, the monstrous excesses of Victor Frankenstein's creation, the hidden side of Dr. Jekyll, the noteworthy horrors of *The Phantom of the Opera*, the unsightly crimes of *The Invisible Man*.

There are few really fine criminals in today's fiction. Perhaps it is because of the world we inhabit, where real-life crime runs so rampant that we are unsympathetic to a gentleman thief. Victorian and Edwardian England was a perfect breeding ground for the proliferation of great crooks because crime was not common, or at least it rarely touched the book-buying populace. Today, it touches or threatens us all each time we venture out of doors at night. But there is a wonderfully rich tradition of memorable crooks in mystery fiction, and it is to be hoped that neither the tradition nor the crooks will die. Even while the best crooks are in the process of taking, they also have a great deal to give.

NOTES

[1] Ellery Queen, ed.: *Rogues' Gallery,* Boston, Little, Brown, 1945.

[2] Anonymous: *Detective Stories;* Told by Ex-Detectives, London, Henderson, ca. 1887.

[3] Frederick Forsyth: *The Day of the Jackal,* New York, Viking, 1971.

[4] Cornell Woolrich: *The Bride Wore Black,* New York, Simon and Schuster, 1940.

[5] John Gardner: *The Return of Moriarty,* New York, Putnam, 1974; *The Revenge of Moriarty,* New York, Putnam, 1975.

[6] Sax Rohmer: *The Mystery of Dr. Fu-Manchu,* London, Methuen, 1913.

[7] In the first three books, the evil doctor's name was hyphenated; in the remaining books in the series, the hyphen was eliminated.

[8] *The Golden Scorpion,* New York, McBride, 1920.

[9] Guy Boothby: *A Bid for Fortune; or, Dr. Nikola's Vendetta,* New York, Appleton, 1895.

[10] Sax Rohmer, *Sumuru,* New York, Gold Medal, 1951.

[11] Sir Arthur Conan Doyle: "The Final Problem," collected in *The Memoirs of Sherlock Holmes,* New York, Harper, 1894.

[12] Sir Arthur Conan Doyle: "The Adventure of the Empty House," collected in *The Return of Sherlock Holmes,* New York, McClure Phillips, 1905.

[13] *Bull-Dog Drummond,* "Sapper" (H. C. McNeile), New York, Doran, 1920.

[14] "Sapper" (H. C. McNeile): *The Final Count,* New York, Doran, 1926.

[15] "Sapper" (H. C. McNeile): *The Female of the Species,* New York, Doran, 1928.

[16] K. and Hesketh Prichard: *The Chronicles of Don Q,* Philadelphia, Lippincott, 1904.

[17] L. T. Meade: *The Sorceress of the Strand,* London, Ward Lock, 1903.

[18] L. T. Meade: *The Brotherhood of the Seven Kings,* London, Ward Lock, 1899.

[19] Melville Davisson Post: *The Strange Schemes of Randolph Mason,* New York, Putnam, 1896; two further collections of stories subsequently appeared—*The Man of Last Resort,* New York, Putnam, 1897, and *The Corrector of Destinies,* New York, Clode, 1908.

[20] Pierre Souvestre and Marcel Allain: *Fantomas,* Brentano, 1916; more than a dozen novels in the series subsequently appeared.

[21] E. W. Hornung: *The Amateur Cracksman,* New York, 1899, Scribners.

[22] E. W. Hornung: *Mr. Justice Raffles*, New York, Scribners, 1909.

[23] Grant Allen: *An African Millionaire*, London, Richards, 1897.

[24] Arnold Bennett: *The Loot of Cities*, London, Alston Rivers, 1904 (one of the rarest first editions in twentieth-century literature).

[25] Clifford Ashdown: *The Adventures of Romney Pringle*, London, Ward Lock, 1902 (another of the great rarities of mystery fiction volumes).

[26] R. Austin Freeman: *The Exploits of Danby Croker: Being Extracts from a Somewhat Disreputable Diary*, London, Duckworth, 1916.

[27] R. Austin Freeman: *The Uttermost Farthing: A Savant's Vendetta*, Philadelphia, Winston, 1914.

[28] David Durham: *The Exploits of Fidelity Dove*, London, Hodder & Stoughton, 1924; reprinted by Newnes in 1935 with the same title but as Roy Vickers, his real name (the Durham volume is an exceedingly rare first edition).

[29] Edgar Wallace: *Four Square Jane*, New York, World Wide, 1929.

[30] Hulbert Footner: *The Under Dogs*, New York, Doran, 1925.

[31] Frederick Irving Anderson: *The Notorious Sophie Lang*, London, Heinemann, 1925.

[32] Frederick Irving Anderson: *Adventures of the Infallible Godahl*, New York, Crowell, 1914.

[33] George Randolph Chester: *Get-Rich-Quick Wallingford*, Philadelphia, Altemus, 1908.

[34] Christopher G. Booth: *Mr. Clackworthy*, New York, Chelsea House, 1926; *Mr. Clackworthy, Con Man*, New York, Chelsea House, 1927.

[35] O. Henry: *The Gentle Grafter*, New York, McClure, 1908.

[36] O. Henry: "A Retrieved Reformation," collected in *Roads of Destiny*, New York, Doubleday Page, 1909.

[37] Jack Boyle: *Boston Blackie*, New York, Fly, 1919.

[38] Percival Wilde: *Rogues in Clover*, New York, Appleton, 1929.

[39] Edward D. Hoch: *The Spy and the Thief*, New York, Davis, 1971.

[40] Edward D. Hoch: *The Thefts of Nick Velvet*, New York, Mysterious Press, 1976.

[41] Robert L. Fish: *Kek Huuygens, Smuggler*, New York, Mysterious Press, 1976.

[42] G. K. Chesterton: "The Blue Cross," collected in *The Innocence of Father Brown*, New York, John Lane, 1911.

[43] Ian Fleming: *Goldfinger*, New York, Macmillan, 1959.

[44] Dashiell Hammett: *The Maltese Falcon*, New York, Knopf, 1929.

NOTE: Publication dates are generally for first American editions, except where there is no American edition, when it appears significantly later than the English, or if the English edition is the essential one for any one of a number of reasons.

FIFTEEN

FRANCIS M. NEVINS, JR.

*Francis M. Nevins, Jr. has been
interested in mystery fiction
since he was thirteen years of age.
In his early thirties, he
has already written many short
stories for* ELLERY QUEEN'S
MYSTERY MAGAZINE *and* ALFRED
HITCHCOCK'S MYSTERY MAGAZINE,
edited THE MYSTERY
WRITER'S ART, *and
coauthored* DETECTIONARY.
In 1975 his book ROYAL
BLOODLINE: ELLERY QUEEN,
AUTHOR AND DETECTIVE *was given
a special Edgar Award by
the Mystery Writers of America.
Mr. Nevins contributes regularly
on the mystery genre to a
wide range of publications and
lectures on mystery fiction.
His first novel,*
PUBLISH AND PERISH,
*appeared in 1975. Mr. Nevins
is associate professor of law
at St. Louis University
School of Law.*

NAME GAMES:
MYSTERY WRITERS AND THEIR PSEUDONYMS

The by-lines that appear on mystery novels often conceal stories within themselves; in the case of certain mediocre mysteries the story behind the by-line may be more interesting than the fiction the author wrote.

The literature of crime and detection is bursting with writers who use more than one name, multiple writers who employ a single by-line, women who write under men's names, and men under women's, and series characters whose adventures hop rabbit-like from one by-line to another. The entire gamut of nomenclatural permutations is represented in the genre.

The reasons for these maneuvers are for the most part grounded in the economics of the writing business. Most hardcover publishers are unwilling to issue more than two or three books a year by the same author for fear of glutting the market. Consequently, a prolific mystery writer is forced to play amoeba and split off into two or more selves, each with a separate by-line and series of books. Philip MacDonald, for instance, became so prolific during the late twenties and early thirties that his British publishers required two pseudonyms for him—Martin Porlock and Anthony Lawless—in addition to his own name. In America all his novels appeared under his own name.

Aaron Marc Stein uses his own name for novels about archaeologists Tim Mulligan and Elsie Mae Hunt, and for the adventures of engineer Matt Erridge. Both series rely heavily on foreign locales and strong antiquarian interest. He has also invented the persona of George Bagby, who narrates the cases of New York City's sore-footed homicide ace Inspector Schmidt, and the additional by-line of Hampton Stone to report the investigations of Assistant District Attorneys Gibson and Mac.

Judson Pentecost Philips calls himself Hugh Pentecost when writing about artist John Jericho or hotel manager Pierre Chambrun, but he switches to Judson Philips when he is relating the adventures of one-legged newsman Peter Styles.

John Creasey, probably the most prolific mystery writer of all time, has employed at least sixteen separate and distinct pseudonyms for his hundreds of mystery novels. In alphabetical order, he has been Gordon Ashe, M. E. Cooke, Norman Deane, Robert Caine Frazer, Michael Halliday, Charles Hogarth, Brian Hope, Colin Hughes, Kyle Hunt, Abel Mann, Peter Manton, Richard Martin, Rodney Mattheson, J. J. Marric, Anthony Morton, and Jeremy York. As if that weren't enough, Creasey also had four lengthy series of crime novels—the Scotland Yard adventures of Roger West, the capers of Richard Rollison (The

Toff), the science-fiction-cum-political thrillers about Dr. Palfrey, and the espionage stories of Department Z—all running simultaneously for several decades under his own name.

Another explanation for certain pseudonyms lies in the orientation of various subgenres of mystery fiction. Gothics are aimed at women readers, hard-boiled novels at men. Few publishers issue Gothics under a male by-line, and the rare exceptions, like Jean Francis Webb and Hillary Waugh, happen to have names that a casual reader could take for female. In fact, however, hundreds of Gothics have been written by men. Evelyn Bond's paperback novels about distressed damsels in dark castles are turned out by Morris Hershman. The prolific Michael Avallone employs a whole arsenal of female pseudonyms for his Gothics: Priscilla Dalton, Jean-Anne de Pré, Dora Highland, Dorothea Nile, and Edwina Noone. (The last of these is a typical Avallone wordplay, for as Avallone he has written several dozen private-eye yarns about detective Ed Noon.) The multitudinous Gothics of Dorothy Daniels are often coauthored by Mrs. Daniels' husband, veteran pulp and paperback writer Norman Daniels. But the king of male Gothic writers appears to be W. E. D. Ross, a Canadian, who in addition to the name he was born with, uses a host of other by-lines consisting of a female first name coupled with his own last name: Clarissa Ross, Marilyn Ross, etc. Any paperback you see on the stands with a Ross in the by-line is almost certain to be his, unless, of course, it's by Ross Macdonald.

The violent hard-boiled type of novel, on the other

hand, is primarily intended for male readers and always carries a male by-line, the tougher-sounding the better. It was for this reason that mild-mannered New York University professor Rudolf Kagey concealed his authorship of the Hank Hyer private-eye novels under the more appropriate by-line of Kurt Steel. But unlike the Gothic, which is frequently written by men, the tough-guy book is rarely authored by women writers. Two female contributors to this subgenre are exceptions: Leigh Brackett happened to be blessed with a suitably ambiguous first name, and Mary Violet Heberden concealed herself under the initials of M. V. Heberden and the spurious maleness of Charles L. Leonard.

Another reason a writer might prefer a pseudonym is a desire to split off his "popular" fiction from his more "serious" work, as is true of many mystery-writing college professors and other intellectuals. When the erudite aesthete Willard Huntington Wright suffered a nervous breakdown in the early 1920s, he diverted himself during his convalescence by outlining three detective novels about another erudite aesthete, Philo Vance, and submitting them to Scribners under the by-line of S. S. Van Dine. The Vance novels hit the best-seller lists, became the basis of more than a dozen detective films, and made a huge fortune for Wright, who was snobbish enough to detest his own popular success but human enough to take the money and live like a king.

A more recent example of an aesthetician doubling as a mystery writer is *The New York Times* art critic John Canaday, whose crime novels appear under the

by-line of Matthew Head. Among the host of literature professors who write learned studies under their
own names and mystery novels under *noms de plume*
we may mention Carolyn Heilbrun (Amanda Cross),
Rudolf Kagey (Kurt Steel), Francis Steegmuller (David
Keith), and J. I. M. Stewart who has written detective
stories for forty years under the name of Michael Innes.

Members of other intellectual groups have also
performed this self-bifurcation, including a composer
(Robert Bruce Montgomery, who becomes Edmund
Crispin when he turns to murder), a poet laureate (the
late C. Day Lewis, better known to mystery lovers as
Nicholas Blake), a British judge (Alfred Alexander
Gordon Clark, whose crime novels as by Cyril Hare
are a joy forever), and an American jurist (Michigan
Supreme Court Justice John D. Voelker, who wrote
Anatomy of a Murder and other novels under the name
of Robert Traver).

A variant of this motivation is the case of the writer
who thinks of himself as a serious novelist, but who
also likes to do popular stuff now and again (or else
needs the money). James Hilton of *Lost Horizon* and
Goodbye, Mr. Chips fame wrote a single detective novel
as Glen Trevor. Fulton Oursler, who made a fortune
from inspirational best-sellers like *The Greatest Story
Ever Told,* created the pseudonym Anthony Abbot for
his detective tales about New York City Police Com-
missioner Thatcher Colt.

Among living writers who fall into this category
are Gore Vidal, who published three amateurish but
highly satiric mysteries as Edgar Box; William Goldman, whose crime thriller *No Way to Treat a Lady* was

published under the name of Harry Longbaugh; Kingsley Amis, who added a novel to the James Bond saga (*Colonel Sun,* 1968) under the mantle of Robert Markham; and Evan Hunter, who has spent a good part of the last twenty years on his 87th Precinct police procedurals writing as Ed McBain. Even Mario Puzo, author of *The Godfather,* has turned out at least one paperback spy thriller behind a disguise (*Six Graves to Munich* by Mario Cleri, 1967).

Then there are those writers who are well-known in another field and who want to remain primarily identified with it. Consequently, when they turn out an occasional mystery they prefer to do so in disguise. Several science-fiction writers fit this category: Dean R. Koontz becomes K. R. Dwyer on suspense novels, and Barry Malzberg writes the Lone Wolf paperback series as Mike Barry. It has long been rumored that Robert A. Heinlein, the dean of science-fiction writers, was guilty of mystery authorship during his salad days, but he has steadfastly refused to reveal the alias he used on those nefarious endeavors. Science-fiction writer Jack Vance indulges in a sort of half-hearted bifurcation by using the short form of his name on science fiction and his full name, John Holbrook Vance, on mystery novels, to the bamboozlement of not a single reader. On the other hand such superstars of science fiction as Poul Anderson, Isaac Asimov, and Ray Bradbury have never had compunctions about putting their own names on crime stories as well.

The writers who do use their own names on mystery novels sometimes desire to create a new literary personality for themselves, or want to introduce a new series character. On such occasions a pseudonym may once again come in handy. Thus John Dickson Carr uses his own name for the bizarre Henri Bencolin novels, the classic detective cases of Dr. Gideon Fell, and his historical crime stories, but used the by-line of Carr Dickson for the single appearance of detective John Gaunt (*The Bowstring Murders,* 1933) and the better-known Carter Dickson persona for the rumbustious adventures of Sir Henry Merrivale. I have yet to meet a reader who has been fooled by these flimsy disguises.

Then there's the case of Erle Stanley Gardner, who spent half-a-dozen years (1933–39) writing the spectacularly successful Perry Mason novels and then decided to create a new series, under a new by-line, to see if anyone would recognize him. The result was the team of Bertha Cool and Donald Lam, whose cases were published as by A. A. Fair from 1939 until Gardner's death in 1970. These novels were so completely different in spirit and structure from the Mason books that it took several years for the dual identity of Gardner and Fair to be revealed.

Perhaps the most famous contemporary mystery writer to adopt pseudonyms for new manifestations of himself is Donald E. Westlake. His first few novels, published under his own name, exhibited the taut, understated toughness of the Dashiell Hammett tradition. Then, in 1961, he split off his hard-boiled side and continued to develop it under the new by-line of Richard Stark, which he used for his tales of a tough thief named Parker. As the decade advanced, Westlake began to reserve his own name for a series of hugely comic crime capers such as *The Hot Rock* and *Bank Shot*. At the same time he launched yet another criminous personality in a group of five novels in the Ross Macdonald vein that deal with disgraced ex-cop Mitch Tobin. These appeared under the name of Tucker Coe.

One aspect of pseudonymology is beginning to be subjected to heavy criticism from the women's liberation movement—and with some justification. Throughout the history of the genre, dozens of female mystery writers have been encouraged or pressured to use male by-lines by publishers who believed that higher sales would result if a man's name were on the cover (a myth little shaken by the success of authors such as Mary Roberts Rinehart and Dame Agatha Christie). An Englishwoman named Elizabeth Ferrars, whose novels were published in Britain under her full name, found herself billed as E. X. Ferrars when her work came out in the United States. Nor is she the only woman to be hidden behind the neutrality of initials: M. V. Heberden, P. D. James, E. C. R. Lorac, D. B. Olsen, R. E. Shimer, and R. B. Dominic are all females. (R. B. Dominic is, in fact, two females, the same ladies who are much better known under their other joint by-line, Emma Lathen.) Lee Blackstock, Clemence Dane, Lesley Egan, Stanton Forbes, Leslie Ford, David Frome, Anthony Gilbert, Paul Kruger, Ellis Peters, Craig Rice, Forbes Rydell, Dell Shannon, Richard Shattuck, John Stephen Strange, Lee Thayer, Michael Venning, Tobias Wells—every single one of these by-lines conceals a woman, and there are dozens more.

When two authors are writing in collaboration they may choose to publish their material under a double by-line—like Maj Sjöwall and the late Per Wahlöö who wrote the superb Swedish police procedurals about Martin Beck—or they may concoct a single joint pseudonym for their work. The most famous mystery writing tandem, of course, consisted of Frederic Dannay and the late Manfred B. Lee. In 1928 these two young cousins decided to enter a $7,500 prize contest for a detective novel. Their submission, which they called *The Roman Hat Mystery,* consumed their nights and weekends for about three months. The detective who unraveled the hat puzzle was given the name of Ellery Queen—a name that would quickly become almost a synonym for a master sleuth. But Dannay and Lee went further and decided to use the name Ellery Queen not only for their detective, but also as their own joint by-line. They reasoned that mystery readers tend to remember the names of the detectives in the books they enjoy more readily than the names of the authors. By employing the same name in both functions, just as the Nick Carter dime novels of their youth had appeared under the by-line of Nicholas Carter, they reinforced reader identification to a stunning degree and earned themselves several million dollars in the process. A few years after launching Ellery Queen the cousins devised a second joint pseudonym, Barnaby Ross, which they used on four classic detective novels about actor Drury Lane, beginning with *The Tragedy of X* (1932).

More commonly, however, the joint pseudonym of two collaborators is an amalgam of elements from each of their names. Thus Robert Wade and Bill Miller turned out the Max Thursday private-eye series and a large number of paperback originals under the by-line of Wade Miller. The novels of the husband-wife team of Frances and Richard Lockridge were published in Britain under the amalgamated name Francis Richards. Emma Lathen, author of the acclaimed detective novels about Wall Street banker John Putnam Thatcher, is actually two women named Mary J. Latsis and Martha Hennissart. Deloris Stanton Forbes and Helen Rydell collaborate as Forbes Rydell; Bill Pronzini and Jeffrey Wallmann, as William Jeffrey; science-fiction writers Thomas Disch and John Sladek, as Thom Demijohn; Audrey Kelley and her husband William Roos, as Kelley Roos; Adelaide Manning and Cyril Coles, as Manning Coles.

But even the pseudonym of an individual mystery writer may have a story behind it, as witness the matter of Cornell Woolrich, one of the supreme masters of the pure suspense tale. After several years of selling countless stories to pulp magazines under his own name, Woolrich branched out in 1940 and began publishing hardcover suspense novels, also under his own name, beginning with the classic *The Bride Wore Black*. Within a few years he'd written so many novels that he had to come up with a pseudonym for some of them. One version of the tale credits editor Whit Burnett with suggesting the name William Irish; others have pointed out that there was a real William Irish who had worked in Hollywood as a title writer for First National Studios in the late 1920s when Woolrich was employed by the same company. (Could *that* William Irish have been a Woolrich pseudonym too?) In any event, some of Woolrich's finest suspense novels—*Phantom Lady, Deadline at Dawn, I Married a Dead Man*—appeared under the Irish name in the forties. When Woolrich needed yet another by-line he simply pulled out his two unused middle names and published perhaps his greatest novel, *Night Has a Thousand Eyes* (1945), as by George Hopley. This novel was later reprinted in paperback under the Irish name and more recently was reissued by a second paperback publisher with Woolrich's own name.

Many an insider's joke is buried within a mystery writer's pseudonym. Dashiell Hammett's initial few short stories, including the first adventure of the Continental Op, appeared under the by-line of Peter Collinson as a sort of ironic self-mockery, since Peter Collins was contemporary underworld slang for a nobody. Major Cecil Street wrote a lengthy series of leisurely British detective novels under the playful pseudonym of John Rhode, then launched a second series as by Miles Burton, carefully choosing a first name that embodied both a travel reference and a hint of his military background (*miles* being Latin for soldier). Van Wyck Mason turned out two crime novels writing as Geoffrey Coffin, and Jonathan Latimer once used the by-line of Peter Coffin. Anthony Boucher (itself a pseudonym—of the late William A. P. White) devised a by-line for his tales of nun-detective Sister Ursula that incorporated his own love of true-crime writing; the name he chose, H. H. Holmes, had actually been used as an alias by a notorious nineteenth-century mass murderer, Herman W.

Mudgett! (Boucher also published some verse under the Mudgett by-line, and used the name of another figure from true-crime, Theo Durrant, for the novel *The Marble Forest,* 1951, on which he and several other California mystery writers collaborated.)

Edward D. Hoch, one of the most prolific of mystery short-story writers, is occasionally published in *Ellery Queen's Mystery Magazine* as R. L. Stevens—a by-line created by editor Fred Dannay because one of Hoch's stories reminded Dannay of Robert Louis Stevenson. Finally, there is that rare aquatic bird, Robert L. Fish, who never strays far from the ancestral waters when he needs a pseudonym, as witness his choices of Robert L. Pike and A. C. Lamprey.

A writer's choice of pseudonym may also conceal a subtle bit of competitive jockeying. It's quite likely, for example, that Fulton Oursler signed his detective novels Anthony Abbot because he knew that libraries frequently arrange reading lists alphabetically by author and hoped to leapfrog to top position by this maneuver. (The fact that the titles of the Abbot novels generally began with *About the Murder of . . .* indicates a further desire to appear at the top of those reading lists that were arranged alphabetically by title.) Helen Reilly may well have had similar intentions in the early 1940s when she attached the by-line of Kieran Abbey to a trio of suspense novels. But both Oursler and Reilly were checkmated when a gentleman whose real name happened to be Edward S. Aarons started writing mystery novels and became king of the mountain without any artificial assistance. (However, he apparently cared little about his alphabetical place since many of his books were published under the pseudonym of Edward Ronns!)

Protests from another writer with prior claim to a name have sometimes forced an author to play the game of pseudonym-hopping. One of John Creasey's pseudonyms, Michael Halliday, turned out to be unusable in the United States because we already had a Brett Halliday (real name, Davis Dresser) who was writing the Michael Shayne private-eye novels. As a result, the Creasey books published in England under the name of Michael Halliday were allocated to other by-lines when issued on this side of the Atlantic. But the most famous pseudonym-hopper, as well as the nimblest, is probably Kenneth Millar. After publishing four crime novels under his own name, in 1949 he created a new detective character, a certain Lew Archer, and a new by-line for the Archer novels, John Macdonald. He didn't know that there was already a man of that name in the mystery field, John D. MacDonald to be precise. When he learned of John D.'s existence, Millar changed the by-line of the Archer novels to John Ross Macdonald, hoping to end reader's confusion. He didn't, and a few books later Millar hopped once more, this time to a simple Ross Macdonald which he has retained to this day and under which all of his books, including reprints of the early Millar titles, are now published.

Once an author has become established, the trend today is to reprint his earlier pseudonymous work under the hybrid by-line of "A writing as B." Dozens of novels by-lined "John Creasey writing as Anthony Morton" or "Erle Stanley Gardner writing as A. A. Fair" can be found on any good-sized paperback rack. Indeed, one can even find instances where the publisher has apparently lost track of the author's real name, as in the case of "M. E. Chaber writing as Christopher Monig" when in fact both Chaber and Monig are pseudonyms of the prolific Kendell Foster Crossen. But if an author becomes notorious enough under his real name, the "writing as" gimmick is dispensed with and the writer's complete works reappear without pseudonym, as happened to the dozens of espionage thrillers by Watergate burglar E. Howard Hunt that had originally appeared under a variety of pen names.

One of the most confusing nomenclatural sagas in mystery fiction surrounds the triple by-line of Patrick Quentin, Q. Patrick, and Jonathan Stagge. In 1931–32, Richard Wilson Webb and Martha Mott Kelley coauthored two mystery novels under the Q. Patrick name. Then Miss Kelley left the partnership and the third Q. Patrick title was written by Webb alone. Thereafter Webb found a new partner, Mary Louise Aswell, and coauthored the fourth and fifth Q. Patrick with her, after which *she* left the team. At this point Webb began an association with Hugh Wheeler, and from 1936 to 1952 the two men did six more Q. Patrick novels, dozens of Patrick novelettes and short stories, nine more novels under the by-line of Patrick Quentin, and an additional nine under the name Jonathan Stagge. In 1952 Webb retired from the partnership and Wheeler wrote seven more Patrick Quentins solo. Then Wheeler abandoned most of his criminous work and concentrated on writing Broadway plays under his own name, including *Big Fish, Little Fish* and *A Little Night Music.*

Although not instances of pseudonyms in the full sense, three more name gambits employed by mystery writers are worth passing mention.

1. The occasional publication of an anonymously authored book. Perhaps the best known mystery titles that qualify are *The President Vanishes* (1934) by Rex Stout and *The Smiling Corpse* (1935) by Philip Wylie and Bernard A. Bergman.

2. The much more common employment of a single "house name" as the by-line for all the adventures of a series character, no matter how many authors have contributed to the series. This ploy was quite common in the hero-pulp magazines of the thirties, in which, for example, the by-line of Maxwell Grant was used for the adventures of *The Shadow* (most of them penned by Walter B. Gibson). The name Grant Stockbridge was used for the exploits of The Spider, Curtis Steel for the Operator 5 espionage thrillers, and Kenneth Robeson for the tales of Doc Savage and The Avenger. Behind such house names lurked a horde of prolific writers, including Lester Dent, Paul Ernst, Frederick C. Davis, and Norman Daniels. Even today, the new Avenger paperbacks are being turned out by Ron Goulart under the old Kenneth Robeson by-line.

3. The also quite common, if not always frankly acknowledged practice of ghost writing. Not even the name of a well-known professional on a book's spine is an absolute guarantee that he wrote the work him-

self, as Leslie Charteris has been frank enough to acknowledge in prefaces in which he gives full credit to the various hands who assisted on the last several adventures of Simon Templar, The Saint. But when a celebrity without literary experience suddenly appears with a mystery manuscript under his or her arm, it has generally been supplied for a fee by a professional. Thus the novels published by Gypsy Rose Lee, George Sanders, and Helen Traubel were in fact written respectively by Craig Rice, Leigh Brackett, and Harold Q. Masur.

What is the point of all these anecdotes? Of course, there needn't be a point at all. Criminous pseudonymology does not have to be justified by some higher purpose, but may be enjoyed for its own sake, like movie trivia. However, if a moral must be drawn, it's simply that just as there are sermons in stones, so there are stories in names, and one can learn much about the mystery story by seeing how and why certain writers in the field chose the by-lines they did. For the true detective, no fact is without significance.

SIXTEEN

E. T. GUYMON, JR.

E. T. Guymon, Jr. is the dean of
American collectors of mystery
books and memorabilia.
As a fledgling bibliophile, Mr.
Guymon began collecting in
the 1920s, concentrating on first
editions in American literature.
He soon found this field too
broad. By 1930, he had narrowed
his acquisitions to detective
and mystery fiction, in
first editions.
By the late 1960s, Mr. Guymon
had amassed a formidable
library numbering some 15,000
items, including some rare
memorabilia from the seventeenth
and eighteenth centuries, and
one rarity dated 1592.
Future generations of mystery-
story students will be in Mr.
Guymon's debt: He has donated
his entire collection to his
Alma Mater, Occidental College,
for the use of investigators
of the genre.

WHY DO WE READ THIS STUFF?

In these pages you have read much concerning detective and mystery fiction. This is proper terminology since it includes just about everything in the category, detection without mystery, mystery without detection, and all the overlapping examples between. Here, however, in discussing this great branch of literature, for simplification we can use the terms mystery story or mystery fiction in a broad sense.

When I say "great branch of literature," I mean just that. It is recognized that Edgar Allan Poe was the father of the detective story as we know it. Disregarding the background of Poe's works (which has been well covered in this book) the fact remains that for some one hundred thirty-five years, interest in this genre has never flagged. There are those who say this interest has been revived, recreated, or increased. Well, when once one becomes an aficionado of mystery fiction, his interest never has to be revived. Only for a novice does it need to be created and any increase in interest can be explained and will be later.

From this book you may have learned much concerning the mystery story, its origins, its history, its categories, its authors, and the characters found among its pages. You have discovered the masks behind which many authors hide their faces. You have scanned a definitive list of titles devoted to a certain classification of fictional detectives. Just about all other categories have been covered. So what remains? Why, to read these books, of course. The newcomer to the field should be inspired. The veteran reader needs no inspiration. Which brings up the question: Why *do* we read this stuff?

The answer comes easily. Mystery fiction is the greatest escape literature of all time. Escape from what? Why, from the reality of problems. We are all armchair detectives and from the safety of that armchair we can identify ourselves with the characters in the book and enjoy the crime, the mystery, the danger, the chase and, very important, the puzzle, the matching of wits and the solution. If interest in the mystery story has increased, as mentioned above, it must be because problems—personal, domestic and foreign—have also increased. In other words, today we have more from which to escape.

To read these books, we must acquire them one way or another, and this is not always easy. Modern books, yes, but many of the classics are out of print, many are scarce, and many are downright rare. Some may be available in libraries but someone once said that a book worth reading is a book worth owning. It is truly amazing how difficult it often is to locate a certain title when many copies do exist.

This brings up a subject of lesser interest to many people, the subject of first editions. There, of course, is where the greatest rarity lies. The collector of first editions must be interested in the bibliography of a book as well as in the story it contains and this applies to comparatively few people. One author said he was more interested in the tenth edition of his book than he was the first and it is certainly unnecessary, and often unwise, to read the text from a first edition. A rare first edition should be handled as little as possible. The fact remains, however, that the bite of the first-edition bug produces an incurable disease.

There are probably as many rarities in the category of mystery fiction as in any other branch of literature. Poe's "Murders in the Rue Morgue" first appeared in 1841 as a frail little pamphlet. Only a few copies are known and it is unlikely another will turn up. Mystery fiction has nothing to compare pricewise with a Gutenberg Bible, but it does have *Beeton's Christmas Annual* of 1887 in which Sherlock Holmes first appeared and this item is scarcer than a Gutenberg. Mystery fiction has nothing to match in value a first folio of Shakespeare, but this collector has vainly sought for over forty years a copy of J. S. Fletcher's first book, *Andrewlina,* 1889. To the best of his frustrated knowledge, there are only two copies known.

Reading should be for pleasure. You may say that we read for knowledge but that, too, should be a pleasure. So now that we know the satisfaction to be found in reading the mystery story, let us descend from the rarified atmosphere of first editions, and concentrate on the text. (Confidentially, I *love* first editions!)

SEVENTEEN   ROBERT E. BRINEY*

(A biographical sketch of Dr. Briney, who contributed two chapters to this book, appears on page 234.)

*With grateful appreciation to Allen J. Hubin and Francis M. Nevins, Jr., for valuable advice and information.

THE LITERATURE OF THE SUBJECT:
AN ANNOTATED BIBLIOGRAPHY

As many an enthusiast has discovered, with delight not unmixed with resignation, reading *about* mystery fiction can be almost as habit-forming as reading the fiction itself. It is virtually impossible to read extensively in the field without experiencing some awakening of curiosity about the genre: its history, its practitioners, what others have thought and written about it. Sometimes it is a simple desire for knowledge: What are the other forty-odd books about Superintendent West? Where will I find the story behind that puzzling reference to "the affair at the Royal Scarlet Hotel"? In other instances we are tempted to play the stimulating game of matching our own opinions and perceptions against those recorded by others. In still other cases, interest blossoms into a fatal fascination with a certain character or *milieu*, leading us down the endless Holmesian paths of speculation and exegesis. Whatever form our interest in mystery fiction may take, there is ample material in print for it to feed on.

The bibliographic guide presented here is in two sections: Part I deals with writings on the mystery genre as a whole, or on significant sub-categories (for example, private-eye novels); Part II covers material on individual authors or characters. Neither section has any claim to completeness, though most of the important works in English are certainly included. (Foreign language material has been excluded, in spite of the existence of a substantial body of critical commentary in Swedish, French, and German, among other languages.) With a few important exceptions, we list only material in book or pamphlet form as opposed to periodicals. Most of those essays in the Haycraft and Nevins anthologies (see Part I) which initially appeared as chapters or introductions in other books are not cited separately. Purely bibliographic works are omitted, as are most of the high school and college textbooks in mystery fiction which have appeared in recent years. (The editorial commentary in some of these books is nevertheless of interest.) Finally, certain topics—Poe, Wilkie Collins, Conan Doyle and Sherlock Holmes, *The Mystery of Edwin Drood,* Gothic novels, and other subjects which belong as much to general literature as to mystery fiction in particular—have generated such a vast secondary literature that their appearance here has had to be restricted to a few representative titles.

PART I

BOOKS AND PAMPHLETS ON MYSTERY FICTION (GENERAL)

Allen, Dick & David Chacko, eds. DETECTIVE FICTION: CRIME AND COMPROMISE. N.Y.: Harcourt Brace Jovanovich, 1974.

Well thought out textbook/anthology for courses in crime fiction. Section IV consists of critical essays on the genre.

Anonymous, ed. MEET THE DETECTIVE. (Introduction by Cecil Madden.) London: Allen & Unwin, 1935; Harrisburg, Pa.: The Telegraph Press, 1935.

Transcriptions of BBC radio talks in which ten crime writers describe their detectives or chief villains.

Adams, Donald K., ed. THE MYSTERY AND DETECTION ANNUAL— 1972. Beverly Hills, Ca.: Donald Adams, 1972.

_____. THE MYSTERY AND DETECTION ANNUAL—1973. Beverly Hills, Ca.: Donald Adams, 1974.

Anthology of new essays, reviews, notes & queries (plus verse and illustrations) on all aspects of mystery fiction. Designed and printed by Grant Dahlstrom at The Castle Press.

Barnes, Melvyn. BEST DETECTIVE FICTION: *A Guide from Godwin to the Present*. London: Clive Bingley, 1975; Hamden, Conn.: Linnet Books, 1975.

A historical survey of the field, structurally similar to *Queen's Quorum* by Ellery Queen (q.v.). This is a smoothly written introductory treatment, useful mainly to beginners.

Barzun, Jacques & Wendell Hertig Taylor. A CATALOGUE OF CRIME. N.Y.: Harper & Row, 1971. Second Impression, Corrected, 1974.

A compilation of critical opinions by the authors on some 7500 works of detective fiction and related genres, based on fifty years of appreciative and informed reading. Once the authors' biases as to what constitutes good detective fiction are recognized, the work can be read with great enjoyment and profit. The bibliographic citations, however, are sometimes incomplete or misleading.

Boucher, Anthony [pseud. of William Anthony Parker White]. BEST DETECTIVE STORIES OF THE YEAR. N.Y.: E. P. Dutton. *18th Annual Collection* (1963) through *22nd Annual Collection* (1967).

Each volume has an introduction, notes on the stories included, and a "Yearbook of the Detective Story" (containing a bibliography of relevant fiction and non-fiction from the previous year, a list of the year's awards in mystery fiction, a necrology, and an Honor Roll of additional stories). The 23rd Annual Collection (1968) was published shortly after the editor's death, and includes only the Honor Roll for that year. See also Hoch, Edward D. and Hubin, Allen J.

Boucher, Anthony. MULTIPLYING VILLAINIES: *Selected Mystery Criticism, 1942–1968.* Edited by Robert E. Briney and Francis M. Nevins Jr. Boston: A Bouchercon Book, 1973.

A representative sample of Boucher's mystery criticism from the *San Francisco Chronicle* and *The New York Times,* plus book introductions and miscellaneous essays. Boucher was arguably the best and certainly the most influential mystery critic of his time. The book also contains a foreword, "Tony Boucher as I Knew Him," by mystery novelist Helen McCloy.

Brean, Herbert, ed. THE MYSTERY WRITER'S HANDBOOK. N.Y.: Harper & Brothers, 1956.

Subtitled "A handbook on the writing of detective, suspense, mystery and crime stories." By members of the Mystery Writers of America.

Burack, A. S., ed. WRITING DETECTIVE AND MYSTERY FICTION. Boston: The Writer, Inc., 1945; revised edition, 1967.

Thirty chapters on the specialized techniques of mystery writing, by such writers as John Creasey, Stanley Ellin, Mary Stewart, Charlotte Armstrong, etc.

Butler, William Vivian. THE DURABLE DESPERADOES. London: Macmillan, 1973.

Excellent survey of British "rogue fiction": Raffles, Bulldog Drummond, Blackshirt, The Saint, The Toff, etc.

Chandler, Frank Wadleigh. THE LITERATURE OF ROGUERY. [Two volumes.] Boston: Houghton Mifflin, 1907.

An early account of the rogue story as a facet of world literature.

Davis, David Brian. HOMICIDE IN AMERICAN FICTION: 1798–1860. Ithaca, N.Y.: Cornell University Press, 1957.

Gilbert, Michael, ed. CRIME IN GOOD COMPANY. London: Constable, 1959.

Essays on crime fiction by members of the Crime Writers Association: Eric Ambler, Josephine Bell, Maurice Procter, Julian Symons, etc.

Goulart, Ron. CHEAP THRILLS. *An Informal History of the Pulp Magazines*. New Rochelle, N.Y.: Arlington House, 1972; paperback, using subtitle, N.Y.: Ace Books, 1973.

Contains one chapter on The Shadow, one on detective pulp magazines in general.

Gribbin, Lenore S. WHO'S WHODUNIT. Chapel Hill, N.C.: University of North Carolina Library, 1968.

A compilation of over a thousand pseudonyms used by mystery writers.

Gruber, Frank. THE PULP JUNGLE. Los Angeles: Sherbourne Press, 1967.

Memoir of Gruber's years as a pulp fiction writer, with information and anecdotes on the mystery pulps, their editors and writers.

Hagen, Ordean. WHO DONE IT? *A Guide to Detective, Mystery and Suspense Fiction*. N.Y.: R. R. Bowker Co., 1969.

The first attempt at a comprehensive bibliography of mystery fiction, together with supplementary checklists: mysteries in film and on stage, principal characters, settings, anthologies, secondary sources, etc. Although riddled with errors, many of them inevitable in such a pioneering effort, the book is still an important source of information and a starting point for further investigations. [See Hubin, Allen J.]

Harper, Ralph. THE WORLD OF THE THRILLER. Cleveland: The Press of Case Western Reserve University, 1969; paperback, Baltimore: Johns Hopkins University Press, 1974.

A study of thriller fiction and its readers from the viewpoint of modern philosophy and psychology.

Haycraft, Howard, ed. THE ART OF THE MYSTERY STORY. *A Collection of Critical Essays.* N.Y.: Simon & Schuster, 1946; paperbound, N.Y.: Grosset & Dunlap, 1961.

In itself an entire library of detective story commentary and criticism, including important essays by R. Austin Freeman, E. M. Wrong, Willard Huntington Wright, Dorothy L. Sayers, Raymond Chandler, James Sandoe, Edmund Wilson, John Carter, Ellery Queen, and many others. An indispensable volume.

Haycraft, Howard. MURDER FOR PLEASURE: *The Life and Times of the Detective Story.* N.Y.: Appleton-Century, 1941. Newly Enlarged Edition, N.Y.: Biblo & Tannen, 1968.

A comprehensive history of the "pure" detective story, covering both British and American practitioners. A treasure-house of information and informed critical opinion.

Herman, Linda and Beth Stiel. CORPUS DELICTI OF MYSTERY FICTION: *A Guide to the Body of the Case.* Metuchen, N.J.: The Scarecrow Press, 1974.

Oversimplified and misleading attempt at a guide for librarians and collectors.

Highsmith, Patricia. PLOTTING AND WRITING SUSPENSE FICTION. Boston: The Writer, Inc., 1966.

Hoch, Edward D., ed. BEST DETECTIVE STORIES OF THE YEAR. *30th Annual Collection.* N.Y.: E. P. Dutton, 1976.

Continues the Boucher and Hubin (qq.v.) tradition of story annotations and "Yearbook of the Detective Story," and adds capsule biographies of authors whose stories are included in the collection.

Hubin, Allen J., ed. THE ARMCHAIR DETECTIVE. A Quarterly Journal Devoted to the Appreciation of Mystery, Detective and Suspense Fiction. 1967—date.

The showcase for much modern writing and research on mystery fiction. Each annual volume (containing four quarterly issues) consists of between 300 and 400 large pages, and features biographies of mystery writers, critical studies, checklists and bibliographies, reviews of books and films, both old and new, notes, queries, quizzes, and a long and lively letter column where readers share their opinions and discoveries. Between January 1971 and February 1976 each issue also contained a healthy installment of the Crime Fiction Bibliography, a revision and up-dating of Ordean Hagen's bibliography in WHO DONE IT? (q.v.).

Hubin, Allen J., ed. BEST DETECTIVE STORIES OF THE YEAR. N.Y.: E. P. Dutton. *24th Annual Collection* (1970) through *29th Annual Collection* (1975).

Each volume contains the editor's Introduction, notes on the individual stories, and a "Yearbook of the Detective Story" (bibliography, awards, necrology, and honor roll). See also Boucher, Anthony and Hoch, Edward D.

Jones, Robert Kenneth. THE SHUDDER PULPS. *A History of the Weird Menace Magazines of the 1930's.* West Linn, Ore.: FAX Collector's Editions, 1975.

Detailed and profusely illustrated survey of a peculiar mystery-related subgenre of pulp fiction. Among the mystery writers who wrote in this backwater are Paul Ernst, Bruno Fischer, Steve Fisher, Frank Gruber, and Richard Sale.

Keating, H. R. F. MURDER MUST APPETIZE. London: Lemon Tree Press, 1975.

Brief (63 pages) reminiscences and commentary, mostly on "Golden Age" British mystery writers.

la Cour, Tage & Harald Mogensen. THE MURDER BOOK. *An Illustrated History of the Detective Story.* London: Unwin, 1971; N.Y.: Herder & Herder, 1971. [Originally published in Danish under the title MORDBOGEN, Copenhagen: Lademann Forlagsaktieselskab, 1969.]

The text consists of eighty-three brief encyclopedia-style articles on various aspects of mystery fiction. Much information on European material is included, in addition to the major English-language books and authors. Hundreds of drawings and photographs, in both color and black-and-white, form the heart of the book.

Lambert, Gavin. THE DANGEROUS EDGE. London: Barrie & Jenkins, 1975; N.Y.: Grossman, 1976.

Essays on nine "crime-artists": Wilkie Collins, Conan Doyle, Chesterton, John Buchan, Eric Ambler, Graham Greene, Simenon, Raymond Chandler, and Alfred Hitchcock. The author emphasizes the psychological underpinnings of the works of these writers, and how their fiction grew out of circumstances in their own lives.

Larmoth, Jeanine. MURDER ON THE MENU. N.Y.: Scribner's, 1972.

Entertaining essays on the English mystery novel, with emphasis on the role of food and drink, and enlivened with appropriate recipes by Charlotte Turgeon.

Madden, David, ed. TOUGH GUY WRITERS OF THE THIRTIES. Carbondale, Ill.: Southern Illinois University Press, 1968.

Introduction and seventeen essays on such topics as *Black Mask* magazine, Hammett, Chandler, James M. Cain, Horace McCoy, and "private eye" films.

Murch, A. E. THE DEVELOPMENT OF THE DETECTIVE NOVEL. London: Peter Owen, 1958; N.Y.: Philosophical Library, 1958; Port Washington, N.Y.: The Kennikat Press, 1968.

Good treatment of pre-World War I books; unsatisfactory on more modern material.

Nevins, Francis M., Jr., ed. THE MYSTERY WRITER'S ART. Bowling Green, Ohio: Bowling Green University Popular Press, 1971 (hardcover and paperback).

Introduction and twenty-one essays on topics ranging from Edgar Allan Poe to science fiction mysteries. Includes John Dickson Carr's "The Grandest Game in the World" and contributions by Philip Durham, Jacques Barzun, Donald A. Yates, Robert A. W. Lowndes, and others.

Nye, Russel B. THE UNEMBARRASSED MUSE: *The Popular Arts in America*. N.Y.: The Dial Press, 1970.

Only one chapter in this massive overview of popular culture deals with mystery fiction—a chapter studded with factual errors.

Prager, Arthur. RASCALS AT LARGE, *or The Clue in the Old Nostalgia*. Garden City, N.Y.: Doubleday, 1971.

A good-humored survey of boys' and girls' book series, including the Hardy Boys and Nancy Drew mysteries. There is also an affectionate and not too inaccurate chapter on Sax Rohmer's Dr. Fu Manchu.

Quayle, Eric. THE COLLECTOR'S BOOK OF DETECTIVE FICTION. London: Studio Vista, 1972.

Large "coffee-table" format, excellent illustrations. Good treatment of selected Victorian and Edwardian mystery writers, but the comments on more recent writers are too often merely paraphrases of Brazun/Taylor or other sources. Plentiful attention to the pleasures and problems of collecting detective fiction, with many mouth-watering color photographs of rare editions.

Queen, Ellery [pseud. of Frederic Dannay and Manfred B. Lee]. THE DETECTIVE SHORT STORY: A BIBLIOGRAPHY. Boston: Little, Brown, 1942; reprint, with new Introduction, N.Y.: Biblo & Tannen, 1969.
Annotated bibliography of anthologies and single-author collections of detective short stories.

Queen, Ellery. IN THE QUEENS' PARLOR *and Other Leaves from the Editors' Notebook*. N.Y.: Simon & Schuster, 1957; London: Gollancz, 1957; N.Y.: Biblo & Tannen, 1969.

Editorial shoptalk (mostly from *Ellery Queen's Mystery Magazine*) and miscellaneous writings on crime fiction and its bibliography.

Queen, Ellery. QUEEN'S QUORUM: *A History of the Detective-Crime Short Story as Revealed in the 106 Most Important Books Published in This Field Since 1845*. Boston: Little, Brown, 1951; London: Gollancz, 1953; new edition, with Supplements through 1967, N.Y.: Biblio & Tannen, 1969.

The subtitle says it all; indispensable to anyone interested in short crime fiction. The 1967 Supplements bring the total up to 125 books.

Randall, David A., compiler & editor. THE FIRST HUNDRED YEARS OF DETECTIVE FICTION, 1841–1941. Bloomington, Ind.: The Lilly Library, Indiana University, 1973. [Lilly Publication No. XVIII]

Annotated, illustrated catalogue issued to accompany an exhibit of detective story milestones.

Rodell, Marie F. MYSTERY FICTION: THEORY AND TECHNIQUE. N.Y.: Duell, Sloan & Pearce, 1943; revised edition, Hermitage House, 1952; London: Hammond, Hammond & Co., 1954.

Routley, Erik. THE PURITAN PLEASURES OF THE DETECTIVE STORY: *A Personal Monograph.* London: Gollancz, 1972.

Excellent chapters on Doyle and Chesterton; distinctive approach to modern British writers; totally unreliable on American writers (even including Poe).

Ruehlmann, William. SAINT WITH A GUN: *The Unlawful American Private Eye.* N.Y.: New York University Press, 1974.

One-sided study of the American private eye story, condemning the entire genre as "vigilante literature."

Sandoe, James. THE HARD-BOILED DICK: *A Personal Checklist.* Chicago: Arthur Lovell, 1952.

Brief but information-packed pamphlet, containing concise and pointed critical annotations on the work of more than thirty writers in the "hard boiled" tradition. The Sandoe chapter in the present book is an amplification of this pamphlet.

Sandoe, James, ed. MURDER: PLAIN AND FANCIFUL, *with Some Milder Malefactions.* N.Y.: Sheridan House, 1948.

Characterized by Barzun & Taylor as a "virtually perfect anthology." Critical and scholarly contributions by the editor include an excellent Foreword and an annotated checklist, "Criminal Clef: Tales and Plays Based on Real Crimes."

Sayers, Dorothy L., ed. GREAT SHORT STORIES OF DETECTION, MYSTERY AND HORROR. London: Gollancz, 1928; as THE OMNIBUS OF CRIME, N.Y.: Payson & Clarke, 1929.

――. GREAT SHORT STORIES OF DETECTION, MYSTERY AND HORROR: SECOND SERIES. London: Gollancz, 1931; as THE SECOND OMNIBUS OF CRIME, N.Y.: Coward-McCann, 1932.

――. GREAT SHORT STORIES OF DETECTION, MYSTERY AND HORROR: THIRD SERIES. London: Gollancz, 1934; as THE THIRD OMNIBUS OF CRIME, N.Y.: Coward-McCann, 1935.

Mammoth compendia of mystery fiction in its widest sense, with superb Introductions by the editor. The Introduction to the first volume is included in Haycraft's THE ART OF THE MYSTERY STORY. Miss Sayers's Introduction to TALES OF DETECTION (London: Dent [Everyman's Library], 1936) is also valuable.

Schwartz, Saul, ed. THE DETECTIVE STORY: An Introduction to the Whodunit. Skokie, Illinois: National Textbook Company, 1975.

Compendium of representative mystery fiction from Poe through contemporary authors, with commentaries, annotations and class "activity" assignments by the editor. Compiled as a textbook for high school-level courses on the detective story.

Scott, Sutherland. BLOOD IN THEIR INK: *The March of the Modern Mystery Novel.* London: Stanley Paul, 1953; Folcroft, Pa.: Folcroft Library Editions, 1973.

Descriptive treatment of modern mystery fiction, with much information on plots, characters, and settings of individual works.

Slung, Michele B., ed. CRIME ON HER MIND. *Fifteen Stories of Female Sleuths from The Victorian Era to the Forties.* N.Y.: Pantheon Books, 1975 (hardcover), 1976 (paperbound).

In addition to the fiction, contains the editor's Introduction, Notes, and "The Women Detectives: A Chronological Survey."

Steinbrunner, Chris, Charles Shibuk, Otto Penzler, Marvin Lachman, Francis M. Nevins, Jr. DETECTIONARY. *A Biographical Dictionary of the Leading Characters in Detective and Mystery Fiction.* Privately published [Lock Haven, Pa.: Hammermill Paper Company], 1971.

An interestingly designed and well-illustrated paperback of almost 600 pages. Entries are arranged in four sections: Detectives, Rogues & Helpers, Cases, and Movies, thoroughly cross-referenced and indexed. A unique compilation.

Steinbrunner, Chris, Otto Penzler, Marvin Lachman, Charles Shibuk. ENCYCLOPEDIA OF MYSTERY & DETECTION. N.Y.: McGraw-Hill Book Co., 1976.

The basic reference work on the mystery genre, both in written form and on film. Author biographies, checklists, plot summaries, descriptions of principal detectives and villains, with more than 300 illustrations.

Symons, Julian. BLOODY MURDER. *A History—From the Detective Story to the Crime Novel.* London: Faber & Faber, 1972. U.S. title: MORTAL CONSEQUENCES. N.Y.: Harper & Row, 1972.

A knowledgeable, entertaining, and sometimes controversial account of the development of the detective story from its beginnings to what Symons views as the natural next step in its evolution.

Symons, Julian. CRITICAL OCCASIONS. London: Hamish Hamilton, 1966.

Collection of critical essays, including discussions of Eric Ambler and Raymond Chandler.

Symons, Julian. THE DETECTIVE STORY IN BRITAIN. London: Longmans, Green & Co., 1962; revised edition, 1969. Published for The British Council and the National Book League. [Writers and Their Work: No. 145]

A thirty-page overview, containing many of the points made at greater length in BLOODY MURDER, plus a twelve-page "select bibliography" of representative works.

Symons, Julian. ed. THE 100 BEST CRIME STORIES. London: The Sunday Times, 1959.

The results of a survey, compiled and introduced by Symons.

Thomas, Gilbert. HOW TO ENJOY DETECTIVE FICTION. London: Rockliff, 1947.

Contributes little to the enlightenment promised by the title, but contains a brief history of the genre and numerous references to specific authors and books, both important and obscure.

Thomson, H. Douglas. MASTERS OF MYSTERY: *A Study of the Detective Story*. London: Collins, 1931; Folcroft, Pa.: Folcroft Library Editions, 1973.

An early attempt at a history and critical survey of mystery fiction, done with wit and verve.

Usborne, Richard. CLUBLAND HEROES. *A Nostalgic Study of Some Recurrent Characters in the Romantic Fiction of Dornford Yates, John Buchan and Sapper*. London: Constable, 1953; revised edition, London: Barrie & Jenkins, 1975.

Watson, Colin. SNOBBERY WITH VIOLENCE: *Crime Stories and Their Audience*. London: Eyre & Spottiswoode, 1971; N.Y.: St. Martin's Press, 1972.

A sharply witty though seriously intended look at thriller fiction (mainly British) as a reflection of, and an influence upon, the social attitudes and prejudices of the reading audience.

Wells, Carolyn. THE TECHNIQUE OF THE MYSTERY STORY. Springfield, Mass.: Home Correspondence School, 1913; revised edition, 1929.

Wilson, Edmund. A LITERARY CHRONICLE: 1920–1950. N.Y. Farrar, Straus, 1950.

Here is the voice of the Opposition, in the form of Wilson's three famous (if not notorious) essays attacking detective fiction.

Winks, Robin W., ed. THE HISTORIAN AS DETECTIVE: *Essays on Evidence*. N.Y.: Harper & Row, 1969.

The parallels between the profession of historian and that of detective are lovingly explored in these essays in investigation. In his introductions and footnotes Winks discusses some of the great and not-so-great detective stories relevant to the historical subjects.

PART II

BOOKS AND PAMPHLETS ON MYSTERY FICTION
(INDIVIDUAL AUTHORS OR CHARACTERS)

[compiled by R. E. Briney & Francis M. Nevins, Jr.]

Amis, Kingsley. THE JAMES BOND DOSSIER. London: Jonathan Cape, 1965; N.Y.: New American Library, 1965.

A witty, enthusiastic look at the reasons behind the popularity of Ian Fleming's secret agent. Includes a chart summarizing the villains, locales, etc., in the Bond books.

Baring-Gould, William S. THE ANNOTATED SHERLOCK HOLMES. [Two volumes.] N.Y.: Clarkson N. Potter, Inc., 1967.

Texts of the complete Holmes canon (four novels and fifty-six short stories), with a one-hundred-page introductory essay and copious annotations, exegeses, and hundreds of illustrations. The cornerstone of any library of Holmesiana.

_____. NERO WOLFE OF WEST THIRTY-FIFTH STREET. *The Life and Times of America's Largest Private Detective.* N.Y.: Viking Press, 1969; paperback, N.Y.: Bantam Books.

A biography of Wolfe in the Baker Street Irregular manner, complete with hypothetical reconstructions of Wolfe's and Archie Goodwin's backgrounds based on discrepancies in the Rex Stout novels.

Boucher, Anthony [pseud. of William Anthony Parker White]. ELLERY QUEEN: A DOUBLE PROFILE. Boston: Little, Brown Co., 1951.

12-page pamphlet published on the occasion of Queen's 25th novel, *The Origin of Evil.*

Boucher, Anthony and Vincent Starrett. SINCERELY, TONY/ FAITHFULLY, VINCENT. *The Correspondence of Anthony Boucher and Vincent Starrett.* Edited by Robert W. Hahn. Chicago: Robert W. Hahn, 1975.

A 17-year exchange of brief notes, with occasional longer letters, most of them reproduced in facsimile, with exegeses by the editor. Topics include Sherlockiana and the perils and pleasures of editing and reviewing mystery fiction. The overall effect is rather like overhearing only portions of a fascinating conversation.

[Boucher, Anthony] A BOUCHER PORTRAIT: *Anthony Boucher as Seen by His Friends and Colleagues,* compiled by Lenore Glen Offord [with] A. BOUCHER BIBLIOGRAPHY, compiled by J. R. Christopher, with D. W. Dickensheet and R. E. Briney. White Bear Lake, Minn.: [Allen J. Hubin], 1969. Offprint from *The Armchair Detective,* vol. 2, nos. 2,3,4.

Collection of brief but cogent memorial statements by a dozen of Boucher's friends and fellow writers, together with an exhaustively annotated bibliography of Boucher's writings in all fields.

Boyd, Ann S. THE DEVIL WITH JAMES BOND! Richmond, Va.: John Knox Press, 1967.

A totally straight-faced attempt to establish that Ian Fleming was a theologian *manqué* and 007 a modern St. George.

[Buchan, John] JOHN BUCHAN by *His Wife and Friends.* London: Hodder & Stoughton, 1947.

Carr, John Dickson. THE LIFE OF SIR ARTHUR CONAN DOYLE. London: John Murray, 1949; N.Y.: Harper & Brothers, 1949; paperback, Garden City, N.Y.: Dolphin Books (Doubleday), n.d.

The definitive biography of the creator of Sherlock Holmes, written with passionate enthusiasm and meticulous attention to detail.

Carr, Nick. AMERICA'S SECRET SERVICE ACE. Oak Lawn, Ill.: Robert Weinberg, 1974.

Detailed analysis of the *Operator 5* pulp magazine novels (most of them written by Frederick C. Davis): heroes, villains, plot summaries, chronology. Illustrated with numerous pulp magazine cover reproductions.

Cole, Dame Margaret, THE LIFE OF G. D. H. COLE. London: Macmillan, 1971; N.Y.: St. Martin's Press, 1971.

Biography of the distinguished teacher, scholar, biographer, and Socialist historian, by his widow. The thirty-odd volumes of detective fiction by G. D. H. and M. I. Cole are dismissed with barely disguised disdain in less than two pages. Although Dame Margaret's brother, Raymond Postgate, plays a prominent role in the book, the fact that he too wrote detective fiction is not even mentioned.

[Creasey, John] JOHN CREASEY—FACT OR FICTION? *A Candid Commentary in Third Person,* by John Creasey [with] A JOHN CREASEY BIBLIOGRAPHY by R. E. Briney and John Creasey. White Bear Lake, Minn.: [Allen J. Hubin], 1968; revised edition, 1969. Offprint from *The Armchair Detective,* vol. 2, no. 1.

In addition to Creasey's own (auto)biographical commentary, the pamphlet contains a memoir of Creasey by Allen J. Hubin. The bibliography, complete as of January 1969, lists 534 books by Creasey, under twenty-six by-lines.

Davis, Nuel Pharr. THE LIFE OF WILKIE COLLINS. Urbana, Ill.: University of Illinois Press, 1956.

Derleth, August. A PRAED STREET DOSSIER. Sauk City, Wis.: Mycroft & Moran, 1968.

Contains extensive notes on the creation of Derleth's Holmes surrogate, Solar Pons, and on the origins of the stories, together with three sample tales.

De Waal, Ronald Burt. THE WORLD BIBLIOGRAPHY OF SHERLOCK HOLMES AND DR. WATSON. Boston: New York Graphic Society, 1974 [1975].

Mammoth compendium (526 pages) listing over 6000 works in all phases of Sherlockiana.

Donaldson, Norman. IN SEARCH OF DR. THORNDYKE. *The Story of R. Austin Freeman's Great Scientific Investigator and His Creator.* Bowling Green, Ohio: Bowling Green University Popular Press, 1971 (hardcover and paperback).

Smoothly written biographical and critical study of Freeman, exponent of scientific detection and of the "inverted" detective story.

Durham, Philip. DOWN THESE MEAN STREETS A MAN MUST GO. *Raymond Chandler's Knight.* Chapel Hill: University of North Carolina Press, 1963 (hardcover and paperback).

The first biographical/critical book on Chandler: knowledgeable, enthusiastic, and charming.

Eisgruber, Frank, Jr. GANGLAND'S DOOM. *The Shadow of the Pulps.* Oak Lawn, Ill.: Robert Weinberg, 1974.

Exhaustive analysis of the pulp magazine novels about The Shadow, with more information than anyone but a fanatic could want; illustrated.

Farmer, Philip Jose. DOC SAVAGE: HIS APOCALYPTIC LIFE. Garden City, N.Y.: Doubleday, 1973; paperback, N.Y.: Bantam Books, 1975.

A "biography" of Doc Savage based on the one hundred and eighty-one pulp magazine novels, plus Farmer's elaborations. This book is part of Farmer's intricate exercise in "creative mythography" which ties together most of the famous characters in popular fiction (including detective fiction) into a single incredible framework.

Feinman, Jeffrey. THE MYSTERIOUS WORLD OF AGATHA CHRISTIE. N.Y.: Award Books, 1975 (paperback). (Distributed in England by Tandem Publishing Ltd.)

Brief biographical sketch; facile survey of Agatha Christie's literary career, including capsule comments on specific books and quotations from reviews and critical commentary by other writers.

Gant, Richard. IAN FLEMING: THE FANTASTIC 007 MAN. N.Y.: Lancer Books, 1966 (paperback). As IAN FLEMING: THE MAN WITH THE GOLDEN PEN. London: Mayflower Books, 1966 (paperback).

Quickie biography of Fleming, obviously written and published to cash in on the James Bond boom of the mid-1960s.

Gardiner, Dorothy and Kathrine Sorley Walker, eds. RAYMOND CHANDLER SPEAKING. Boston: Houghton Mifflin, 1962.

A skillfully arranged volume of Chandler's correspondence, providing fresh evidence on every page that he was one of the last great letter-writers. Also included are a previously unpublished Chandler short story and a fragment of an unfinished Philip Marlowe novel.

Grindea, Miron, ed. ADAM *International Review*. Nos. 328–330. Rochester, N.Y.: University of Rochester, 1969.

This issue of ADAM is devoted largely to Georges Simenon: his life style, views on what it means to be a novelist, correspondence with André Gide (in French), and a fine essay on Maigret by George Grella. Claude Menguy provides a 30-page Simenon bibliography, covering French-language publications only.

Harrison, Michael. PETER CHEYNEY, PRINCE OF HOKUM. London: Neville Spearman, 1954.

The life and times of a prolific British thriller-writer who set many of his novels in the United States (although his America is purely a figment of his imagination) and won most of his popularity in France.

Hawke, Jessica. FOLLOW MY DUST! *A Biography of Arthur Upfield*. London: Heinemann, 1957.

Much information on Upfield and his adventurous life, which provided the background for most of his detective novels, but little specific data or commentary on the books themselves or on Upfield as a writer.

Hellman, Lillian, ed. THE BIG KNOCKOVER: *Selected Stories and Short Novels by Dashiell Hammett*. N.Y.: Random House, 1966.

This collection offers a generous helping of Hammett's pulp mystery tales and the opening chapter of an unfinished novel. The introduction is an intimate memoir of Hammett by playwright Lillian Hellman, with whom he lived for most of the last thirty years of his life. Much material on Hammett (some of it duplicating the contents of the present Introduction) appears also in Miss Hellman's *An Unfinished Woman* (Boston: Little, Brown, 1969) and *Pentimento* (Little, Brown, 1973).

Hinckle, Warren, ed. CITY OF SAN FRANCISCO MAGAZINE. Vol. 9, no. 17 (4 Nov. 1975).

This "souvenir edition" is devoted almost exclusively to Dashiell Hammett, including features on San Francisco as

Hammett knew it, interviews with his first wife and two men who worked as Pinkerton detectives with him, and the unfinished first draft, set in San Francisco, of *The Thin Man*.

Hitchman, Janet. SUCH A STRANGE LADY: *A Biography of Dorothy L. Sayers*. London: New English Library, 1975; As SUCH A STRANGE LADY: *An Introduction to Dorothy L. Sayers*. N.Y.: Harper & Row, 1975.

Ms. Hitchman loves Dorothy L. Sayers for her creation of detective Lord Peter Wimsey, but her disinterest in everything else that fired Sayers' intellectual passions—the history of detective fiction, theology, Dante—combines with the non-cooperation of the Sayers estate to make this a disappointingly superficial biography.

Hoffman, Daniel. POE POE POE POE POE POE POE. Garden City, N.Y.: Doubleday, 1972; paperback, Garden City, N.Y.: Anchor Books (Doubleday), 1973.

One of the best books on Edgar Allan Poe: impeccable scholarship and sound critical sense combined with fascinatingly idiosyncratic presentation.

Hoyt, Charles Alva, ed. MINOR AMERICAN NOVELISTS. Carbondale, Ill.: Southern Illinois University Press, 1970.

This irrelevant-sounding anthology includes an essay by Roger Herzel on John Dickson Carr, the only sustained discussion in print of this locked-room specialist.

Johnston, Alva. THE CASE OF ERLE STANLEY GARDNER. N.Y.: William Morrow & Co., 1947.

A superficial but entertaining little book, based on *Saturday Evening Post* articles, relating many of Gardner's courtroom battles which eventually became the basis for the forensic maneuvers of Perry Mason.

Lane, Margaret. EDGAR WALLACE. *The Biography of a Phenomenon*. London: Heinemann, 1938; revised edition, 1964. Garden City, N.Y.: Doubleday, 1939.

Lengthy and superbly written life of one of the crime genre's most prolific and popular entertainers. The revised edition has a foreword by Graham Greene.

Lewis, C. Day. THE BURIED DAY. London: Chatto & Windus, 1960; N.Y.: Harper & Brothers, 1960.

Autobiography of the British poet-laureate who wrote detective novels under the name Nicholas Blake; passing references to his detective fiction (esp. Chapter III).

Lofts, W. O. G. and Derek Adley. THE SAINT AND LESLIE CHARTERIS. London: Hutchinson Library Services, 1971; Bowling Green, Ohio: Bowling Green University Popular Press, 1972 (hardcover and paperback).

An amateurish but enthusiastic little book on one of the great rogues of crime fiction, Simon Templar (The Saint), and his creator. Contains a Charteris bibliography covering only British appearances. [The British edition contains a note saying "First published in Great Britain by Howard Baker Ltd. in 1970"; the Howard Baker edition was in fact never published.]

Ludlam, Harry. A BIOGRAPHY OF DRACULA: THE LIFE STORY OF BRAM STOKER. London: Foulsham, 1962.

Thoroughly researched and fascinating account of the actor, theatre critic and writer who created the most famous vampire in literature. There is also a brief survey of Gothic romances in general, placing *Dracula* in its proper literary context.

Macdonald, Ross [pseud. of Kenneth Millar]. ON CRIME WRITING. Santa Barbara, Calif.: Capra Press, 1973. [Yes! Capra Chapbook Series, No. 11; hardcover and paperback.]

Two essays: "The Writer as Detective Hero" (included in Nevins, ed., *The Mystery Writer's Art;* see Part I) and "Writing *The Galton Case*" (included in AFTERWORDS: NOVELISTS ON THEIR NOVELS, ed. Thomas McCormack. N.Y.: Harper & Row, 1969).

MacShane, Frank. THE LIFE OF RAYMOND CHANDLER. N.Y.: E. P. Dutton, 1976.

The definitive, authorized biography of Chandler, but quite limited as a literary study. MacShane's distaste for pulp detective magazines and his unfamiliarity with 1940s crime movies prevents him from seeing Chandler in his proper context as a writer.

Morse, A. Reynolds. THE WORKS OF M. P. SHIEL. *A Study in Bibliography*. Los Angeles: Fantasy Publishing Company, Inc., 1948; paperback, 1971.

The bulk of this work consists of meticulous descriptions of all editions of Shiel's books, with plot summaries and copious annotations. Many of the titles are mystery fiction, including the collaborations with Louis Tracy under the by-line "Gordon Holmes."

Narcejac, Thomas. THE ART OF SIMENON. London: Routledge & Kegan Paul, 1952.

English translation of *Le cas Simenon* (Paris, 1950); a critical study of Simenon, with several chapters on his Maigret stories.

Nevins, Francis M., Jr., ed. NIGHTWEBS: *A Collection of Stories by Cornell Woolrich*. N.Y.: Harper & Row, 1971; revised edition, paperback, N.Y.: Equinox Books (published by Avon Books), 1974.

This huge collection of all-but-forgotten stories by a master of suspense includes a long introductory essay on Woolrich by the editor, and a full checklist of Woolrich's multitudinous writings (compiled by Nevins, Harold Knott, and William Thailing). (The revisions in the paperback edition are in the introduction and checklist.)

————. ROYAL BLOODLINE: ELLERY QUEEN, AUTHOR AND DETECTIVE. Bowling Green, Ohio: Bowling Green University Popular Press, 1974 (hardcover and paperback).

A guided tour through the adventures of Ellery Queen and the lives of Frederic Dannay and Manfred B. Lee, the cousins who created Ellery in 1929 and wrote of him until Lee's death in 1971. A complete EQ checklist is included.

Nolan, William F. DASHIELL HAMMETT: A CASEBOOK. Santa Barbara, Calif.: McNally & Loftin, 1969.

An all-too-brief account of the life and work of the hard-boiled genre's leading performer. Emphasis on biography and bibliography rather than in-depth analysis, with a 50-page annotated checklist of writings by and about Hammett.

Nordon, Pierre. CONAN DOYLE: *A Biography*. London: John Murray, 1966; N.Y.: Holt, Rinehart & Winston, 1967.

First published in French (Paris, 1964). Nordon's study is drier, more detached, and less well organized than the rumbustious Doyle biography by John Dickson Carr, but provides more insight into Doyle's spiritualistic activities (a subject slighted by Carr) and five full chapters on Sherlock Holmes.

Norton, Charles A. MELVILLE DAVISSON POST: MAN OF MANY MYSTERIES. Bowling Green, Ohio: Bowling Green University Popular Press, 1973 (hardcover and paperback).

A diligently researched but awkwardly written study of the man whose Uncle Abner tales made him the foremost American writer of detective short stories between Poe and Hammett. Extensive bibliography (Warning: Norton reveals the endings of several stories in the course of his discussion.)

Overton, Grant. CARGOES FOR CRUSOES. N.Y.: D. Appleton & Co., 1924.

A collection of florid but informative essays on popular writers of the early part of the century, including mystery authors Melville Davisson Post, E. Phillips Oppenheim, and Frank L. Packard.

Pearson, Hesketh. CONAN DOYLE: HIS LIFE AND ART. London: Methuen, 1943; N.Y.: Walker & Co., 1961.

A robust life of Doyle by one of the deans of the art of biography.

Pearson, John. THE LIFE OF IAN FLEMING. London: Jonathan Cape, 1966; N.Y.: McGraw-Hill, 1966.

The most comprehensive biography of 007's alter ego.

Pearson, John. 007 JAMES BOND. London: Sidgwick & Jackson, 1973; N.Y.: Wm. Morrow & Co., 1973.

[Queen, Ellery] A SILVER ANNIVERSARY TRIBUTE TO ELLERY QUEEN FROM AUTHORS, CRITICS, EDITORS AND FAMOUS FANS. Boston: Little, Brown, 1954.

A 31-page pamphlet published to celebrate EQ's twenty-fifth anniversary in the mystery field.

Ramsey, G. C. AGATHA CHRISTIE: MISTRESS OF MYSTERY. N.Y.: Dodd Mead, 1967; revised, London: Collins, 1968.

A slight, diffuse, poorly organized study that does not come close to doing justice to its subject, but does at least provide sixteen pages of photographs and a useful annotated checklist of Christie's fiction and plays.

Raymond, John. SIMENON IN COURT. London: Hamish Hamilton, 1968; N.Y.: Harcourt, Brace & World, 1969.

The first book on Simenon to appear in the United States. Raymond argues cogently and concisely that Simenon is one of the great European novelists. The checklist of Simenon's writings was omitted from the American edition.

Sayers, Dorothy L. LORD PETER: *A Collection of All the Lord Peter Wimsey Stories.* N.Y.: Harper & Row, 1972.

Compiled and with an informative introduction by James Sandoe, this collection deserves its subtitle only in the second printing, which contains a newly discovered Lord Peter story not known at the time the book was first published. The book also contains Carolyn Heilbrun's loving and perceptive essay, "Sayers, Lord Peter and God," reprinted from *The American Scholar* (1968).

Sladen, N. St. Barbe. THE REAL LE QUEUX. London: Nicholson & Watson, 1938.

The life of that flamboyant and today almost forgotten writer of lurid thrillers, William LeQueux.

Snelling, O. F. 007 JAMES BOND: A REPORT. London: Neville Spearman, 1964; N.Y.: Signet Books, 1965 (paperback).

A neat yet loving dissection of Ian Fleming's super-spy in the manner of Richard Usborne's *Clubland Heroes.*

Standish, Robert. THE PRINCE OF STORY-TELLERS. London: Peter Davies, 1957.

The life of that tireless chronicler of polite international intrigue, E. Phillips Oppenheim.

Sullivan, John, ed. CHESTERTON: A CENTENNIAL APPRAISAL. N.Y.: Barnes & Noble, 1974.

Contains "Father Brown and Others" by W. W. Dobson, and other essays.

Turner, Robert. SOME OF MY BEST FRIENDS ARE WRITERS, BUT I WOULDN'T WANT MY DAUGHTER TO MARRY ONE! Los Angeles: Sherbourne Press, 1970.

Hard-nosed, relentlessly honest memoirs of a professional pulp writer, with many sidelights into the hard-boiled detective genre and some of its practitioners.

Tuska, Jon [et al.]. PHILO VANCE: THE LIFE AND TIMES OF S. S. VAN DINE. Bowling Green, Ohio: Bowling Green University Popular Press, 1971. [Popular Writers Series, No. 1]

A brief chapbook containing three essays on Van Dine (by Tuska, Leonard Maltin, and David R. Smith): his troubled life, his Philo Vance detective novels, and the many movies based on his work. Also contains a filmography and 17 photographs.

Van Ash, Cay and Elizabeth Sax Rohmer. MASTER OF VILLAINY: *A Biography of Sax Rohmer.* Bowling Green, Ohio: Bowling Green University Popular Press, 1972 (hardcover and paperback); London: Tom Stacey Ltd., 1972.

Entertaining reminiscences of the life and times of the creator of Dr. Fu Manchu, edited by Robert E. Briney from material written by Sax Rohmer himself, his widow, and his protégé. Foreword, notes, and bibliography by the editor.

Van Dine, S. S. [pseud. of Willard Huntington Wright]. PHILO VANCE MURDER CASES. N.Y.: Scribner's, 1936.

The Introduction to this omnibus collection of three Vance novels is an autobiographical essay by Van Dine. The book also contains a miscellany of articles and notes about Van Dine.

Wallace, Edgar. PEOPLE: *A Short Autobiography.* London: Hodder & Stoughton, 1926; reissued under the title EDGAR WALLACE: *A Short Autobiography,* 1929. As PEOPLE: *The Autobiography of a Mystery Writer.* Garden City, N.Y.: Doubleday (The Crime Club), 1929.

Chatty, informal reminiscences covering Wallace's life and career through 1920. (Note: The subtitle appears only on the spine of the book, not inside.)

Walsh, John. POE THE DETECTIVE: *The Curious Circumstances Behind the Mystery of Marie Rogêt*. New Brunswick, N.J.: Rutgers University Press, 1968.

An important study of how Poe came to write "The Mystery of Marie Rogêt" and of the story's relation to the famous Mary Rogers murder case.

Waugh, Evelyn. THE LIFE OF THE RIGHT REVEREND RONALD KNOX. London: Chapman & Hall, 1959. As MONSIGNOR RONALD KNOX. Boston: Little, Brown, 1959.

Biography of the distinguished theologian, pioneer of Sherlockian scholarship, and mystery novelist.

Weinberg, Robert, ed. THE MAN BEHIND DOC SAVAGE. *A Tribute to Lester Dent*. Oak Lawn, Ill.: Robert Weinberg, 1974.

Eight essays on Lester Dent, covering not only his Doc Savage pulp novels (written under the house pseudonym of Kenneth Robeson) but also his stories for *Argosy* and *Black Mask,* and his "straight" mystery novels. The booklet also contains reprints of two Dent pulp stories, and is illustrated with reproductions of 39 *Doc Savage* pulp covers plus other drawings and photographs.

Wolfe, Peter. GRAHAM GREENE: THE ENTERTAINER. Carbondale, Ill.: Southern Illinois University Press, 1972.

A careful literary study of Greene's spy thrillers, or "entertainments," from *Orient Express* to *Our Man in Havana.*

Wynne, Nancy Blue. AN AGATHA CHRISTIE CHRONOLOGY. N.Y.: Ace Books, 1976 (paperback).

A catalogue of all of Christie's books, with plot summaries, annotations, and a detailed bibliography of hardcover editions. Little attempt at critical commentary.

Zeiger, Henry A. IAN FLEMING: THE SPY WHO CAME IN WITH THE GOLD. N.Y.: Duell, Sloan & Pearce, 1966; paperback, N.Y.: Popular Library, n.d.

Biography of Fleming, with two chapters (more than a third of the book) devoted to Fleming as a writer. Lengthy critique of the James Bond novels and speculations on the causes of their popularity.

There are, of course, numerous biographical and autobiographical works on writers of mystery fiction which have not been listed in Part II. Many of these, while being interesting and worth reading on their own merits, share the disappointing characteristic of slighting or ignoring their subjects' involvement with mystery fiction. For example, G. K. Chesterton's *Autobiography* (1936) contains not a single mention of the author's Father Brown detective stories. In the autobiography of Dick Francis, *The Sport of Queens* (1969), the author's crime novels receive a four-line mention on the last page of the book. A similar situation holds in varying degrees for the autobiographical works of Elizabeth Daly, Ngaio Marsh, and other writers. For this reason, the books have been omitted from the present checklist.

Further bibliographies, covering material in newspapers and magazines as well as in book form and including some foreign language works, are to be found in Haycraft's *Murder for Pleasure* and the books by Barzun & Taylor, Hagen, and la Cour & Mogensen cited in Part I. In addition, "A Bibliography of Secondary Sources," compiled by Walter Albert, is an annual feature of Allen J. Hubin's journal *The Armchair Detective*. The supplements for 1972, 1973, and 1974 appeared, respectively, in v7#1 (November 1973), v7#4 (August 1974) and v8#4 (August 1975).

TYPOGRAPHY BY CHAPMAN'S PHOTOTYPESETTING
TEXT WAS SET IN BASKERVILLE

*

PRINTED AND BOUND BY HADDON CRAFTSMEN

*

DESIGN/PRODUCTION BY HENRY RATZ

*

ILLUSTRATIONS BY DARREL MILLSAP